FAMILY HISTORY
for Fun and Profit

Vincent L. Jones, B.A.
Arlene H. Eakle, M.A.
Mildred H. Christensen

This book originally appeared under the title *Genealogical Research: A Jurisdictional Approach*. It is reprinted here with a new cover and title but no substantial change in content.

Revised Edition
1972

Library of Congress Catalog Number: 72:075075
Third Printing
Printed in the United States of America
by Community Press, Provo, Utah
for The Genealogical Institute

FAMILY HISTORY
for Fun and Profit

About the authors —

Vincent L. Jones, a professional genealogist of wide experience, has conducted numerous seminars and classes in basic
research techniques and American genealogy throughout the
United States. He holds a B.A. in American history from
Brigham Young University and has completed several years of
post-graduate work. He now resides in New Hampshire and is
Vice President, Manufacturing, for Potter Instrument Company of Plainview, New York. *Arlene H. Eakle,* a member of
the Utah Genealogical Association, the Maryland Genealogical
Society and the Organization of American Historians, holds
an M.A. in British history. She is presently an NDEA Fellow
at the University of Utah where she is completing her doctoral
studies. She has taught American and English genealogical research in formal methods classes and through personal consul-
tation. *Mildred H. Christensen,* a former city clerk and court
reporter for the United States District Court of New Mexico,
has more than 20 years experience in genealogical research. She
has taught many classes in basic research methods and pedigree
analysis. At the present time, she is credit manager for South
Davis Community Hospital in Bountiful, Utah.

Errata

p. 76.   Add to bibliographies, Filby, P. William. *American and British Genealogy and Heraldry: A Selected List of Books*. Chicago: American Library Association, 1968.

p. 272.   Add to bibliography, *National Union Catalog of Manuscript Collections*. Several volumes. Washington D.C.: Library of Congress, 1963-1973.

p. 305.   Chapter Twelve, footnote 1, read Dr. Louis Marks for Dr. Lewis Marx.

p. 306.   Appendix One, footnote 6, read Rulings for Ratings.

p. 314.   Add to bibliography, Williams, Dr. Ethel W. *Know Your Ancestors: A Guide to Genealogical Research*. Rutland, Vt.: Charles E. Tuttle Co., 1960.

Foreword

Genealogical researchers will benefit from two significant contributions the authors of this text have made to the field of genealogy. First, they have presented a *system* of research. This is not a series of disconnected chapters of standards and definitions, important as they may be, but a real, down-to-earth, practical research *system* which anyone can follow. Second, they have provided an excellent notekeeping system appropriately placed at the beginning.

This is how-to-do-research in the true sense of the term. The authors outline, for the first time, a step-by-step procedure. The net effect is to give us what we need, when we need it. We know that a child learns first to crawl, then to walk and later to run. Only the extraordinary child diverts from this sequence. Most of us are not extraordinary; we need step-by-step instruction.

While the course is designed primarily with the beginning researcher in mind, it is the experienced genealogist who will appreciate it most. Those who have done research are only too aware of the need of such a comprehensive system. I consider the *Jurisdictional Approach*® to be a most significant step in the right direction. The early telephone was not as fully perfected as the phone of today, yet the principles discovered by Alexander Graham Bell remain the same. I fully expect that the elements of this systematic approach to genealogy will remain basically unchanged as they undergo rigorous testing by broad usage and application.

Rulon T. Burton
Attorney at Law

TABLE OF CONTENTS

INTRODUCTION

STEP ONE: PRELIMINARY SURVEY

STEP TWO: PRE-SEARCH ANALYSIS

STEP THREE: OUTLINED RESEARCH

STEP FOUR: POST-SEARCH ANALYSIS

STEP FIVE: RE-SURVEY

CONCLUSION

APPENDIXES

BIBLIOGRAPHIES

Preface

Family history is the fastest growing hobby in America and one of the newest interests of the historical profession. As more and more people become involved in the pursuit of ancestry, it is important that techniques and procedures be standardized to prevent confusion and to alleviate the need to re-do what each generation of genealogists or historians has done. Conclusions should always be subjected to scrutiny, but the research of the past should stand such re-examination. *Family History for Fun and Profit* is a how-to-do-it book offered as a guide to the production of fully documented, accurate family records. It applies the proven scientific method, used in other research disciplines, to the field of genealogy. But theory is not all it discusses. The practical procedures of notekeeping, collecting data from source materials, evaluating evidence and compiling the information into reliable family records are also discussed, *in the order in which they should be followed* for maximum success with a minimum expenditure of time and money. Emphasis is on procedure—indicated in each chapter by marginal asterisks.

The researcher, using the book for the first time, should become familiar with the table of contents and the overall organization of the book. Study and apply one chapter at a time. When the concepts and procedures of one chapter have been mastered and applied, go on to the next. In this way research will proceed step-by-step in proportion to knowledge and experience. The key advantage of a step-by-step approach is to keep the genealogist out of research mischief. The system is organized so that each step is important in its own right but if any step is incorrect or lacking, all subsequent steps will be based on incorrect assumptions. Such control ensures that the genealogist will proceed in a logical and systematic fashion without going off on tangents which may prove detrimental to his research objectives. When the last chapter is reached, the researcher, if he has applied the procedures outlined, will be both knowledgeable and experienced in scientific research.

Since this system was first developed in the early 1960's, we have come under obligation to many people. To the teachers and students of numerous classes held throughout the West we owe a debt of gratitude for applying these principles to their own research and for criticisms which have led to its improvement. We would like to thank especially Dr. Davis Bitton, Professor of History at the University of Utah, Ronald Bremer of the Research Department of the Genealogical Society of Utah, Roger Flick, Instructor in Genealogy at Brigham Young University and Arthur T. Challis, Librarian of the College of Southern Utah. Rulon T. Burton, Attorney at Law, graciously consented to write the foreword. We also thank Claud Russell, Maxine Belnap, Kathryn E. Miller and Kendall Williams for their many contributions.

We encourage all constructive criticism and suggestions from those who use the material that we might further improve and refine the approach.

Vincent L. Jones
Arlene H. Eakle
Mildred H. Christensen

INTRODUCTION

CHAPTER ONE
RESEARCH STANDARDS

During the past few years genealogy has moved steadily away from amateurism and taken on the aspects of a professional discipline. It has won growing recognition and approval. Genealogy and family history are now accepted as valid scholarly studies for graduate degrees in French, English, Canadian and American universities. In 1968, William Manchester's *Arms of Krupp, 1587-1968*, the history of a famous German industrial family, was selected for international book club distribution. In 1963, Sumner Chilton Powell's genealogically based, *Puritan Village: The Formation of a New England Town* was awarded the Pulitzer Prize in History. More recently, "A Discovery Concerning the Towneley and Warren Families of Virginia," by Mary B. McCurdy was published in the *Virginia Magazine of History and Biography* (1969) and the part played by the Wentworth family of New Hampshire in the years just prior to the American Revolution was treated in the *Journal of Social History* (1970). Local and family history had never enjoyed such respectability.

At the same time there were significant efforts to upgrade genealogical research standards. The National Genealogical Society (Washington, D.C.), the New England Historical and Genealogical Society (Boston) and the Genealogical Society of the Church of Jesus Christ of Latter-day Saints (Salt Lake City) established accreditation programs. Several technical manuals and how-to-do-it books appeared.[1] Seminars and courses in genealogical research and local history are now offered at American University (Washington, D. C.), Stanford University (California) and Leicester University (England). Associate of Science and baccalaureate degrees in genealogical technology are granted by Brigham Young University (Provo, Utah).

Also symptomatic of growing professionalism is the desire to share information and the increasing mutual dependence and cooperation among genealogists. Most genealogical periodicals and many local newspapers publish query or exchange sections where genealogical data are listed at nominal advertising rates. Genealogists are encouraged to help each other for the price of a stamped, self-addressed envelope.

A final earmark of increasing professional awareness is the recognition of the need for a code of ethics to which genealogists can subscribe. Derek Harland and Dr. Ethel Williams are among recent genealogists to outline the ethical practices and research standards which they themselves have been willing to follow scrupulously and which they have hoped others would also adopt.[2]

Research Methods

Although genealogy has made many strides toward true professional status, its reputation among students and scholars of other fields is still not what it should be. Too many look upon genealogy as of minor importance, the work of ill-trained and often uneducated dilettantes. To a certain degree this reputation is deserved. The haphazard manner in which many genealogists have approached their work and their lack of concern for accuracy or completeness have made their conclusions suspect[3]. Yet genealogical research need not be haphazard for scientific methods are as applicable to genealogy as to other fields of research. Table One illustrates this application.

Table One.

Discipline*	Science	History	Genealogy
Definition	Systematic pursuit and use of truth and knowledge to master oneself and one's environment	Systematic study and interpretation of the relationships between human experience and the events of the past to construct a written narrative of them for posterity	Systematic study of the descent of persons and families to form a continuous chain of complete, correct and connected family units from the present back in time to the common ancestor
Methods Used	1. Observation— One's own or another's if it is reliable 2. Hypothesis— State the problem Define objectives 3. Experimentation— Collect evidence Test hypothesis 4. Evaluation— Evaluate evidence Draw conclusions Report findings	1. Bibliographic Survey— What others have done What sources exist 2. Hypothesis— State the problem Define objectives 3. Gather Data— Collect all relevant data 4. Evaluation— Evaluate evidence Draw conclusions Write narrative	1. Preliminary Survey— What others have done 2. Pre-Search Analysis— Evaluate Survey Define objectives 3. Outlined Research— Collect data from all existing relevant sources 4. Post-Search Analysis— Evaluate evidence Compile family units Extend pedigree 5. Re-Survey— What others have done on newly identified ancestors

*Absolute certainty is impossible in all three fields; probability and reason must suffice. But if any step is incorrect or lacking, all subsequent steps will be incorrect or based on incorrect assumptions.

Based on F. Ashley, "The Scientific Method and Historical Research," *Industrial Arts and Vocational Education,* XXVI (1937), 173-75; Fred M. Fling, *The Writing of History* (New Haven: Yale University Press, 1920); Paul Freedman, *The Principles of Scientific Research* (New York: Pergamon Press, 1960); Derek Harland, *Genealogical Research Standards* (Salt Lake City: Bookcraft, 1963).

A doctor discovering a new means of operating on the heart, an engineer at Cape Kennedy sending a manned project to outer space, an historian recreating a picture of the past — each one uses the same basic research techniques. Each one is dedicated to the discovery of truth and each one makes a real contribution to knowledge. Genealogists must accept the challenge to adopt the methods used by researchers in other scientific disciplines if they are to produce conclusions which can be relied upon.

Research Ethics

Individual adherence to a code of research ethics for the genealogical researcher is prerequisite to the establishment of genealogy as an endeavor equal in stature and comparable in discipline to any of the other professions pursued by men.

Have an Open Mind. The genealogist should give attention to new ideas, new approaches and new data regardless of the effect that data might have on prior conclusions, published volumes or family traditions. Most persons beginning new research are soon confronted with information which conflicts with established family traditions. Accept this as a challenge to establish the truth through your own efforts. A closed mind cannot be relied upon to compile complete or correct family records. You should permit no preconceived notions to stand in the way of new information. Personal biases and prejudices are present in all researchers; but objectivity demands they be controlled in the decision making processes.

Critical analysis of data often requires the use of techniques for which a beginning researcher has no background. If research methods are sound, they are based on common sense and are not beyond your grasp. With an open mind you can learn them. All that is needed is the willingness to try. The critical acumen needed to evaluate genealogical data is but an extension of the critical judgments which you make each and every day as you go about your daily affairs.[4]

Document Your Sources of Information. Concern for your own research integrity should make the adage, "Give credit where credit is due," a fundamental requirement. If you copy ideas or sources from the work of another, you must give full credit. There is more to this than mere professional courtesy.

A genealogical conclusion, though it may prove to be accurate, inspires little confidence and is considered unacceptable unless it is carefully documented. The finished family history must indicate through footnotes and other annotations the sources from which the conclusions have been drawn. The single family group form must have a fully documented case history (see pages 20-21) containing the supporting evidence upon which it is based. If these substantiating data are lacking, the research must be redone. Sir Anthony R. Wagner, noted English genealogist and member of the College of Arms, advises professional genealogists to recheck all previous work to avoid following erroneous pedigree lines.[5]

It is often difficult to convince oneself that research must be critically analyzed for accuracy and completeness before proceeding further. But you cannot afford to accept undocumented conclusions. They are of dubious worth without supporting evidence. During the course of research, you will come upon records which represent the conclusions of someone else — authentic in appearance but poorly annotated and impossible to evaluate. The choice is clear: such records must be treated as hearsay evidence only, the ultimate worth of which can be ascertained only by thorough re-research. This does not minimize their value as clues, indirect sources, which may lead to original sources upon which reliance is justified. To the layman who tinkers in research this may seem a harsh and arbitrary standard. The hobbyist may accept the results of his efforts in accordance with his own standards, and justify himself as having performed his task for the pleasure of doing. But the genealogist who takes pride in the professional standards upon which his discipline is based will not be satisfied with anything less. A compromise of principle is a breach of professional ethics. By carefully annotating the records you compile and bequeath to posterity, you can assure that those who follow will not have to re-do the work on which you spend time and effort.

Always Be a Scholar. You should realize that differences of interpretation are necessary for productive research. They should not lead to name-calling or casting aspersions on another's professional ability. Such below-the-belt tactics debase scholarship to the level of a street brawl.[6] If you challenge another's research conclusions, justify your action in a scholarly way. If your own are questioned, accept the criticism in a similar manner.

Do Not Compromise Your Research. Genealogical problem should be defined and solved systematically.[7] Selective or haphazard searching of sources will not provide all of the data needed. In any kind of research, all of the data should be gathered and carefully analyzed before attempting to draw conclusions. If conclusions are formed prematurely, research is compromised. Such compromise in another profession resulted in thousands of deformed babies: recall the drug Thalidomide, developed to relieve nervous tension and other discomforts of expectant mothers. The drug was placed upon the market for public consumption before scientists fully realized the terrible side-effects it could have on unborn children. Compromises in genealogy, like compromises in drug research are of little value to anyone, and usually detrimental to the consumer.

You can never know all that there is to know concerning your ancestors. All you can hope is that your conclusions will be as complete and correct as "existing records permit." This is an exacting standard. You should not promulgate unwarranted conclusions which might then become accepted without question in the future. Error becomes more difficult to weed out the longer it is perpetuated. Each conclusion must be based upon exhaustive examination of all existing sources pertinent to your pedigree and careful, responsible evaluation.

Use Primary and Original Sources Wherever Possible to Compile Family Units. Copying from the work of others only, while necessary in the beginning stages of a project, will lead to the perpetuation of errors already compiled. It is your responsibility to use the work of others as a foundation for your own to prevent unnecessary duplication. But you must then search primary sources before your project is completed and ready for analysis.[8] Past neglect of primary evidence has contributed to the poor reputation of family history. The only way to reverse this is to base genealogical research firmly on primary source materials wherever possible.

Be Willing to Share Information with Others. Research is a cumulative work. You build on the foundations laid by others; subsequent researchers will use your contributions. In other scholarly fields, the interchange of ideas and data have made cooperation an integral part of the discipline. Genealogical researchers should foster the same cooperative spirit by generously sharing their findings. "A candle loses nothing when it lights another candle."[9]

Establish Your Fees Commensurate to Services Rendered. If you do research for hire, your experience, type of search performed and type of report submitted should determine the charge. Obviously, a beginner working in well-indexed records in an air-conditioned library should not charge the same rates as an experienced researcher wading through unindexed court files in a hot, dirty attic. A genealogist who plans, searches, evaluates and compiles a pedigree is entitled to a larger fee than one who performs only searches. But share your knowledge of source materials and procedures without charge if the occasion warrants it. Never let the desire to please a client prompt you to fabricate evidence or sacrifice principles of sound research.[10] Always produce quality work and charge accordingly.

It is the responsibility of those who teach, practice or consult in genealogical research to exemplify these standards. To these ends this course of study has been written. We leave it to our students to stand upon our shoulders for a clearer view. Reason assures us they will.

CHAPTER TWO
RESEARCH NOTEKEEPING

Before using records beginning researchers should learn how to organize research data. Even experienced researchers need to overcome the confusion and disarray that often typifies genealogists' files. Too much time is now spent determining what has already been accomplished. Most of us are interested in economy of time and money. If keeping notes requires all of your time, there will be no time for research. If money is spent on expensive files, notebooks and photographic equipment, it will be unavailable for research. Research notekeeping tools can be kept simple and restricted to items which are inexpensive to acquire in the necessary quantity, efficient to use and designed to serve the researcher.[1] With these tools, large amounts of data can be organized with minimum effort, making it easy to find specific items in a minimum amount of time.

Pedigree Chart

Systematic research is completely oriented around the pedigree. You must become familiar with the simplest methods for charting a pedigree and understand its proper application. The most commonly used pedigree presents the common ancestor at the top with descent by family unit. Such a chart effectively shows collateral (non-direct) ancestors — brothers, sisters, aunts, uncles and cousins — as well as direct lineage.

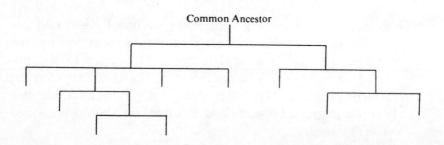

12

Other pedigree charts begin with the present generation and move back in time depicting direct ancestors only, who double in number with each generation.

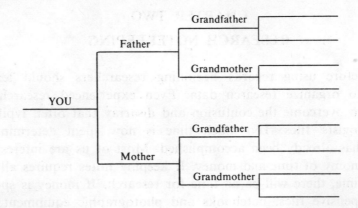

The second type of pedigree chart is the best one to use as a research tool. Research properly begins with the present generation — YOU — and moves back in time, following blood lines.[2] Like a road map, it serves as a guide to genealogical activity; it reflects at a glance, the progress being made. It lists the pedigree ancestors from whom you descend in a direct line and those for whom you should compile complete, correct and connected family units.

Two charts are actually needed during the course of research, a work chart and a permanent record chart. Each should be appropriately labeled:

Pedigree work chart. This chart contains the names and associated information of those assumed to be pedigree ancestors. Until the necessary research has been thoroughly performed, *all* names appearing on this pedigree chart are *assumed* ancestors only.

* Fill out the chart placing your name on line 1, then add the data for your parents and grandparents, and so on up the pedigree.[3] As this is a work copy, it is proper to list unverified or unproven information even though there may be reason to suspect it is inaccurate. Filling in data on this chart is a perpetual process and information should be added as it is obtained.

* *Enter the names* in the order in which they are written: given name, middle name, last name. *Enter the date:* day, month, year. Write the month out or use standard abbreviations; never use a number to designate the month in genealogy. Omit all punctuation marks in dates. *Enter the place:* town, village, county or its equivalent, state or its equivalent.[4] Such items as occupation, title, place of residence or change of name can also be noted on this work chart.

PEDIGREE CHART

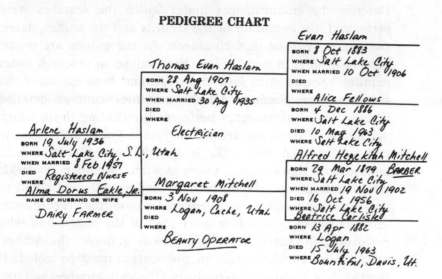

Permanent Pedigree Chart. This chart contains only those pedigree ancestors which have been *proven* through research. When a completed research case history (see below) substantiating a pedigree ancestor has been completed, that individual may be added to the permanent pedigree chart. There is to be no record of assumed ancestors on this permanent chart.

Research Calendar or Log

This is a sheet of paper, conveniently ruled in columns, on which a description of all research activities is recorded in sequence. If filled out properly, it presents a blow-by-blow account of every action taken in research and provides a table of contents to the documents accumulated.

---

*Asterisks signal procedures to be followed.

CALENDAR
(COPYRIGHT 1972, GENEALOGICAL COPY SERVICE)

ENC. NO.	S NO.	DATE OF SEARCH	SOURCE: Description, Condition, Unusual Circumstances, How Searched.	JURISDICTION OR LOCALITY	PERIOD OF TIME	SURNAME OR NAME	RE-SULT

* Describe the circumstances under which the searches were performed, the condition of the records and the names, dates, and places involved in each search. As the entries are made, keep two things in mind. First, the analysis of research notes requires knowledge of how thorough and how extensive the searches were. Second, unless your files contain detailed descriptions of all searches performed, including those which did not yield data, researchers in future years will conclude that you omitted them. The inevitable consequence will be unnecessary duplication. Every search, whether it yields information or not, should be described in sufficient detail to convey exactly what was covered, how the record was searched (word by word or brief scan of the pages) and who performed the search. If the source is a book, the author, title, publisher and the year of publication must be noted. If located in a library or depository, the call number and the name and address of the library must be included. The condition of the book or document must be clearly described. Missing, torn or blurred pages and entries, foreign language, incomplete indexes and other important items must be noted. When interviewing elderly contacts, memory clarity and general physical condition must be recorded. All research actions must be reported honestly if the research is to be properly evaluated.

* Indicate the results of the search by writing "ws" (worksheet, i.e., notes taken) or "nil" (no information located). In this way, every search regardless of result, is systematically recorded.

* Cross-reference the calendar. Each record category consulted is a separate search. Number each search chronologically by date of search in the proper column. This same number is placed on all worksheets (notes) compiled during

that search. If an enclosure (a document in your possession) is involved, the enclosure number is also entered on the calendar, thus providing a table of contents to your document files.

CALENDAR

(COPYRIGHT 1972, GENEALOGICAL COPY SERVICE)

ENC. NO.	S NO.	DATE OF SEARCH	SOURCE: Description, Condition, Unusual Circumstances, How Searched.	JURISDICTION OR LOCALITY	PERIOD OF TIME	SURNAME OR NAME	RE-SULT
	35	2 May 1965	Life sketch of Eli Brumm Rodgers written after his death by his wife Loretta in her own hand. Original in possession of Betty Eakle, 934 West 1500 South Woods Cross, Utah.	Home	May 1957	Eli B Rodgers	ws

A separate calendar for each ancestral surname or each family unit is not recommended. This is an unnecessary complication. Most sources will give information on more than one surname and, as each search must be described in detail on a calendar, maintenance of surname calendars would require duplicating the entry on calendars for each surname. Too time-consuming! Similarly, document files should be consolidated. Sources giving data on several surnames would require duplication if you tried to provide a document file for each separate surname. Such procedures enslave you to a system. As you will see below, all notes must be alphabetically arranged and cross-referenced to calendars and document files, eliminating the need for separate surname files.

Worksheets

A vital feature of effective research is the way in which notes are taken. They should be written on some uniform-size card or sheet so that they can be systematically arranged and made readily accessible. For this purpose some researchers prefer 3 X 5 or 5 X 8 index cards. Some use inexpensive scratch pads; others prefer notebooks in which extracts are made, numbered, then cut apart and mounted on paper of uniform size. These are all temporary — requiring organization later. A better and less costly approach is to use a specially designed family group worksheet upon which each piece of genealogical data concerning an individual or a family may be placed.[5]

HUSBAND .... of ....
Birth .... Place ....
Chr. .... Place ....
Death .... Place ....
Burial .... Place ....
Mar. .... Place ....
Father .... Mother ....

WIFE .... of ....
Birth .... Place ....
Chr. .... Place ....
Death .... Place ....
Burial .... Place ....
Father .... Mother ....

DOCUMENT DATED: .... RECORDED: ....

Enc # .... Search # .... Family Line ....

Home .... Institution .... Township .... Parish .... County ....
Municipal .... Local .... District .... State .... National ....

Personal Papers   Census   Financial   Interview
Family Records   Land   License   Correspondence
Pedigree   Probate   Church   Researcher
History   Court   Employment   Original
Biography   Tax   Cemetery   Trans. Copy
MSS Colls   Military   School   Photo Copy
Coat of Arms   Poor Relief   Newspaper   Manuscript
Oral History   Birth   Profession   Printed
Periodical   Marriage   Estate   Extract
Membership   Death   Insurance   Legible
Other   Election   Shipping   Foreign Lang.

Call # .... Vol. .... Page .... Date of Search ....

Male or Female	CHILDREN	WHEN BORN			WHERE BORN			DIED				MARRIED		
		Day	Mo.	Yr.	Town	County	State or Country	Day	Mo.	Yr.	Place	Date	Place	To
1														
2														
3														
4														
5														
6														
7														
8														
9														
10														
11														
12														

Approaches to the field of genealogy are almost as varied as the number of people who are involved in the science. Some prepare pedigrees of the male lines only, some make tables of descent based upon a few family units. We conceive of genealogy as the identification of complete families. After all, the family is the basic unit of society. Everyone born on this earth in the past or who will be born in the future is a member of a family unit. Therefore, the end result of genealogical research should be complete, correct and connected family groups depicting each marriage union involving a pedigree ancestor. If your great-grandfather was married three times, a separate family group should be compiled for each of those marriages, although you may only trace earlier lineages of the woman through whom you descend. Research conclusions will be placed on family group forms at the end of the research process. The use of such a form, as data is collected, will facilitate final analysis and compilation of each family unit.

* Extract the data from each source directly onto worksheets. If the information fits the blanks on the worksheet, enter it in the proper place. If if does not, use the worksheet as you would any ordinary lined paper.

* Extract data honestly without any change of meaning. Retain the same spelling, the same grammar, the same words as the original. Write the dates exactly as they appear in the record. Retain the same abbreviations of names, places and words. Every source should be considered on its own merits. Some genealogists make the mistake of deciding prematurely whether the source is right or wrong. In extracting data from the sources, they copy only the information which *they think* is correct. Or, even worse, they alter the source and record the data as *they think* it should be. This is dishonest research. An exact transcription of the pertinent material should be made including all errors, actual or supposed. If there is reason to believe that the record is wrong, indicate your thoughts about it. This can be done by first copying the data exactly as they appear in the record. Then, somewhere on the sheet, write any ideas or opinions which come to mind and place them in brackets [ ]. Hunches and snap judgments will often be forgotten by the time you

are ready to evaluate your work if they are not promptly recorded. Brackets indicate to other readers that the original source did not contain the enclosed material. In every instance there must be clear distinction between the notes taken from the records and the evaluation of those notes which you make yourself.

* Re-check your notes against the source at the time you make the abstract. Check for accuracy and completeness the spelling of names and places, dates and relationships. Re-check all clues you extracted and annotated. This step, to prevent errors, takes a little longer at the time, but in the long run you will not have to re-check sources to which you no longer have ready access. Finally, indicate on the worksheet that the data has been proof-read against the source.[6]

* Carefully check the proper record category in the reference corner of the worksheet and briefly describe the record and its condition on the lines provided. Note the date of search and be sure to list the volume and page of the source giving the information. Data are of questionable worth if they cannot be identified with their sources.[7] When preparing evidence from data it must be classified in a good, better, best fashion which can be done only when all of the circumstances are present. Therefore, any notekeeping system must clearly state the identity of each source from which each piece of data comes. Files must be maintained in such a condition from day to day, that should you be removed from research for any reason, someone else could continue. Succeeding generations will then never have to re-do the research you have done. (See the following example).

HUSBAND Thomas H. Woodbury

Birth .... Place ....
Chr. .... Place ....
Death .... Place ....
Burial .... Place ....
Mar. 1872. Place ....
Father .... Mother ....

held at Wells Ward, 1890 South 5th East
Salt Lake City, Utah.

WIFE Mrs [Mary Alice Lambert]

Birth .... Place ....
Chr. .... Place ....
Death .... Place ....
Burial .... Place ....
Father .... Mother ....

DOCUMENT DATED: 10 June 1922   RECORDED: ....

Enc # .... Search # 116 .... Family Line Woodbury

Home ✓ Institution.......... Township.......... Parish.......... County..........
Municipal.......... Local.......... District.......... State.......... National..........

......Personal Papers   ......Census   ......Financial   ......Interview
......Family Records   ......Land   ......License   ......Correspondence
......Pedigree   ......Probate   ......Church   ......Researcher
......History   ......Court   ......Employment   ......Original
......Biography   ......Tax   ......Cemetery   ......Trans. Copy
......MSS Colls   ......Military   ......School   ......Photo Copy
......Coat of Arms   ......Poor Relief   ......Newspaper   ......Manuscript
......Oral History   ......Birth   ......Profession   ✓Printed
......Periodical   ✓Marriage   ......Estate   ......Extract
......Membership   ......Death   ......Insurance   ✓Legible
......Other   ......Election   ......Shipping   ......Foreign Lang.

Golden Wedding Invitation

Call # .... Vol. .... Page. .... Date of Search 29 May 1965

Male or Female	CHILDREN	WHEN BORN Day Mo. Yr.	WHERE BORN Town	County	State or Country	DIED Day Mo. Yr. Place	MARRIED Date Place	To
1	Thomas L. Woodbury							
2	Maria W. Ross							
3	Mary Alice Woodbury					dec'd		
	Charles K. Woodbury							
4	George L. Woodbury					dec'd		
5	Ella F. W. Osborne							
6	Catherine L. Woodbury							
7	Loretta W. Rodgers					dec'd		
8	Richard L. Woodbury							
9	Myrtle W. Doelle					dec'd		
10	Irene L. Woodbury							
11	Annie W. Jensen							
12	Elias L. Woodbury							

(COPYRIGHT 1972, GENEALOGICAL COPY SERVICE)

* Never record information pertaining to more than *one family* on a single worksheet. If a source ties one family to some other family unit, note the relationships, in brackets, on the worksheet so the information is not lost, but do not combine the two families on the same sheet. Use additional worksheets for each additional family. Information relating to

one family should be available for analysis, separate from data relating to a different family. If the family Bible contains records of five families, for example, five separate worksheets should be made. The process of analysis is easily the most difficult phase in research but adherance to this principle will make it much easier to assemble all data on any given family.

* Record data from *one source only* on each worksheet. Data, like the pieces of a jig-saw puzzle, must be compared for fit. When information from one source is mixed with that from another, the identity of the data is lost. In order to properly evaluate the information, it must be kept separate. It takes no longer to copy notes onto separate worksheets and the cost of paper is a minor part of the cost of research, especially when you attach a value to the amount of time spent. (Incidently, worksheets, page for page, are less expensive than notebooks.) The use of bound or spiral notebooks makes it impossible to sort and arrange notes into any order unless they are cut into pieces, whereas separate sheets can be quickly organized into family units.

* Maintain worksheets in order, alphabetically by names of heads of households, and chronologically by their birthdates where worksheets share common names.

* Cross reference each worksheet to the other components of your notekeeping system by recording the search number and document numbers from the calendar in the proper blanks on the worksheet. The alphabetical arrangement of the worksheets provides a detailed index to the entire system.

Case Histories. When all existing records have been searched and the data extracted onto worksheets, analyses and evaluations will be performed to complete family records. All of the worksheets which contribute to the compilation of a given family will be retained together to constitute a completed research *case history*. The only additional element needed in the case history is an evaluation of different pieces of evidence, especially if there are conflicting statements. One source must be weighed against another. A brief narrative summary can explain **reasons** for the judgment rendered. This is the part of the work most properly scrutinized by future researchers. You are under full obligation to include in each case history, a summary of your reasoning in support of your decisions. These comments should also be entered in brackets on the worksheets involved. The case history should then be filed permanently in a safe, accessible place.

The case history is gradually created during the research process. It is not a product of any subsequent laborious task, which it might otherwise be, if worksheets are used as note-keeping media. If the sources from which the data came have been clearly recorded on each worksheet, and if the information has been honestly extracted by the researcher, the worksheets will tell the story of the research behind that family unit. If the search number is recorded on each worksheet, the examiner of the completed file has easy access to the rest of the story through the description of the searches and the conditions of the sources on the calendar. Through the enclosure number a fellow scholar has access to the documents in your possession. The next generation of researchers can confidently build upon a work properly done.

Enclosure (Document) File

Required in your notekeeping system is a simple means for maintaining and preserving the documents you accumulate during research. A manila folder with a prong fastener, a loose-leaf binder or a manila envelope can be used to preserve such documents.

* Preserve every certificate, letter, scrap of paper, notebook, news clipping, picture, report from a field researcher or any other document in your possession containing pertinent genealogical data. Punch each document, number it in sequence of searching and permanently file it in a manila folder or other enclosure file. Documents, in which you do not want to punch holes, may be placed in manila envelopes or plastic protective sheets which are also punched, numbered and filed.

* Extract all genealogical data from these enclosures onto separate worksheets. This is necessary if all data concerning a given problem are to be accessible for effective organization

and analysis. Evaluation will be done by using the worksheets, not the enclosure files which are intended merely to preserve source materials in an orderly way.

* Consider scrapbooks, books of remembrance, family record books, Treasures of Truth, baby books and wedding books as parts of the enclosure files. The certificates, newsclippings and pictures or other items of genealogical value already mounted and placed in these books need not be removed and filed in manila folders in order to be consistent with the system. Extract all genealogical information from them onto worksheets and describe them on the calendar. A reference to the appropriate book and page makes these items part of the enclosure files and accessible to the researcher.

* Do not punch or number current legal papers — deeds, identification papers, licenses, passports, birth certificates and other current legal documents which must be used by the researcher himself in his legal activity. This invalidates them. Extract the pertinent data from them onto worksheets and describe them on the calendar indicating where they are located — safety deposit box, wallet or other location.

* Cross-reference the enclosure files. It makes no difference in what order the documents are filed. Number each one as you search it and file it in sequence. Enter this same document number on the calendar for the appropriate search and on the worksheets which contain the data extracted from it.

There will not be an enclosure for each search described on the calendar. When searching in original records or during personal interviews, the information obtained should be extracted directly to worksheets without intermediate copying. The action should be carefully described on the calendar giving the name and address of the person or record depository in which the documents are located. Inasmuch as the documents are not in your own possession, there will be no enclosure or document number. If extracts are made properly and proofread at the time they are made, there is no need to have the actual documents or photocopies of them in the researcher's possession. The extract will be sufficient.[8]

Each of the foregoing tools is different and has a distinct function; yet the different elements are interrelated to form one unified system. The *pedigree chart* shows at a glance the extent of your genealogical activity and what remains to be done. It is cross referenced to the other parts of the system through names which appear on it. A description of each search is recorded chronologically, by date of search, on the *calendar*. Each entry is cross referenced to both the worksheets (notes) and the enclosure (document) files associated with the search, by the search and enclosure numbers. It serves as a table of contents to the enclosure files. Data are extracted from the records directly onto *worksheets* with care to insure against any change in meaning. The worksheets are cross referenced to both the calendar and enclosure files by the search and enclosure numbers. Worksheets are arranged alphabetically by surname thus providing a name index to the entire system. All documents or sources which are in your possession are filed in numerical sequence in the *enclosure file*. This file is cross referenced to the calendar and worksheets by the enclosure number.

This system lends itself easily to any number of refinements to suit the individual personality. However, to omit any part of it, as here outlined, would severely lessen its effectiveness, if not destroy its usefulness entirely.

Procedure

* Obtain a supply of worksheets (family group forms, index cards, IBM cards or plain sheets of paper), calendar forms (plain or ruled paper), and enclosure file (folder, looseleaf or envelope).[9] Plastic sheets may be used to protect old or easily damaged documents.

* Begin by collecting into one big pile all of the genealogical records which you have in your own home. Clean out buffet drawers, boxes, closets, trunks and the attic. There is no need to sort. Starting at the top of the pile, examine the first item. Read it. Extract its genealogical contents onto worksheets. Completely describe the record and its condition on the calendar. Punch the document, give it an enclosure number and file it in the enclosure file. Enter the enclosure number on the calendar and place the search number and enclosure number on the worksheets taken from that record. Take item 2 from the top of the pile. Examine, read, extract,

describe on the calendar, punch, number and file it in the
enclosure file. Add search and enclosure numbers to the
worksheets. Do the same with the remaining items.

This is the procedure to follow in converting genealogical
collections into orderly, manageable research data. An amazing
amount of information will be "discovered" once it is arranged
onto worksheets, properly described and filed. It does not matter
in what order the records are entered as the system is adequately
cross referenced, indexed and alphabetized for easy access. Pedigree, research notekeeping and genealogical research itself begin
with YOU!

STEP ONE: PRELIMINARY SURVEY

CHAPTER THREE
STEP ONE: PRELIMINARY SURVEY

Chapters One and Two present an introduction to the field of systematic genealogical research; they formally outline the elementary notekeeping skills and the ethical basis for the concepts and procedures which follow. Research consists of five steps, each distinct and important on its own, but each dependent upon the one preceding it. If any step is incorrect or lacking all subsequent steps will be based on incorrect assumptions. These five steps will be considered in detail in the following chapters but let us first give a brief overview of the system as a whole to provide a frame of reference for the discussion of each step.

Step One: Preliminary Survey. The *preliminary survey* is the systematic collection of genealogical information relating to pedigree ancestors and their families which has been previously compiled by others. It is wise to survey the entire pedigree before new research is undertaken. If properly completed, the *survey* will prevent unnecessary duplication, it will provide the foundation for new research and it will discipline you, temper your judgment and season you in the science. Armed with this experience and knowledge, you can properly seek additional evidence on your ancestors.

Step Two: Pre-Search Analysis. Upon completion of the survey, analyze the data collected, decide which pedigree families are complete and correct and divide the pedigree into geographic segments. In the *pre-search analysis,* you define research objectives and outline thoroughly the means of logically reaching them.

Step Three: Outlined Research: A well prepared research outline is the guide to follow for executing searches in all of the sources produced by, for or about ancestoral families. In this step, you carefully gather all of the existing information which pertains to your progenitors.

Step Four: Post-Search Analysis. When the searches, as outlined during the pre-search analysis, have been completed, you perform careful evaluations of the information collected. You compare it with other data in your possession, resolve discrepancies which have arisen and record the conclusions on standard family group forms and pedigree charts. The evidence to substantiate those conclusions is placed in completed case history files.

Step Five: Re-Survey. Pedigree ancestors, newly identified during the post-search analysis are *re-surveyed* in order to outline the next set of research objectives. The whole process begins again.

Throughout these steps, disciplined *research notekeeping* provides the foundation for the entire system. There can be no system without this base; each step is performed by comparing and evaluating the data collected and organized (notekeeping) in the preceding step.

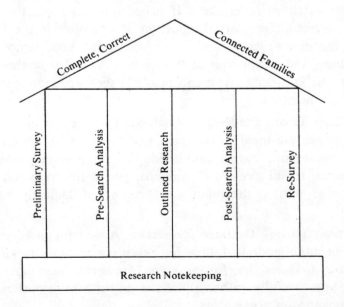

The Preliminary Survey

The first step is the systematic collection of genealogical information on pedigree ancestors and their families compiled by others. You will need names, dates, places, relationships and other identifying facts to establish that these ancestors belong to you.[1]

Survey Objectives

The first and most obvious reason for the *survey* is *to eliminate unnecessary duplication of research.* You determine what others have already collected or compiled relating to your pedigree ancestors. It is most discouraging to perform extensive and often expensive research, only to discover that Uncle Willie had the same data in his possession and would willingly have shared it had he been asked to do so. It is disturbing to pay several hundred dollars to have research performed on one or two ancestral families, only to discover later that other lines come from the same area and the same amount of money must be spent again to gather information on these families. A thorough *preliminary survey,* performed on all pedigree lines before new research is undertaken, will eliminate these problems.

Unfortunately, much effort must be duplicated because others have not preserved the evidence from which their conclusions were drawn. Genealogical information without proper reference to sources of origin is of questionable worth. Unless you can evaluate the conclusions drawn, you should remain skeptical and suspend judgment until they are proven to be true or false. Many ancestral families previously considered complete and correct will be the very ones which demand the greatest amount of research.

A second function of the survey is *to examine printed and manuscript secondary sources* — family and local histories, biographies, historical journals, pedigrees and genealogies. They represent a composite of genealogical conclusions some of which are the result of painstaking research and fully documented. To neglect these would be unwise. Others offer little documentation and little evidence of real research. Too many genealogists, amateur and professional, base their "research" on these secondary sources only, with no attempt to determine the validity of the conclusions set forth. Copying the work of others is important *survey* work, but it is not research.

The third and most important objective of the *preliminary survey* is to provide the researcher with a sound basis upon which a successful research program can be built. You work from the known to the unknown in research, and the *survey* provides the first known data. Only after a thorough *survey* has been completed are you in a strong enough position to outline an effective research program.

Each search of the *preliminary survey*, is defined in terms of jurisdiction, pedigree ancestors and search procedure. The jurisdiction is the creating authority of the records which provide genealogical data. Two kinds of jurisdictions produce *survey* sources — the home jurisdiction and institutional jurisdictions (genealogical societies, hereditary societies and other groups). Both of these must be consulted. Pedigree ancestors are defined as father, mother, grandfather and grandmother — those from whom you are directly descended. The entire family unit of husband, wife and children, however, is also included because these are needed to identify the pedigree ancestors. There are two types of search procedures in genealogy — particular and general. *Particular searches* are selective because they seek individual ancestors in specific sources. *General searches* are comprehensive because they seek all persons bearing the same surname in all the sources within a given, carefully defined geographical area. *Particular search* procedures only are used during the *preliminary survey*. NEVER MAKE A GENERAL SEARCH IN A SURVEY JURISDICTION. Table Two illustrates these dimensions.

Table Two.

Step	Jurisdiction	Names	Search Procedure
Preliminary Survey: Systematic collection of genealogical information concerning pedigree ancestors and their families which has been previously compiled by others	**Home:** Immediate family and friends Close relatives and associates **Institution:** Genealogical societies Hereditary societies Historical societies Archaeological societies Record societies	All pedigree ancestors All pedigree ancestors	Particular searches Particular searches

"Where do I begin my preliminary survey?" With yourself. The *survey,* like *research notekeeping* begins with YOU and is performed on every family represented on the pedigree chart before new research is undertaken.[2] Many genealogists perform surveys piecemeal, visiting relatives and searching sources for one ancestor at a time. This is unnecessarily time consuming. You should obtain data on every pedigree family to which a source refers in one sitting. To search one record six different times for six different pedigree ancestors is unwise, when one search would do for all six. Harrassed relatives and busy record keepers will appreciate such efficiency as well.

"When is my survey complete?" The very notion of re-survey, mentioned earlier as one of the steps in the research cycle, suggests that the *survey* process — locating and searching previously collected and compiled data — never ends. This being the case, how do you know when to end the first *survey* phase and begin the pre-search analysis? There is no absolute indicator; there are, however, several helpful guidelines.

1. Have I exhausted the sources of my immediate family and friends?
2. Have I fully explored the potential of my close relatives and associates?
3. Have I made full use of composite records, indexes and files preserved by institutional jurisdictions with which my ancestors were connected?

4. Have I consulted family and local histories, genealogies and pedigrees located in jurisdictions where my pedigree ancestors lived?

When you can answer these questions in the affirmative, the *survey* is sufficiently completed to permit analysis of the data collected preparatory to research. Perhaps some sources will have been overlooked in the investigation, but a point of diminishing returns should have been reached. Loose ends will become apparent during the pre-search analysis and can be picked up at that time or during the re-survey later.

Survey Outline

Each search undertaken during the *preliminary survey,* no matter how trivial it may seem, should be thoroughly planned *before* it is executed. This plan is called a survey outline. You should list the relatives, friends and associates you plan to visit and the institutions (genealogical societies, hereditary societies, etc.) which are most likely to contain data on your ancestors. You should outline the types of records they have and how you can obtain them. The survey outline pictured below[3] is organized in the proper order for successful searching, with the kinds of records which should be found, already written in. Blanks are left for additional sources you may discover. Armed with this outline, you will accomplish what you desire in an orderly and effective way. Procedures for planning and carrying out *survey* searches as well as detailed instructions on the use of the survey outline as a genealogical tool can be found in Chapters Four and Five.

SURVEY OUTLINE

PEDIGREE ANCESTORS: BIRTH DATE AND PLACE

_____

_____

_____

_____

_____

_____

_____

HOME JURISDICTION: (Immediate Family, Friends, Close Relatives, Associates)

Those I Can Personally Visit	Those I Must Correspond With

HOME SOURCES:

This checklist is a guide to the records you should find in the homes of your relatives. Check (✓) each record you search. Write additional sources you may discover in the empty blanks.

Personal Records —

___Journal
___Diary
___Biography
___Patriarchal Blessing
___Letters
___Seal
___Photographs
___Autograph Album
___Personal Knowledge
___Baby Book
___Wedding Book
___Scrapbooks
___Funeral Book
___Guest Register
___Travel Account
___Treasures of Truth
___Book Plates
___
___
___

Legal Papers —

___Will
___Deeds
___Land Grants
___Water Rights
___Mortgages
___Leases
___Bonds
___Loans
___Contracts
___Summons
___Subpoena
___Tax Notices
___Guardian Papers
___Abstracts of Title
___
___
___

Certificates —

___Birth
___Marriage
___Death
___Divorce
___Adoption
___Graduation
___Christening
___Blessing
___Baptism
___Confirmation
___Ordination
___Transfer
___Ministerial
___Mission Release
___Membership
___Apprenticeship
___Achievement
___Award
___
___

Military Records —

___Service
___Pension
___Disability
___Discharge
___*National Guard*
___Selective Service
___Bounty Award
___Service Medals
___Ribbons
___Sword
___Firearms
___Uniform
___Citations
___Separation Papers
___
___
___

Citizenship Papers —

___Naturalization
___Denization
___Alien Registration
___Deportment
___Passport
___Visa
___Vaccination
___
___
___

School Records —

___Diplomas
___Report Cards
___Honor Roll
___Awards
___Transcripts
___Yearbooks
___Publications
___
___
___

Employment Records —

___Apprenticeship
___Awards
___Graduation
___Citations
___Severance Papers
___Social Security
___Retirement Papers
___Pension
___Union
___Income Tax
___
___
___

Family Records —

___Bible
___Books of Remembrance
___Family Group Sheets
___Pedigrees
___Genealogies
___Temple Record Books
___Family Bulletins
___Family Histories
___Printed Histories
___MS Histories
___Local Histories
___Family Traditions
___"Birth Briefs"
___
___

Announcements —

___Wedding
___Birth
___Death
___Funeral
___Graduation
___Divorce
___Anniversary
___Memorial Cards
___New Job
___Travel
___New Home
___Birthday
___Professional
___Engagement
___
___
___

Newspaper Clippings —

___Announcements
___Obituaries
___Special Events
___Vital Statistics
___Home Town Papers
___Professional
___Trade
___
___
___

Membership Records —

___Cards
___Publications
___Programs
___Uniforms
___Awards
___Certificates
___
___
___

Financial Records —

___Accounts
___Bills
___Receipts
___Check Stubs
___Estate Records
___
___
___

Health Records —

___Xrays
___Insurance Papers
___Hospital Records
___Medical Records
___Immunizations
___
___
___

Licenses —

___Business
___Occupation
___Professional
___Hunting
___Firearms
___Drivers
___Motor Vehicle
___
___
___

Household Items —

___Silverware
___Needlework
___Sampler
___Tapestries
___Dishes
___Friendship Quilt
___Coat of Arms
___Insignias
___Souvenirs
___Clothing
___Tools
___Memorial Rings
___Engraved Jewelry
___
___
___

Books —

___Atlases
___Yearbooks
___Textbooks
___Prizes
___Treasured Volumes
___Vocational
___Foreign Language
___
___
___

INSTITUTIONAL JURISDICTIONS: (Genealogical Societies, Hereditary Societies, Historical Societies, Archaeological Societies, Record Societies)

Consult published indexes and guides to determine which ones have data pertinent to your pedigree ancestors.

INSTITUTIONAL JURISDICTIONS: (Societies, Associations, Libraries, etc.)

INSTITUTION	LOCATION OR ADDRESS	METHOD OF SEARCH (Personal, Researcher Correspondence)	FEES RESTRICTIONS

INSTITUTIONAL SOURCES:

This checklist is a guide to the records you should find in institutional libraries. Check (____) each record you search. Write additional sources you may discover in the empty blanks.

Composite Records:

Always search as part of **survey.**

____Special Indexes
____Family Histories
____Local Histories
____MSS Histories
____Printed Histories
____Genealogies
____Pedigrees
____Biographies
____Heraldry Collections
____Coats of Arms
____Personal Papers
____MSS Collections
____Printed Collections
____Oral History Files
____Periodicals
____Journals
____Proceedings
____Transactions
____
____

Archival Records:

Search only if ancestor was a member of the society.

____
____
____

Membership Records —

____Lists
____Enrollment Books
____Admissions
____Transfers
____Removals
____Terminations
____Disciplinary Proceedings
____Biographies
____Bequests
____Yearbooks
____Bulletins
____Newspapers
____Directories
____Memorials
____Alumni
____
____
____

Administrative Records —

____Minutes
____Histories
____Donations
____Disbursements
____Accounts
____Correspondence
____Charitable Funds
____Insurance Funds
____Scholarship Funds
____Migration Funds
____Refugee Records
____Immigrant Files
____Displaced Persons
____
____

CHAPTER FOUR
PRELIMINARY SURVEY: THE HOME JURISDICTION

Efforts to find information about ancestors and to extend the pedigree should begin in the home jurisdiction. Those who search deepest in home sources have the most success in their research. Records in possession of immediate family members and close relatives are usually the most accessible, the most relevant and the most easily evaluated materials which you can obtain. How often does a family genealogist spend long hours and hundreds of dollars to locate the place of origin of an ancestor when, had he browsed through a relative's attic, he would have found an old letter, journal or diary disclosing the forgotten information? Relatives, both living and dead, have been actively interested in genealogy and possess or have left records of their ancestors. Profit by the information they have collected.

Home jurisdiction research should be done in three stages: immediate family and friends, close relatives and associates and distant relatives and old-timers. Closeness of relatives is based on familiarity, not degree of relationship. Obviously a researcher may be close to a third cousin with whom he grew up while he may be a stranger to his father's brothers and sisters.

The third stage — dealing with distant relatives and old timers who often have little interest in genealogy — should *not* be explored during the course of the *preliminary survey*.[1] There are two reasons: First, the memory needs to be primed like the old hand pump — water must be put in before water will come out. Second, memory is subject to imagination. Unless you have certain facts regarding the family, you have no way to gauge the accuracy of the information you are given. Detailed instructions for consulting distant relatives can be found in Chapter Thirteen, Re-Survey.

The home jurisdiction includes friends and associates of the family. Many genealogists overlook this rich source of information about their people. Think carefully a minute — how much information do you have in your possession about your friends? It is surprising what you know about them. The same thing is true of associates. They often possess information of value for your family history. Consult them in this phase of your research project.

Tradition

Personal knowledge and family traditions, handed down from generation to generation, are essential in solving pedigree problems but they must be used with care. Relationships, traditions and character of family members are considered valid evidence in a court of law. A child usually knows his own parents, brothers and sisters, often aunts, uncles and grandparents. While his knowledge is good evidence of relationship it is unreliable as to dates and events. Such data should always be corroborated with additional information.

Personal knowledge is best obtained through personal contact (interview). Much valuable information is committed to memory and never written down. Get it now! This data is partially lost when memory becomes dim and is completely lost when a person dies. "There is, by God's grace, an immeasurable distance between late and too late." If you wait, you have no way of knowing when it is too late.

Family tradition is an "oral transmission of information, customs, etc., from ancestors to posterity, without written memorials. Something that is handed down from the past." Usually, tradition is enlarged upon and changed, sometimes intentionally, until it becomes entirely different. Tradition is like the parlor game of gossip — passing a message from one person to another. Each telling of the message adds or omits small details until it is totally unlike the original story. Many of these stories through the years become accepted facts.[2] The original story may be affected by language and dialect. Emphasis may be placed on position, wealth or education, while less favorable characteristics or traits are covered up. For these reasons, be careful in accepting Aunt Minnie's account as gospel; she may be repeating an interesting but exaggerated family legend or concealing an old scandal.

Most traditions do contain particles of truth but no matter how accurate and feasible they may seem, they should not be accepted until verified. Record and preserve each family tradition until sufficient evidence exists to evaluate it intelligently, but do not base comprehensive research on such a foundation.

* Evaluate each tradition with the following questions:

    1. Is the time element correct?

    2. Does the tradition conform to data from other sources?

    3. Did the claimed parentage have children?

    4. Do names and localities agree with known facts?

If each question can be answered yes, the tradition is probably based on fact. Use the clues which the tale contains but corroborate the details with other evidence.

Clues

Researchers often overlook valuable clues because they fail to recognize their importance. Genealogically, this can be fatal.[3] A clue is an indirect source which can guide you to additional information or direct sources which will assist in the solution of pedigree problems. In and of themselves, they have no place on a family group form, but they often lead to information that does belong there. Every clue is important and should be duly recorded and preserved. Take them all the first time if possible so the record will not have to be searched again. In extracting data from a source, note that which is actually stated in the record and that which is suggested or implied. These implications are the clues usually overlooked:

    1. Names of relatives interested in genealogical research — family record books, reports and letters to and from paid researchers, receipts and check stubs of payments for documents and searches, family group records, pedigree charts and other records.

    2. Occupation and profession — textbooks, tools, uniforms,

---

*Asterisks signal procedures.

diplomas, certificates, licenses to practice, clothing, education.

3. Reasons for unusual gaps in the births of children — illness, military service, travel, occupation.

4. Military service — medals, ribbons, insignias, swords, firearms, uniforms, pictures.

5. Religious affiliations — crucifix, palm leaves, Bible editions, letters from missionaries, statuary, receipts or check stubs of contributions, bequests, funeral services, friends and associates.

6. Addresses of residence — postmarks, return addresses, deeds, water rights, news clippings, pictures, paintings.

7. Country of origin — letters, language, passports, flags, seals, photographs, paintings, clothes, traditions.

The following document contains many clues which do not fit the names, dates and places slots on a family group record, but they are extremely valuable for identification and further research. Examine the items which are italicized.

To Mrs. Jane Young of Denver, Colorado, April 23, 1863.

Dear Jane,

I promised you *I'd write a bit about my life* and give it to you *for your birthday*. So I am enclosing my attempt. I hope that you have a very happy occasion, my dear.

Rebecca comes about once a week to prepare my laundry and clean the house. She has been a dear. Her *family is growing* and keeps her so busy, I don't know where she gets the time to *care for me too*. But I'm grateful to her.

Spring is here and I must be *getting old* because as I *sit in court* I find my mind wandering and I long to be out in the sun. *Tell the family hello* and *happy birthday*.

Your father,

A. F. Young.

I was born in Augusta County, Virginia in the *Fall* of 1801. My mother, Margaret Kennedy was a *beautiful woman with light brown hair always worn in the latest style.* My father, James Young, whom she married in Virginia, was an *Irishman.* He could *read and write* remarkably well for a man of his day, but he *spoke with a thick brogue.* I remember him as an *affectionate, playful person, extremely kind and compassionate.* He taught us all to be *God-fearing and religious.* He felt *slavery was unjust* and *treated the slaves given him by his father-in-law,* as he *treated the members of his family.* In fact, he *wanted to free them all,* but the economic conditions of the *South* and the plight of those negroes who were freed made this impractical.

As I began to approach manhood, I became obsessed with the *desire to go West. Glorious reports* of the beauties and abundance to be found *in Ohio* were received from many of our *friends and neighbors* who, one by one had left for "greener pastures." When I could stand it no longer, I *sought my father's permission* to go. *Not being 21,* I felt I should not go without it. My mother was quite upset and not easily persuaded. *Uncle* James had some *land in southwestern Ohio* which he wanted *to sell to me.* This was beyond my wildest dream, and finally when father saw he could not change my mind, he agreed to my venture. He insisted that I take his *most able negro* with me to look out for me and to help with work. He also *gave me two horses and money.* With this start and hope in the future *which most youngsters possess,* I was on my . . . (From here to the bottom of the page was so blurred it was not possible to read any further.)[4]

Each of the clues indicated are important and should be noted. As experience is gained, recognition of clues will become almost second nature.

Home Sources

While many sources found in the home are widely known, there are some not so common and therefore, not so widely used.

Let us describe in detail some of the documents found most often and the clues they contain and some which are often overlooked by genealogists or considered to be unimportant.

Family Histories. Researchers are usually careful to spot and use printed histories on their families, but they often neglect to ask for manuscript histories in the possession of family members. Some of these are brief biographical sketches of one husband or wife, others are lengthy folio volumes giving extensive details of the family for several generations. Rare is the family about which at least one history, printed or manuscript, does not exist. Always ask for such materials in each home contact.

Bulletins of Family Organizations. Many families have copies of the bulletins published by their family organizations. These bulletins contain historical and genealogical information on both living and dead relatives. They may be highly secondary but valuable to *survey* work.

Family Bibles. The Bible is the most read, best selling book ever printed. Years ago, it was the prize possession of the family. From it the children were entertained, taught and educated. In it were recorded the important dates and events of family life. Many times this information included data on aunts, uncles, brothers and sisters-in-law as well as immediate family members. Stories of heroism are told in connection with protecting and preserving this valuable record. If a family Bible exists, every means should be used to gain access to it. Extract the data from the regular genealogical section to be sure, but take care not to overlook other items recorded in the margins and on the flyleaves. Scan the book page by page. In this way, you'll be able to get all the data it contains. Always copy the date of publication and note different handwriting and ink. Enter this information on your calendar under description of sources (see following example). These clues indicate when the various items were recorded and will be needed for evaluation.

CALENDAR

(COPYRIGHT 1972, GENEALOGICAL COPY SERVICE)

ENC. NO.	S NO.	DATE OF SEARCH	SOURCE: Description, Condition, Unusual Circumstances, How Searched.	JURISDICTION OR LOCALITY	PERIOD OF TIME	SURNAME OR NAME	RE-SULT
29	31	11 Mar 1962	Personal visit to Dr. George W. Diehl, pastor of Oxford Presbyterian Church, Lexington, Va. He copied Johnston family Bible, property of Miss Roberta Johnston in possession of Mrs. Nettie Huffman. No date, old and worn. Written by several hands. I believe earlier entries added after events, later entries as they occurred.	Home	1770- 1896	Johnson Kennedy	wS nil
	,						

HUSBAND _James Johnston, Sr._

Birth _30 Apr. 1780_ Place ....

Chr. .... Place ....

Death _5 Apr. 1835_ Place ....

Burial .... Place ....

Mar. _17 Dec. 1801_ Place ....

Father .... Mother ....

WIFE _Jane Montgomery_ of ....

Birth .... Place ....

Chr. .... Place ....

Death .... Place ....

Burial .... Place ....

Father .... Mother ....

DOCUMENT DATED: .... RECORDED: ....

Enc # _21_ Search # _31_ Family Line _Johnson_

Home _✓_ Institution.... Township.... Parish.... County....

Municipal.... Local.... District.... State.... National....

Personal Papers ....Census   ....Financial   ....Interview
....Family Records ....Land   ....License   ....Correspondence
....Pedigree   ....Probate   ....Church   ....Researcher
....History   ....Court   ....Employment   ....Original
....Biography   ....Tax   ....Cemetery   _✓_Trans. Copy
....MSS Colls   ....Military   ....School   ....Photo Copy
....Coat of Arms   ....Poor Relief   ....Newspaper   ....Manuscript
....Oral History   _✓_Birth   ....Profession   ....Printed
....Periodical   _✓_Marriage   ....Estate   ....Extract
....Membership   _✓_Death   ....Insurance   ....Legible
....Other   ....Election   ....Shipping   ....Foreign Lang.

Family Bible. Copied by Dr. George
W. Diehl.

Coll # .... Vol. .... Page. .... Date of Search _11 Mar._
_1962_

Male or Female	CHILDREN	WHEN BORN Day Mo. Yr.	WHERE BORN Town	WHERE BORN County	State or Country	DIED Day Mo. Yr.	DIED Place	MARRIED Date	MARRIED Place	MARRIED To
1										
2	[I believe birth date added after event									
3	perhaps marriage also due to									
4	use of "Sr." in birth and marriage									
5	entries]									
6										
7										
8										
9										
10										
11										
12										

Temple Record Books. Before the development of family group sheets, L.D.S. members engaged in research and temple work, made record of the names and other necessary data in temple record books. These were identical to the books used by the temples to record the early ordinances. Sometimes the names were organized in family units, sometimes they were listed individually with the males in one section and females in another. Even though identifying data may be incomplete and in many cases, scanty, these records are extremely valuable. In addition to names of pedigree ancestors, birth dates and places, relationships to family representatives, and other data, the following clues should be noted: date and temple of ordinances, proxies who stood for the persons listed, localities and relationships of other family members, newsclippings, letters, temple slips and other items that may be pasted in the book or loose among its pages. These data will provide information for further searches. Some books contain special sections for endowment records, sealings, patriarchal blessings, church positions held, missions filled and other remarks. Be sure to check the entire book for data. No two are alike in the amount of detail they contain on any one individual and most L.D.S. families have them somewhere.

Family Record Books, Books of Remembrance. These contain the family records and pedigree charts of previous research. You should always ask to see the evidence behind each sheet. Unless the compilor has sufficient evidence to substantiate conclusions on the sheet, the data should be placed on worksheets and saved for analysis when the survey is completed. If such evidence is available examine it carefully to see if the conclusions in the records are warranted. Make note of your investigation on your calendar.

Journals, Diaries and Biographies. The keeping of diaries became generally popular about the sixteenth century, but some have survived from antiquity. A diary is a written account of daily thoughts and passing events usually contemporaneous with their occurrence. Their existence may not be learned until long after the death of the writer.

Diaries are of three types: the regular record kept daily, the periodic record written at intervals and the record written later with the idea of publication in mind. The third kind is often called memoirs. Daily writing differs from periodic recording. The impulsive mood of the moment may cause the writer to make certain observations, which, with the passing of time, are forgotten or dismissed as unimportant. Consider these examples:

12 Feb. 1768: I cannot express the pleasure I have in writing

down my thoughts at the very moment — my opinion of people when I first see them and how I alter or how confirm myself in it — there is something to me very unsatisfactory in passing years without even a memorandum of what you did.

21 June 1810: Thomas Roberts age 17 and Anna King age 14 were married today in Christ Church, and they both ought to be spanked.[5]

Subjects discussed in diaries include: health, food, weather, domestic relationships, religion, travel, social life, celebrities met, gossip and scandal. Each one is different depending upon the personality and interest of the person. To avoid missing clues read a diary carefully, word by word, entry by entry. Note different colored ink, changes in handwriting and irregular periods of entry on your calendar.[6]

Old Letters and Letterbooks. When transportation was costly and difficult, the only contact many family members had was through correspondence. These letters may still exist in someone's drawers, attic or trunk. Letterbooks were convenient "carbon copies." Where both are preserved, the researcher has original letters and replies at his disposal. The envelope, usually thrown away as useless, may be just as important as the letter itself. The date and place from which the letter was written can lead to other sources of information. These appear on the postmark (dating from the sixteenth century), the wax seal, the return address, the back of the letter itself or on a separate sheet of paper in which the letter was wrapped. Ancient clay tablets containing letters and business contracts of early Mediterranean peoples had special clay envelopes to prevent alteration of the original text.[7]

Letters also mention localities and activities of other family members. This information may help trace temporarily lost relatives or retired pedigree ancestors living in the homes of married children many miles from their own place of residence.

Financial Records. These records are most often destroyed as worthless — but they may contain some of the most valuable data and clues found anywhere. Watch for: payments to doctors, mortuaries, hospitals, insurance companies, clubs and organizations, schools, jewelry companies, travel agencies, abstractors and many more. Accounts, donations, premiums and dues are also recorded in an ancestor's papers. The account or receipt does not belong on a family group record but material in the files of these agencies does. Receipts for court fees can often be found and court records, usually unindexed and difficult to search, contain data of value. With the date of the receipt, you can turn quickly to the pertinent case. An account book may contain lists of items bought. In one old ledger was an itemized listing of all the shoes purchased for the family. By studying the sizes and the type of shoe ordered, it was possible to calculate an approximate age for each of the individuals listed.[8]

Daybooks are account-diaries kept by artisans, public officials, storekeepers and others. Their contents vary depending upon the needs and interests of the compilor. For example, the daybook of a physician will contain the names of patients treated, medicines prescribed, money collected and debts outstanding. The daybook of a carpenter-joiner will contain a record of the coffins he makes, the money charged and the payments made. Since these entries are usually dated, they constitute a death register of the members of the community. Vital statistics are difficult to find before state registration begins making these records especially valuable.

Scrapbooks, Babybooks and Wedding Books. These records provide information for complete and correct families. Old scrapbooks will contain newsclippings, pictures, accounts of trips taken and clues for additional searches. Such records are sometimes referred to as commonplace books.

Photographs and Paintings. Photos and paintings can provide clues from which other searches will result, as well as add interest to the drybones of pedigrees. A famous example is Jan Van Eyck's *Wedding of Giovanni Arnolfini* (1434), a wedding certificate in oil. Watch for names and birthdates of subjects inscribed by the artist on the reverse side or displayed subtly on the painting itself.

Names and addresses of photographers and painters, dates when the work was done, names of subjects, physical background of the picture — locality where the picture was taken or the painting made, manner of dress — all these can be important clues to determining military service, profession, service organizations or schools attended. Some paintings, however, have a fabricated background and may not always be indicative of the areas where your ancestors lived. Be sure to look *on the backs* of such sources.

Old Atlases, Yearbooks, Sunday School Prizes, Favorite Books. The bookcases of ancestors and family members hold genealogical treasures too often overlooked by genealogists. Many localities publish atlases at periodic intervals. Local officials sell subscriptions to the inhabitants of the area and obtain advertising and historical data to publish in them. Your relatives have copies of these old and often rare books. Schools and other organizations publish yearbooks. They contain pictures of the individuals but also addresses of residence. Church organizations of all faiths have long rewarded service with special books. In the front of the book will be found the name of the recipient, the year of the award and the organization or individuals presenting the award. This information may help establish religious affiliation of the person involved. Always check books page by page for notations in the margins or on the fly-leaves. If your ancestor loved books and read them often, he may have jotted notes or events of interest to himself and other valuable information on the margins of his books.

Memorial Cards. The custom of announcing the death of an individual with a memorial card is common to most countries. Many items of genealogical value are printed on these cards.

Wedding, Anniversary, Birthday Announcements. Announcements of open houses commemorating special events are popular and have been for some years. Divorce, annulment and breach of engagement are also announced in this way. Watch for these.

Household Items. Silverware, needlework, souvenirs, dishes and other household items provide valuable clues to genealogists as well as archaeologists. Keepsakes are handed from generation to generation with stories behind them. Traditions usually contain a germ of truth and should be noted and preserved. Identifying labels such as insignias, seals, coats of arms and monograms are also important. Legends embroidered on linens for table and boudoir may prove valuable. One of the first items a girl learned to make was a sampler. These contain designs, flowers, scenes and other items today, but a few years ago they contained biographical data as well. For example: "Mary Campbell, age 11. Born July 17, 1804, Hartford, Connecticut. Daughter of Micheal and Martha Campbell" (see example following). Friendship quilts and pillows were also common with the names, dates and often addresses of those who made the individual blocks.

CALENDAR
(COPYRIGHT 1972, GENEALOGICAL COPY SERVICE)

ENC. NO.	S NO.	DATE OF SEARCH	SOURCE: Description, Condition, Unusual Circumstances, How Searched.	JURISDICTION OR LOCALITY	PERIOD OF TIME	SURNAME OR NAME	RE-SULT
	5	10 Apr 1951	Personal visit to Margaret A. Thatcher 410 West 2nd North, Salt Lake City, Utah. Examined sampler made by Mary Campbell. Well preserved under glass in a frame.	Home	17 July 1804	Mary Campbell	ws

HUSBAND Michael Campbell

Birth .... Place ....
Chr. .... Place ....
Death .... Place ....
Burial .... Place ....
Mar. .... Place ....
Father .... Mother ....

WIFE Martha .... of ....

Birth .... Place ....
Chr. .... Place ....
Death .... Place ....
Burial .... Place ....
Father .... Mother ....

DOCUMENT DATED: Apr. 11 [1851] RECORDED:

Enc # .... Search # S .... Family Line Campbell

Home ✓ .... Institution .... Township .... Parish .... County ....
Municipal .... Local .... District .... State .... National ....

Personal Papers .... Census .... Financial .... Interview ....
Family Records .... Land .... License .... Correspondence ....
Pedigree .... Probate .... Church .... Researcher ....
History .... Court .... Employment .... Original ✓
Biography .... Tax .... Cemetery .... Trans. Copy ....
MSS Colls .... Military .... School .... Photo Copy ....
Coat of Arms .... Poor Relief .... Newspaper .... Manuscript ....
Oral History .... Birth ✓ .... Profession .... Printed ....
Periodical .... Marriage .... Estate .... Extract ....
Membership .... Death .... Insurance .... Legible ✓
Other .... Election .... Shipping .... Foreign Lang. ....

Sampler made by Mary Campbell.

Call # .... Vol .... Page .... Date of Search 10 Apr 1851

Male or Female	CHILDREN	WHEN BORN Day Mo. Yr.	WHERE BORN Town	County	State or Country	DIED Day Mo. Yr. Place	MARRIED Date Place To
1	Mary Campbell	17 July 1804	Hartford		Conn		
2							
3							
4							
5							
6							
7							
8							
9							
10							
11							
12							

(COPYRIGHT 1972 GENEALOGICAL COPY SERVICE)

Tools. The tools left behind on the death of an ancestor can be just as valuable as his wife's handwork. They indicate occupations. Places of origin can be determined by the name of the manufacturer or the mark of the artisan. Accounts of the purchase of tools not made locally are also valuable.

Mission Records. Every missionary, regardless of the denomination for which he serves, receives a ministerial certificate or identification of some kind. Upon his release or death, a certificate of release is issued stating the conditions under which he was released and the reason. Letters, pamphlets and newsletters sent home are also valuable.

Health Records. These include dental and medical X-rays, insurance policies, medical examinations, immunization records, hospital records and others. Insurance companies date from the sixteenth century. Social and fraternal units handled insurance or welfare accounts for their members. Vaccination certificates (from the eighteenth century on) contain name, address, signature, date of birth, sex and sometimes marital or professional status. They were issued for smallpox, yellow fever, cholera, typhoid, plague and polio. They may also contain next of kin and general health of the person.

Vital Statistics Certificates. These certificates contain varying amounts of information according to the locality in which the event occurred. Even though they are usually prepared at or near the time of the event they frequently contain errors. Finding them in the home will save trying to locate them later.

Church Sacrament (Ordinance) Certificates. Christening, blessing, baptism, confirmation, membership, transfer from one congregation to another and many others are available in home jurisdictions. They supply exact dates of birth, marriage and death, when vital statistics are not available.

Newsclippings. Items from newspapers found in the home are clipped because of their reference to family members or friends. Notices of births, marriages, deaths, appointments to important positions, affiliations with organizations and removal from the area are the items most frequently found. Be sure to watch for old newspapers used to line drawers, pad mattresses and rugs. Family members often subscribe to newsheets and papers published in the areas where they previously resided so watch the identification of the papers which you find.

Legal Papers. Wills, land grants, deeds, abstracts of title, mortgages, leases, bonds, water rights, tax notices, court summons, adoption papers and others are to be found in the home. They have legal significance and are carefully preserved. You have heard the cry: "The courthouse burned down and there are no records." For the most part, the records found in the county courthouse are *recorded copies* only. Only these copies have been destroyed; the originals exist, or did exist, in someone's home. Particularly valuable are unrecorded wills and deeds made by an ancestor but unacceptable to the court for filing.

Military Records. Many kinds of military records are to be found in the homes of servicemen. Watch for service records, pension records, disability records, discharge records and bounty papers. Valuable clues are service ribbons, insignias, medals, uniforms and pictures. Clues to regiments, service files and dates of service are obtained from these and provide for easier access to government military files.

Apprenticeship Records. In most countries of the world, apprenticeship provided training for young boys in skilled trades and young girls in domestic pursuits. The training usually lasted seven years and included reading, writing and ciphering. Documents created by this program contain occupations, ages, parents, schooling and other valuable items. Frequently, boys ended their service by marrying the master's daughter. Missing maiden surnames can sometimes be found by investigating records pertaining to the master with whom a boy served apprenticeship.

Citizenship Records. Passports, visas and naturalizations are valuable for establishing countries of origin of ancestors. Since 1906, in the United States, they are confidential records and sometimes difficult to obtain. Originals are in the home and will provide the needed information.

Licenses. Professional and business licenses issued by churches and by civil authorities can be most valuable. Originals are to be found in the home.

School Records. An indication of the extent and type of education that your ancestors received will be found in diplomas (charters), textbooks, yearbooks, alumni bulletins, report cards, scholastic and athletic awards, transcripts of credit, sliderules and other items. Most families preserve these. Watch for handwritten textbooks and workbooks designed for teaching, made or written by a schoolmaster or teacher.

Procedure

The researcher engaged in a *preliminary survey* should proceed with home jurisdiction searches in a systematic way.

* Search your own home for all items of genealogical value first. Organize these materials so they are readily accessible and you know what you have (see Chapter Two). Use the list of home sources in the survey outline (pages 35-37) as a guide.

* List the names and birth dates of your pedigree ancestors at the top of the outline. Then list the names and addresses of immediate family members and close relatives with whom you have had previous contact. Divide the list into "those whom I can personally visit" and "those with whom I must correspond." Be sure to include friends and associates of the family who might possess pertinent genealogical data.

Personal Visits

Personal visits to relatives are more successful than correspondence and should be made whenever possible. Seeing the records in person will enable you to get more information because a relative, unaware of what is important, may overlook data of value. Visits to relatives living many miles away can often become a regular part of family vacations. Mutual affection and stronger family ties usually result.

* Plan your visit in advance. Contact the relative and arrange a definite time to call. Explain the reason for coming so he can be prepared to help you.

* Outline the information you need and the sources most likely to yield that data. The survey outline can serve as a guide. The following questions can be used for interviewing relatives about themselves or about the lives of your ancestors.[9]

1. History and Family Background:

Who was the first immigrant? When and from what country?

Did any family members serve in the military? War? Rank?

What Church did your family attend?

Who was the first convert to the Church? When? Where?

Do you know of any family members who have done genealogy?

Was any temple work performed for the family? By whom? When?

What family traditions do you know?

Do you know of any special family celebrations or gatherings?

2. Parents:

When and where were your parents born?

How did they meet? When and where were they married?

What occupation did your father pursue?

What type of education did they have?

When and where did your parents die? Where are they buried?

Who were their brothers and sisters? Order of their birth?

3. Childhood and Home Life:

When and where were you born? Incidents connected with birth?

Who are your brothers and sisters and when were they born?

Do you have any special remembrances of your grandparents?

How many times have you moved and where have you lived?

Who were your neighbors? Playmates?

What responsibilities did you have in the home?

What was your home like?

Have you ever been involved in a fire, flood, accident? What?

What illnesses have you had?

4. Education:

What schools did you attend? How many years? College?

Who were your favorite teachers and subjects?

What school activities did you participate in?

5. Church Activities:

Where do you go to Church? How long have you
attended?

What positions have you held? Mission filled?

Have you had any faith promoting incidents? Prayers
answered?

6. Marriage and Family Life:

Where and how did you meet the one you married?

What kind of person is your spouse? When and where
born? Parents?

When and where were you married?

Where was your first home?

Where have you lived since your marriage and for how
long?

How many children do you have? What are their names
and ages?

What special events have occurred in their lives?

What were your thoughts when your first child was
born?

7. Business and Social Life:

What special talents or hobbies do you have?

What is your occupation? Do you like your work?

How did you feel when you received your first pay check?

Did you take any remembered trips or vacations?

What do you think is the most important incident or
achievement in your life?

What do you want out of life? What are your goals?

What successes and failures have you had?

What person, more than any other, has influenced your
life?

* Take a good supply of worksheets and a tape-recorder. Be
sure you know how to operate it properly. Nothing is more
discouraging than to depend upon a recorder and later to
discover it was not working. Recorders can be rented very
reasonably by the day, week or month if you do not have
one of your own. There is no need to take previously compiled family group records, calendars, or documents with
you. The reason for going is to get information, not to compare it. Nothing should be accepted or rejected at this
point. This will be done later when the *survey* is completed.

* Remember that the personal knowledge of the relative is different from the documents in his possession. As you talk with your relative ask him, "Do you have any documents to support your comments?" Preserve both his answers and the data from his documents separately, each with its own calendar entry and its own worksheets.

* Extract the genealogical data on your pedigree families directly onto worksheets or record them on tape. Preserve these notes for future analysis. You never know when some obscure statement becomes the key item in identification. Do not trust your memory. When you return home, file your worksheets alphabetically, describe all of the sources searched on the calendar, carefully distinguishing between personal knowledge and documentary information. Then file any documents, pictures or other material that you may have been given in the enclosure file. If the interview was recorded on tape, transcribe it, extract pertinent data to worksheets, describe on calendar and file the transcription as an enclosure.

* Watch for every possible clue. Try not to overlook anything. The successful researcher is a master detective.[10]

* Don't overtire your relatives. It is better to hold several short sessions than one long one. If the relative is an elderly person, there is more likelihood that his memory may lose its sharpness; yet he may know much information of value. Ample time should be given to recall this data. An association with historical dates and events may help to provide the required link with the past.

* Ask your relatives for names and addresses of other family members and friends whom you can contact for information and add these to your survey outline. Home jurisdiction contacts should not become exhausted. In this age of chain reactions, you should do everything possible to create a chain reaction in your contacts. If names and addresses of others are obtained in every instance, it is almost impossible to exhaust the potential of this jurisdiction.

* Conduct the visit with friendliness and a spirit of cooperation. Your relatives will be more willing to share what they

have. 1) Be more interested in the living than the dead. Realize that you are making an imposition with even the smallest request; your relatives do not have to help you. It does not flatter anyone's ego to begin prying into all the family closets without making any inquiry at all concerning the living person or his family. Such an attitude conveys to the relative, that to become a point of interest, he must be dead and in his grave. This is very poor psychology. Why should people be interested in you if you are not interested in them? 2) Make them more curious than suspicious. Genealogical data are the most private and confidential items in a relative's life. Realize that the gathering of such data will be difficult without first obtaining the confidence of the person. People react to every situation with curiosity or with suspicion. Just as the suspicious person will leave no facility unused to insure his security, so the curious person is often foolhardy when seeking to satisfy his curiosity. 3) Offer to share whatever information you have now or you may fall heir to in the future. And keep that promise. People are more willing to cooperate if they think they might get something in return. 4) *Do not ask to borrow their treasures.* Put yourself in the place of the family member. What would your reaction be under similar circumstances? You would not think of allowing him to take your records, so do not ask to take his.

Corresponding with Relatives

Corresponding with relatives you are unable to visit requires many of the rules outlined above, but some special suggestions may help you get better results.[11] The first rule of correspondence is *put yourself in the place of the person to whom the letter is sent.* Ask yourself, "What kind of letter would I be likely to answer?"

* Make letters clean and attractive in their appearance. Letters written in pencil or colored ink, scribbled in haste on crumpled paper, naturally create a bad impression. A typewritten letter or one written legibly in black or blue-black ink on a good grade of paper is likely to command the respect of the person reading the letter. Avoid letterheads when contacting persons unknown to you. They may scare the elderly, backwoods relative whom you wish most to contact.

* Be courteous in your letters. Do not demand information. Ask politely, in such a way as to indicate to the reader that you are asking a favor and express appreciation for any cooperation given. Enclose an addressed envelope and sufficient postage for a reply. In the United States and Canada, stamps will do; for foreign countries, buy international reply coupons from the post office which can be redeemed for the proper postage in that country.

* Be clear and concise. If your reader doesn't understand what you want, he cannot help you. Ask for what you want in unmistakable terms. Relatives have little time to read rambling letters, several pages long; they usually end up in the wastebasket, unanswered. Be concise but not abrupt.

* Be helpful. If you ask for several items of information, number the items: 1, 2, 3. This will make the letter much easier to read and answer. Make it convenient for even the busiest person to acknowledge your letter.

* Be reasonable. Know what your request involves. Do not ask for the impossible. Do not expect a relative to send you all the information he has. Know something about your request before you make it.

* Plan your letter carefully. Write an outline, then a rough draft and finally, a final copy. Go over it item by item before you type the final version. People will judge you by your letters. Use correct form, punctuation, spelling and sentence construction.

* *Do not use form letters.* They lack warmth and personality and they limit the amount of information that you receive. Letters that produce results are those that make the recipient feel important — essential to the success of your endeavor — and this cannot be done with a dittoed, mimeoed, or lithoed letter. Personal letters take more time but they get better results.

* Keep a carbon copy of all letters in a suspense file. When a reply is received, clip it and any accompanying data to this carbon, punch it, number it in sequence and file it in the enclosure file. All genealogical data it contains should be extracted to worksheets and a complete description of the

action entered on the calendar. The suspense file should be checked periodically and all correspondence older than 60 days should be followed-up with a second reminder or marked "unanswered" and permanently filed in the enclosure file.

Unknown Relatives Actively Engaged in Genealogical Research

Relatives, unknown to you, who are actively engaged in genealogy and who may have done extensive research on common ancestry lines should be contacted at this point. To reserve this group for the re-survey would result in unnecessary duplication.

* Check query sections of local publications discussed in greater detail in Chapter Six. Collective genealogical groups often serve as clearing houses for work being done. The American Institute of Genealogy, organized in Chicago a few generations ago, was one of these. Check Frederick A. Virkus, *Handbook of American Genealogy,* for who was who in Genealogy and for lists of genealogists doing research in the 1930's. The Genealogy Club of America (Mendon, Utah) and the International Genealogical Directory, founded by Charles A. Bernau in 1907, are current clearing houses.[12] The *Genealogical Helper* (Logan, Utah), May and November issues, lists genealogists and the families they are working on. The Pedigree Referral Service of the Genealogical Society of Utah (Salt Lake City) was instituted to prevent duplication of research by bringing people working on lines of common ancestry together. The response was not as great as expected and the service has been discontinued. Those registrations which were sent, however, are available in computer print-outs at the Genealogical Society Library.

CHAPTER FIVE
PRELIMINARY SURVEY:
INSTITUTIONAL JURISDICTIONS

The second step in the *preliminary survey* encompasses the use of composite and archival collections preserved by genealogical societies, hereditary or lineage societies, historical, archaeological and record societies. Some of these are nationally organized with local units on state, district, county or town level; others are international in scope. Some are organized as commercial ventures and some by subscription on a private basis. Their functions and membership lists include people from all backgrounds and walks of life and they frequently overlap with persons belonging to more than one society at the same time. The published indexes to their records and publications are easily accessible in most research libraries.

We owe institutional jurisdictions a tremendous debt for their preservation efforts. In many cases, they are the only detour between the creator of the records and the local dump. Unfortunately, their mortality rate, especially local societies, is appalling. It would be appropriate for anyone making an imposing request on a local society, which does not have the backing of government funds, to enclose a contribution. This need not apply to letters of general inquiry concerning the source potential or physical facilities provided by the group where a stamped, self-addressed envelope is usually sufficient.

Genealogical Societies compile and preserve pedigrees, genealogies and family histories. They sponsor instruction classes, informative lectures and visits to record archives. They maintain rosters of persons currently active in genealogy to bring those with common lines of ancestry together for cooperative effort. Two notable examples are the Genealogical Society of Utah (Salt Lake City) and the Society of Genealogists (London).

Hereditary (Lineage) Societies require pedigrees for membership. The burden of proof is placed on the applicant but claims are allowed on the knowledge of the organizational staff. They are found throughout the world. The Daughters of the American Revolution (U.S.A.) and the Order of the Crown of Charlemagne (International) are well known. Not so well known are numerous family organizations. An outstanding one is the Thomas Tolman family with some 10,000 members scattered throughout the United States. It employs several family members as full time genealogists to gather the history of the family.

Historical Societies preserve and perpetuate the history of the area. They are supported by funds from the civil government, from church organizations and from private sources. The members collect and preserve historical records, mark historical sites and graves, and publish books and periodicals. The Virginia Historical Society (Richmond, Va.) and the Historical Society of Lancashire and Cheshire are examples. Church, ethnic and racial historical societies are oriented more narrowly toward a specific field or cultural group.

Archaeological (Antiquarian) Societies are dedicated to the collection and preservation of material remains of past human life. They conduct digs and restore ancient dwellings to as near their original condition as they can. They maintain libraries and publish bulletins. Some have been instrumental in discovering valuable records long hidden and thought to be non-existent. The Nauvoo Restoration Committee, organized to restore the city of Nauvoo, Illinois to nineteenth century Mormon glory, is one such group. Another is the Society of Antiquaries of London which dates from 1707.

Record societies publish numerous volumes of indexed records. Examples include the British Record Society (London) which publishes indexes and calendars to English probate records and the Monumental Brass Society which prints transcripts and facsimiles of numerous brasses in the churches of England.

Institutional Sources

The records preserved by institutional jurisdictions are divided into two categories for convenience in study: composite records and archives.

Composite Records

Genealogical data compiled by others and assembled for reference in libraries of genealogical and historical societies are called composite records. They include both printed volumes and manuscript collections. These records are second-hand accounts of people and events compiled after the deaths of the people and events described. There is a tendency to avoid secondary materials because of their reputation for inaccuracy and error. It is true that many deserve such an evaluation but many are compiled after careful research and are meticulously documented. In either case, secondary sources do have specific value for genealogy: First, secondary works often contain verbatim transcriptions or extracts of documents which have been destroyed. These represent the only existing copies. H. M. Wilson's *Tinkling Spring: Headwater of Freedom*, contains a list of monumental inscriptions from the cemetery adjoining the Tinkling Spring Church in Augusta County, Virginia. Some of the stones are now missing; these printed inscriptions are all that remain. The evidence which they give should be evaluated as a transcription or extract and corroborated by other evidence before they are accepted as valid, but to omit them because of possible error is unwise.

Second, genealogists must work from the known to the unknown. Secondary accounts contribute to the first known information. If these known data are incorrect or based on shoddy research, all succeeding searches are jeopardized. If they are carefully documented, you can use them to begin your own work. Be careful, however, not to read into evidence already compiled, conclusions that it will not support, just to avoid re-doing the work. Let secondary accounts contribute to the known data from which you move into the unknown, but do not let them be the deciding element. If warranted, be willing to duplicate previous research to provide the soundest possible base.

Third, secondary sources can serve as partial indexes to otherwise unindexed collections of original sources. Most histories include indexes to the transcriptions of sources they contain. Use them to understand the sources but realize that such indexes are rarely complete guides to the originals.

Finally, histories and biographies provide a setting in which to place contemporary documents. They give detailed descriptions of the area and the people who lived there. Documents cannot be readily located for searching without knowledge of creating authorities nor can they be understood when separated from the context in which they were produced. Let secondary sources provide this basic understanding.

Pedigrees and Genealogies. Today, pedigrees and genealogies are distinct types of lineage but a few generations ago, they were used interchangeably. Pedigrees record lines of ancestry. They frequently show one line of descent only, the male or female line. The following is an example:

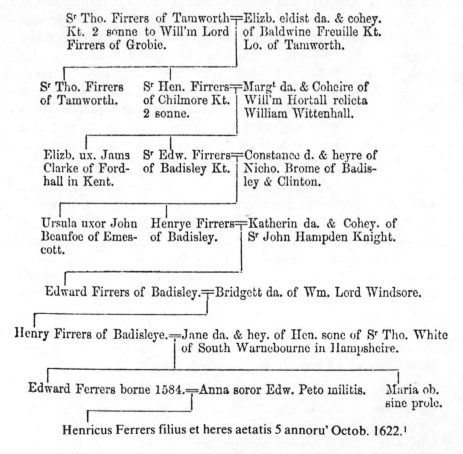

Sʳ Tho. Firrers of Tamworth⹀Elizb. eldist da. & cohey.
Kt. 2 sonne to Will'm Lord │ of Baldwine Freuille Kt.
Firrers of Grobie. │ Lo. of Tamworth.

Sʳ Tho. Firrers   Sʳ Hen. Firrers⹀Margᵗ da. & Coheire of
of Tamworth.   of Chilmore Kt. │ Will'm Hortall relicta
                 2 sonne. │ William Wittenhall.

Elizb. ux. Jams   Sʳ Edw. Firrers⹀Constance d. & heyre of
Clarke of Ford-   of Badisley Kt. │ Nicho. Brome of Badis-
hall in Kent. │ ley & Clinton.

Ursula uxor John   Henrye Firrers⹀Katherin da. & Cohey. of
Beaufoe of Emes-   of Badisley. │ Sʳ John Hampden Knight.
cott.

Edward Firrers of Badisley.⹀Bridgett da. of Wm. Lord Windsore.

Henry Firrers of Badisleye.⹀Jane da. & hey. of Hen. sone of Sʳ Tho. White
                          │ of South Warnebourne in Hampsheire.

Edward Ferrers borne 1584.⹀Anna soror Edw. Peto militis.   Maria ob.
                                                            sine prole.

Henricus Ferrers filius et heres aetatis 5 annoru' Octob. 1622.[1]

Pedigrees have been required since the fifteenth century for membership in hereditary and lineage societies and to determine the right to own a coat of arms. Many of these are available in print; many still exist only in manuscript. For example, the lineage records of the National Society of the Daughters of the American Revolution and the National Society of Mayflower Descendants are published in many volumes. They are easy to consult because they are well-indexed and found in most research libraries. Even though they appear in print, the ancestors on such pedigrees are *assumed* ancestors only until they are verified with other sources. During the sixteenth and seventeenth centuries, families newly enriched from commercial enterprises and exploitation of the New World, sought genealogical support for their new position and numerous pedigrees were compiled. Most of these have never been published. Collections of these manuscript pedigrees are to be found in the College of Arms (London), in the British Museum (London), in the Bodleian Library (Oxford) and in the Society of Genealogists Library (London).[2]

Genealogies compiled a few generations ago may show the descent of families from a common ancestor or they may be in the form of short narratives, cross-referenced from one to the other. The following is an example:[3]

John Tindal, B.D., native of Kent, rector of Beer Ferris, Devon. *Bur.* Jan. 25, 1674.

Matthew, LL.D., Fellow of All Saints, Oxford, author of *Christianity as Old as the Creation*. *B.* circ. 1657. *D.* 1733.

John, of Cornwood, Devon, Clerk. = Elizabeth, da. of Nicholas Prideaux, President of the Council of Barbadoes.

   Elizabeth, = Robert Forster, rector of Plymstock, Devon.

   Nathaniel, D.D., and others.

NICHOLAS TINDAL (subject of this memoir). *B.* 1687. *D.* 1774. = (1) Anne, da. of John Keate, of Hagborn, Berks. = (2) (Aug. 11, 1753) Elizabeth (?), da. of I. Gugelman, Capt. of Invalids.* (No children.)

John, rector of Chelmsford. *D.* Feb. 2, 1774. = (May 9, 1738) Mary, eldest da. of Rev. Oliver Pocklington, rector of Chelmsford.

George, Capt. R.N. = (Mar. 14, 1748) Diana, 3rd da. of same Rev. O. Pocklington.

James, Capt. 4th Dragoons. = Lucy, da. of Sam. Shenton, Clerk.

Nicolas, *Bapt.* Feb. 18, 1741. *Bur.* Aug. 20, 1741.

Anna Maria, *Bapt.* Feb. 18, 1750. *Bur.* April 29, 1810. = John Morgan, rector of Chelmsford. (Eight children or more.)

Thomas, *Bapt.* July 25, 1752. *Bur.* April 14, 1753.

George, *Bapt.* Jan. 12, 1749. *Bur.* Oct. 18, 1777.

Robert, *Bapt.* June 2, 1750. Attorney. = Sarah, da. of John Pocock, of Greenwich.

Diana, *Bapt.* May 8, 1751. *Bur.* April 30, 1806.

Catherine, *Bapt.* June 15, 1753.

Nicolas, *Bapt.* May 31, 1756. *Bur.* April 17, 1757.

Thomas, *Bapt.* June 17, 1759, 11, 1760.

William, *Bapt.* June 8, 1756. *Bur.* Feb. 21, 1800.

Anne. Louisa.

Marianne Elizabeth, *Bapt.* Sept. 5, 1775.

Nicholas Cunningham,† *B.* Dec. 12, 1776. *D.* July 6, 1846. Lord Chief Justice.

Robert, *Bapt.* Dec. 18, 1778. *Bur.* Aug. 31, 1785.

Sarah, *Bapt.* Mar. 18, 1780.

John Pococke, *Bapt.* Aug. 27, 1781.

Thomas, *B.* 1783. *Bapt.* April 26, 1784.

Jane, *Bapt.* April 26, 1784.

George, *Bapt.* Feb. 11, 1785.

Charles, *Bapt.* Oct. 31, 1786.

Sally, *Bapt.* Mar. 27, 1789.

Robert,‡ *Bapt.* Nov. 10, 1790.

Clariana Isabella, *Bapt.* Oct. 1, 1792.

"Aug. 11, 1753, Nicholas Tindal, rector of Alverstoke, Hants, a chaplain of Greenwich Hospital, and Judith Gugelman, *mar.* at the Chapel of the Royal Hospital."—Greenwich Register.
† So spelt in Chelmsford Register. ‡ Mary, an infant, *bur.* May 29, 1772, possibly comes in here.

These genealogies are usually indexed with pedigrees or listed with family histories in standard bibliographies. Genealogies compiled today are organized into family units. Unless they show clearly the sources from which they were compiled, they should not be accepted as valid until they have been proved.

The following select list will provide access to pedigree and genealogy collections (printed and manuscript) in England. Those for America are included in the references on pages 74–79 below.

Bridger, Charles. *An Index to Printed Pedigrees Contained in County and Local Histories, Heralds' Visitations and in the More important Genealogical Collections.* London: John Russell Smith, 1867.

Nicolas, Sir Nicholas Harris. *Catalogue of the Heralds' Visitations with References to Many Other Valuable Genealogical and Topographical Manuscripts in the British Museum.* 2nd ed. London: James Taylor, 1825.

Cope, S. T. "Heraldry, Flags and Seals: A Select Bibliography with Annotations, 1920-45," *Journal of Documentation,* IV (1948-49), 92-146. Also printed separately, London: Aslib, 1948.

Geijer, E. N. "Printed Visitations and County Pedigrees," *Genealogists Magazine,* VI (1933), 194, 258, 314, 350.

"Handlist of Sources for Heralds' Visitations Pedigrees," *Family History,* I (1962), 19-30.

Harleian Society. Heralds' Visitations. Many Volumes.

"Index to Names to the Pedigrees in Harleian Manuscripts in the British Museum." Add. Mss 9805.

Lancour, Harold. "Heraldry: A Guide to Reference Books," *New York Public Library Bulletin,* XLII (1938), 851-56.

Moule, Thomas. *Bibliotheca Heraldica Magnae Britanniae: An Analytical Catalogue of Books on Genealogy, Heraldry . . . with a List of Provincial Visitations, Pedigrees . . .* London: 1822. Reprinted, London: Heraldry Today, 1966. Supplement printed in *Herald and Genealogist,* II and III. Moule's copy in the British Museum has his numerous handwritten additions.

Sims, R. *Index to the Pedigrees and Arms Contained in the Heralds' Visitations in the British Museum.* London: John Russell Smith, 1849. Reprinted, Baltimore: Genealogical Publishing Co., 1970.

Wagner, A. R. *The Records and Collections of the College of Arms.* London: For the Author, 1952.

——————————————. "The Dictionary of British Arms," *Antiquaries Journal,* XXI (1941), 299-322; XXIII (1943), 42-47.

Histories. Genealogical researchers should examine printed and manuscript histories related to the pedigree during the *preliminary survey.* These histories can be valuable genealogical sources *when used properly*, but they represent conclusions and must be evaluated as such.

There are two main types of histories: *Local histories* containing historical data on the jurisdiction itself and genealogical data on the inhabitants of the area. Many people overlook historical material during the *survey,* but they are cheating themselves of essential information when they do.[4] Most local histories give valuable biographical material on the people of the area, living and dead. National, state, shire, county, district, parish, town, church, monastic, cathedral, hospital, honor, manor, university, castle, hundred, district and palace histories pertinent to the pedigree should be consulted. Many are multi-volume sets with the historical treatment in the first volume or two and the remaining volumes devoted to biographies of the people. *Family (surname) histories* are compiled in several ways: 1) story form with genealogical data included as part of the biographical and historical narrative, 2) family group form with each family separately listed in chronological order and with brief genealogical details on each member and 3) pedigree form with only the line of descent shown.

Histories have been written to settle tithe disputes; to spread propaganda for the government or a wealthy patron; to glorify a family of humble origins; to outline improvements needed by a town — paving, lighting or draining of swampland; to provide a heritage as old and illustrious as the Italian cities founded by Rome; to publicize the products and beauty of a local area; to defend one's home, family or university against attack by other writers; to provide a tourist guide for a local castle, palace or country seat; to establish greater antiquity; or simply to describe one's affection or pride for family or locality.

The titles selected for histories vary and are often confusing but they usually contain similar information. Such words as cosmography, chorography, antiquity, topography, natural history, survey, description, account and view are used for local histories. They include descriptions of manners and customs, agricultural and trade production, physical features and geography, government origins and practices, statistics and population figures, curiosities of nature and art, cultural and religious heritage, historical events and legends.

Local and family histories also contain many unexpected surprises: manuscript histories compiled by others are transcribed and indexed; glossaries of terms, long since forgotten; catalogues and calendars of manuscript collections; rolls of arms, pedigrees and visitations. Transcripts of civil and ecclesiastical documents, deeds, wills and monumental inscriptions, parish registers, monastic cartularies and numerous other documents, many no longer in existance, are included (see sample calendar following). Many early histories are quite often the materials from which history is written — documents — rather than history itself. Local historians and genealogists of a few generations ago, could include these items in their publications because of lower costs of printing. They deserve recognition for preserving these materials.

CALENDAR
(COPYRIGHT 1972, GENEALOGICAL COPY SERVICE)

ENC. NO.	S NO.	DATE OF SEARCH	SOURCE: Description, Condition, Unusual Circumstances, How Searched.	JURISDICTION OR LOCALITY	PERIOD OF TIME	SURNAME OR NAME	RE-SULT
22	31	18 May 1970	Tinkling Spring: Headwater of Freedom by Howard M. Wilson, published by the Tinkling Spring and Hermitage Presbyterian Churches, Angusta County, Va. 1954. Call # 975.5 B4 Genealogical Society Library, Salt Lake City. Well documented. Gives locations of records used.	Angusta County Va.	1752- 1952	Johnson Kennedy Berry Eakle	ws ws ws nil
			→ Note: Mss Collections (176 pieces) for history of Zachariah Johnston are located in Virginia State Library. 626 items and 7 Volumes of papers of Zachariah and Thomas Johnston in Duke University Library. Ms 63-102. Have searched or get copies.		1717- 1858		

HUSBAND William Johnston of ....

Birth........................ Place........................

Chr........................ Place........................

Death........................ Place........................

Burial........................ Place........................

Mar........................

Father........................ Mother........................

[Father and Mother of Zachariah Johnston]

WIFE Ann .... of ....

Birth........................ Place........................

Chr........................ Place........................

Death........................ Place........................

Burial........................ Place........................

Father........................ Mother........................

DOCUMENT DATED: 1 June 1747 .... RECORDED: ....

Enc # ... 22 ...... Search # ... 31 ... Family Line .... Johnston ......

Home........ Institution........ Township........ Parish........ County.✓

Municipal........ Local........ District........ State........ National........

Transfer to Tinkling Spring Church.

Figure XXIII. Facing Pag. 226.

Call # .... Vol .... Page .... Date of Search 18 May 1970

Male or Female	CHILDREN	WHEN BORN Day Mo. Yr.	WHERE BORN Town	County	State or Country	DIED Day Mo. Yr. Place	MARRIED Date Place To
1	[signed] John Caldwell						
2	James Bohanen						
3	David Patterson						
4							
5	lived in Notingham [Pa.] Congregation for 2 years						
6	in full Christeen priveleges						
7	departure from al guiltie Scandall or Church Cens'a knoen						
8							
9							
10							
11							
12							

Some volumes were "grangerized;" that is, pictures, wood cuts and prints were cut out of one volume to enrich another. These grangerized copies (named after James Granger) are often to be found in local libraries and other record depositories. Some histories were published with blank pages (called interleaving) so owners could add manuscript comments, criticisms, corrections and additions as they studied the work. Some local histories are the products of the historical tour — a field trip taken into the countryside to personally observe topography, buildings, monuments, industrial and farm activities and to interview local inhabitants. These can be extremely valuable, especially if the original notes taken on the tour are preserved. In several instances, the local historian did not live long enough to write a finished work and all that is left are his raw notes. Examples include John Leland (d. 1552), and his *Itineraries*, William Worcestre (d. 1484) and his *Itineraries* and Sampson Erdeswicke (d. 1603) and his *Observations of Cumberland and Northumberland.*[5]

Victoria County Histories. This project was begun in 1899. Bedfordshire, Berkshire, Buckshire, Hampshire, Hertfordshire, Huntingdonshire, Lancashire, Northamptonshire, Rutland, Surrey, Warwickshire, Worcestershire and Yorkshire (North Riding) are complete. Northumberland and London have their own projects — several volumes have been issued to date for these two counties. The other counties have partial coverage or are still to be started. Each county is a separate unit with sections on geology, natural history, topography, archaeology, prehistory, Domesday Book (English translations are included in each case), place-names, general political and social background, agriculture, industry, population, genealogies and land holdings of the major families of the county. Accuracy and emphasis depend upon the contributors because it is a massive cooperative venture of several hundred volumes. Nevertheless, it is a true monument of English research and considered to be generally accurate and quite thorough.[6]

Locating histories is sometimes a problem.[7] Some were published serially in numbers (weekly installments of five to twenty pages each) for a few pence a number and then issued in book form. They were published in monthly installments in local periodicals or newspapers. Some family histories were privately printed by the family and circulated only to family members. These must be found in family collections (home sources). Some exist in a single manuscript copy from which the title page and other portions are often missing. Many were printed in limited editions and only a few copies have survived. Some were printed in part only, because the task which the author set for himself was so large it took a lifetime to complete, and his lifetime was too short. It is not unusual to find an author spent some ten to forty years collecting data to write a county history.[8]

The following guides and indexes will be helpful in locating both family and local histories. Remember the many histories quoted in part or completely transcribed in local periodicals (see below).

General Bibliographies

Beers, Henry P. *Bibliographies in American History: Guide to Materials for Research.* New York: H. W. Wilson Co., 1942.

Berkowitz, David S. *Bibliographies for Historical Researchers.* Trial ed. N. p., The Compiler, 1969. Preliminary publication of his *Bibliotheca Bibliographia Britannica: A Manual of Bibliographies of Bibliography.* 5 vols. Waltham, Mass.: Privately Printed, 1968.

Besterman, Theodore. *A World Bibliography of Bibliographies.* 5 vols. London: Theodore Besterman, 1947. Several subsequent editions.

British Museum. *Catalogue of Printed Books.*

——————————. *Subject Catalogue.* 1888 to date.

British National Bibliography. A List of all books published in Great Britain. Annual since 1950.

Coulter, Edith M. and Gerstenfeld, Melanie. *Historical Bibliographies: A Systematic and Annotated Guide.* Berkeley: University of California, 1935.

Library of Congress. *National Union Catalogue.*

——————————. *Printed Card Catalogue.*

——————————. Subject Catalogues. 1950 to date.

Pownall, David E. "English-American Serial Bibliographies," *RQ,* VIII (1968), 75-105.

Taylor, Archer. *Book Catalogues: Their Variety and Uses.* Chicago: Newberry Library, 1957.

——————————. *Catalogues of Rare Books.* Lawrence: University of Kansas Press, 1958.

Walford, Albert J., *et. al. Guide to Reference Material.* London: Library Association, 1959. Supplement, 1963.

Wilson, H. W. Co. *Bibliographic Index: Cumulative Bibliography of Bibliographies.* New York: H. W. Wilson, Co., 1938 to date.

Winchell, Constance M. *Locating Books for Interlibrary Loan with a Bibliography of Printed Guides which Show Locations of Books in American Libraries.* New York: H. W. Wilson Co., 1930.

——————————. *A Guide to Reference Works.* 8th ed. Chicago: American Library Association, 1964. First *Supplement,* edited by Eugene P. Sheehy. Chicago: American Library Association, 1968.

Specialized Bibliographies

American Historical Association. *Writings on American History.* 1902 to date.

Anderson, John P. *A Book of British Topography.* London: W. Satchell, Co., 1881. Reprinted, Baltimore: Genealogical Book Co., 1970.

Bradford, Thomas L. *The Bibliographers Manual of American History.* 5 vols. Philadelphia: S. V. Henkels, 1907-10.

Cox, Edward G. *A Reference Guide to the Literature of Travel, Volume III: Tours, Descriptions, Histories and Antiquities, Surveys, Ancient and Present State.* Seattle: University of Washington, 1949.

Culleton Genealogical Agency of London. *Research Notes on English Families.* London: Culleton Genealogical Agency, 1955.

Daughters of American Revolution. *Catalogue of the Genealogical and Historical Works in the Library of the National Society.* Washington: Daughters of American Revolution, 1940.

Davies, Godfrey. *Bibliography of British History: Stuart Period, 1603-1714.* 2d ed. by Mary F. Keeler. Oxford: Clarendon Press, 1970.

Durrie, Daniel S. *Index to American Genealogies.* 5th ed. Albany: J. Munsell's Sons, 1908.

Ferguson, Joan P. S. *Scottish Family Histories Held in Scottish Libraries.* Edinburg: Scottish Central Libraries, 1960.

Filby, P. W. *A Basic List of Books on American and British Genealogy and Heraldry.* Chicago: American Library Association, 1966.

Frewer, L. B. *Bibliography of Historical Writings Published in Great Britain and the Empire, 1940-45.* Oxford: Blackwells, 1947.

Gatfield, George. *Guide to Printed Books and Manuscripts Relating to English and Foreign Genealogy and Heraldry.* London: Mitchell & Hughes, 1892. Reprinted, Detroit: Gale Research Co., 1966.

Glenn, Thomas A. *A List of Some American Genealogies which Have Been Printed in Book Form.* Philadelphia: 1897. Reprinted, Baltimore: Genealogical Book Co., 1969.

Goldentree Bibliographies in American History. 25 vols. New York: Appleton-Century Crofts, 1969.

Griffin, Appleton P. C. *Index of Literature of American Local History in Published Collections, 1890-95.* New York: Argonaut Press, 1966. Reprint of 1896 edition.

Grose, Clyde L. *Select Bibliography of British History, 1660-1760.* Chicago: University of Chicago Press, 1939. Reprinted, New York: Octagon Books, 1967.

Gross, Charles. *A Bibliography of British Municipal History.* 2d ed. Leicester: Leicester University Press, 1966.

——————————. *Sources and Literature of English History to 1485.* London: Longmans, Green, Co., 1900. 2d ed. 1915. Reprinted, New York: F. P. Smith, 1951.

Gough, Richard. *British Topography.* 2d ed. 2 vols. London: J. Nichols, 1780.

Handlin, Oscar, *et. al. Harvard Guide to American History.* Cambridge: Harvard University Press, 1954. Reprinted many times.

Hanson, Laurence W. *Contemporary Printed Sources for British and Irish Economic History, 1701-1750.* Cambridge: Cambridge University Press, 1963.

Harrison, H. G. *A Select Bibliography of English Genealogy.* London: Phillimore, 1937.

Hepworth, Philip. *How To Find Out in History: A Guide to Sources of Information.* Oxford: Pergamon Press, 1966.

Historical Association. *Annual Bulletin of Historical Literature.* 1911 to date.

Howe, G. F., ed. *Guide to Historical Literature.* 2d ed. New York: American Historical Association, 1961.

Kaminkow, Marion B. *Genealogical Manuscripts in British Libraries: A Descriptive Guide.* Baltimore: Magna Carta Book Co., 1967.

Kellaway, William. *Bibliography of Historical Works Issued in the United Kingdom, 1957-1960.* London: London University Press, 1962.

——————————. *Bibliography of Historical Works Issued in the United Kingdom, 1961-1965.* London: London University Press, 1967.

Kuhlicke, F. W. and Emmison, F. G. *English Local History Handlist*. London: Historical Association, 1965. Revised ed. 1971.

Lancaster, Joan C. *Bibliography of Historical Works Issued in the United Kingdom, 1946-56*. London: University Press, 1957.

Library of Congress. *American and English Genealogies in the Library of Congress*. Washington: Government Printing Office, 1919. Reprinted, Baltimore: Genealogical Book Company, 1967. Microcard Supplement to 1954 by C. K. Jones. Up-to-date manuscript additions at the American Antiquarian Society, Worcester, Mass. New edition under preparation.

Lowndes, William T. *Bibliographers Manual of English Literature*. 6 vols. London: Henry G. Bohn, 1857-64.

Marshall, George W. *The Genealogists Guide: A Comprehensive Index to Printed Pedigrees*. London: 1879. Other editions, 1893 and 1903. Continued by John B. Whitemore, 4 vols. London: Harleian Society, 1947-53. Reprinted, Baltimore: Genealogical Book Company, 1967.

Morgan, William T. and Morgan, Chloe S. *A Bibliography of British History, 1700-1715*. 5 vols. Indianapolis: University of Indiana Press, 1939-41.

Munsell, Joel and Sons. *The American Genealogist: Being a Catalogue of Family Histories Published in America from 1771 to Date*. Albany: Joel Munsell and Sons, 1900.

——————————— *Index to American Genealogies and to Genealogical Material Contained in all Works Such as Town, County, Local Histories, Historical Society Publications, Biographies, Historical Periodicals and Kindred Works*. 5th ed. rev. Albany: Joel Munsell and Sons, 1900. Supplement, 1900-1908. Reprinted, Detroit: Gale Research Co., 1966.

Nicolson, William. *English Historical Library*. London: Timothy Childe, 1714. Volumes for Scotland and Ireland also.

Pargellis, S. and Medley, D. J. *Bibliography of British History: Eighteenth Century, 1714-1789*. Oxford: University Press, 1951.

Peterson, Clarence S. *Bibliography of County Histories of the 3111 Counties of the Forty-Eight States*. Baltimore: n.p., 1946. Rev. Ed. Baltimore: Genealogical Publishing Co., 1961.

Read, Conyers. *Bibliography of British History: Tudor Period, 1485-1603*. 2d ed. Oxford: University Press, 1959.

Rawlinson, Richard. *The English Topographer*. London: n.p., 1720.

Royal Historical Society. *Writings on British History. 1901-1933*. 5 vols. in 7 parts. London: Royal Historical Society, 1968. *1934-1945*. Edited by A. T. Milne. 9 vols. London: Jonathan Cape, 1937-1953.

Rubincam, Milton. *Genealogy: A Select Bibliography*. Birmingham, Ala.: Banner Press, 1967.

Stuart, Margaret. *Scottish Family History: A Guide to Works of Reference on the History and Genealogy of Scottish Families*. Edinburgh: Oliver & Boyd, 1920.

Thomson, T. R. *A Catalogue of British Family Histories*. London: John Murray, 1928. 2d ed. London: Edward O. Black, Ltd., 1935. Addenda published in *Genealogists Magazine* VII (1937), 645-48. Manuscript Supplement to 1956 in the Society of Genealogists Library, London.

78

Wallis, P. J. *Histories of Old Schools: A Revised List for England & Wales.* Newcastle-upon-Tyne: University of Newcastle, 1966.

Williams, Judith B. *A Guide to the Printed Materials for English and Economic History, 1750-1850.* 2 vols. New York: Columbia University Press, 1926.

Virkus, Frederick A. *The Compendium of American Genealogy.* 7 vols. Chicago: American Institute of Genealogy, 1928-1937. Manuscript records from which the printed volumes were compiled, including many which did not get into print, are available for sale from the Genealogical Publishing Company, Baltimore, Md.

There are other finding aids available for genealogical and historical materials but they too are rarely consulted by genealogists. University students and faculty members have produced biographies, local and family histories which should be checked during the *preliminary survey.* Guides to theses and dissertations are the tools to use to locate these studies.

American Historical Association. *List of Doctoral Dissertations in History in Progress or Completed at Colleges and Universities in the United States.* Published every three years.

Aslib. *Theses Submitted to Universities in the United Kingdom for Higher Degrees.* Published Annually.

Forbes, Anthony H. *Current Research in British Studies by American and Canadian Scholars.* Marquette, Mich.: North Michigan University Press, 1964.

Gilchrist, David B. *Doctoral Dissertations Accepted by American Universities.* New York: H. W. Wilson Co., 1934-1955.

Institute of Early American History and Culture. *Research in Progress in Early American History.* Williamsburg: College of William and Mary. Issued periodically.

Institute of Historical Research. *List of Theses in Progress and Those Completed in British Universities.* Annual Supplement to *Bulletin of the Institute of Historical Research* at London University. 1933 to date.

Kuehl, Warren. *Dissertations in History: An Index to Dissertations in History Submitted to Universities in the United States and Canada, 1873-1960.* Lexington: University of Kentucky Press, 1965.

Library of Congress. *List of American Doctoral Dissertations Printed.* 27 vols. Washington: Government Printing Office, 1913-1940.

Palfrey, T. R. and Coleman, H. E. *Guide to Bibliographies of Theses in the United States and Canada.* Chicago: American Library Association, 1936. 2d ed. 1940. Reissued, Ann Arbor: University Microfilms, 1969.

Rosenburg, Ralph P. "Bibliographies of Theses in America," *Bulletin of Bibliography,* XVIII (1945), 181-82, 201-03.

University Microfilms. *American Doctoral Dissertations.* Annual since 1957.

_____ *Dissertation Abstracts.* Annual since 1938. Each abstract gives a 600 word summary of those dissertations microfilmed and available from

University Microfilms, Ann Arbor, Michigan. Datrix, a new service, provides a computer search for dissertations on a given subject or locality. Within a few days a bibliography of dissertations available on microfilm will be sent with order blanks for positive film or xerox bound copies of any or all of those listed.

Biographies. Biographical material, ranging from lengthy, multi-volume works to brief autobiographical sketches, is numerous. Some of these are detailed and written with the highest standards of accuracy while others are sloppily compiled. They should be included in the *preliminary survey* and evaluated as secondary material. The following references will help to locate them.

British Record Society. *Index to Biographical and Obituary Notices in the Gentleman's Magazine. 1731-1780.* London: British Record Society, 1891.

Hanham, H. J. "Some Neglected Sources of Biographical Information: County Biographical Dictionaries, 1890-1936," *Bulletin Institute of Historical Research,* XXXIV (1961), 55-66.

Riches, Phyllis M. *An Analytical Bibliography of Universal Collected Biography: Comprising Books Published in the English Language in Great Britain, Ireland, America and the British Dominions.* London: Library Association, 1934.

Slocum, Robert B. *Biographical Dictionaries and Related Works: An International Bibliography.* Detroit: Gale Research Co., 1967.

Be sure to watch for biographical information printed in periodicals and local histories.

Collections Dealing with Titled Persons. Reference works dealing with the nobility, peerage, and landed aristocracy have been compiled by government agencies since medieval times. Some are compiled by commercial or private concerns and date from the early nineteenth century. They are to be found in most countries of the world except the United States, which rejected hereditary and honorary titles from its beginning.

It is estimated that perhaps half of the families of British descent will find a peer or nobleman somewhere on their pedigree. This stems from the open social status of England and the law of primogeniture which permits the title to be held only by the oldest living male heir in each family. All other members of the family are commoners. For example, Sir Winston Churchill, the great English Prime Minister was the grandson of the Seventh Duke of Marlborough. The title, however, descended through his Uncle George and his father, Randolph, was a commoner until he received a "life" title later. This life title died with him.[10] Families of the blue blood are often anxious to possess pedigrees to support their claims and families not presently considered gentle are just as anxious to tie their own pedigrees to titled families. Some of these claims of descent are valid and proven, many are not. Most research libraries possess collections of this kind.[11]

Periodicals and Publications of Institutional Jurisdictions. Since the seventeenth century, institutional jurisdictions have published journals, proceedings and transactions in which biographies, local and family histories, genealogical queries, extracts and transcripts of original documents and record analyses of genealogical value have appeared. This source is *largely untapped* by researchers who, blissfully unaware they exist, duplicate the research which is published in these volumes. Many research libraries subscribe to these publications. Numerous guides and indexes have been prepared to make their contents easily accessible. Use these research aids to tap this valuable secondary source during the *preliminary survey. Be sure to watch for correction pages* published in the same volume or in later issues.

Baer, Eleanor A. *Titles in Series Published Prior to January 1953: A Handbook for Librarians and Students*. Washington: Scarecrow Press, 1953. 2d ed. 1964. Supplements at regular intervals.

Boeham, Eric H. and Adolphus, Lalit, *Historical Periodicals: An Annotated World List*. Santa Barbara: Clio Reference Publishers, 1961.

Clift, Glenn. "Indexes to American Historical Society Publications", *Kentucky Historical Society Register*, XLVIII (1950), 121-27.

Cappon, Lester J. *American Genealogical Periodicals: A Bibliography with a Chronological Finding List*. New York: New York Public Library, 1962. 2d ed. 1964.

Cranfield, G. A. *A Handlist of English Provincial Newspapers and Periodicals 1700-1760*. Cambridge: Cambridge University Press, 1952.

Fisher, Carleton E. *Topical Index to National Genealogical Society Quarterly*, Volumes 1-50, 1912-1962.

Freitag, Ruth S. *Union Lists of Serials: A Bibliography*. Washington: Library of Congress, 1964.

Gandilhow, Rene. *Bibliographie generale des travaux historiques et archeologiques publies par les societes savantes de la France*. 3 vols. Paris: Imprimeria Nationale. 1952.

Gomme, George L. *Index of Archaeological Papers. 1665-1890*. 2 vols. New York: Burt Franklin, n. d. Originally published 1907. Published annually, 1891-1901 as a supplement to major English historical journals and issued separately.

Gray, Richard A. *Serial Bibliographies in the Humanities and Social Sciences.* Ann Arbor: Pienan Press, 1969.

Gregory, Winifred L. *Union List of Serials in the Libraries of the United States and Canada.* 2 vols. New York: H. W. Wilson Co., 1925-26. 2d ed., 1943. 3d ed., 1965.

Griffin, Appleton P. C. *Bibliography of American Historical Societies in the United States and Canada. Annual Report of the American Historical Association,* 1905, II (1907), 1374 pp. Reprinted, Gale Research Co., 1966.

Gummer, H. Margaret. "Catalogues and Bibliographies of Periodicals: A Survey of the More Important Works Published in the British Commonwealth and the United States of America Since 1945," *Journal of Documentation,* XII (1956), 24-38.

Halverson, Frank D. *Genealogical Index.* Salt Lake City, n.p., 1954.

Houghton, Walter E. *The Wellesley Index to Victorian Periodicals, 1824-1900.*

J. Reuben Clark Library. *Index to L.D.S. Church Periodicals.* Provo, Utah: Brigham Young University Press, 1966 to date.

Jacobus, Donald Lines. *Index to Genealogical Periodicals.* 1932-1953. Reprinted, 3 vols. Baltimore: Genealogical Book Co., 1963. Vol. 4 to 1957 currently being compiled.

Lancaster, Joan C. "Recent Record Publications of Local Societies," *Archives,* No. 9 (1953), 11-19.

Milne, A. T. "Indexes to Periodicals," *Bulletin Institute of Historical Research,* XI (1934), 165-80.

Mullins, E. L. C. *A Guide to the Historical and Archaeological Publications of Societies in England and Wales, 1901-1933.* London: London University Press, 1968.

_____. *Texts and Calendars.* London: Royal Historical Society, 1958.

Rider, Fremont. *American Genealogical Index.* 48 vols. Middletown, Conn.: Committee for Subscribing Libraries, 1942-52. Continued as *American Genealogical-Biographical Index,* 1952, in progress. 73 vols. to date.

Rodabaugh, James H. "Historical Societies: Their Magazines and Their Editors," *Wisconsin Magazine of History,* XLV (1961-62), 115-23.

Rogers, Ellen S. *Genealogical Periodical Annual Index.* Bladensburg, Md.: 1962-65. Continued by George E. Russell, 1966 to date. Begun by Walden, 1956-62.

Stewart, James D., *et. al. British Union Catalogue of Periodicals: A Record of the Periodicals of the World from the Seventeenth Century to the Present Day in British Libraries.* London: Butterworths Scientific Publications, 1955-58. *Supplements* to 1962.

Ward, W. S. *Index and Finding List of Serials Published in the British Isles, 1789-1832.* Lexington: University of Kentucky, 1953.

Manuscript Collections of Genealogists and Historians. These collections represent the raw data from which printed or manuscript histories and genealogies were compiled. Some are well indexed and preserved, others are difficult to locate and to decipher. They usually contain lengthy transcripts of documents which have never been printed and have since been destroyed. The British Museum and the Bodleian Library abound in such collections. They can also be found in the College of Arms, the Libraries of the Inns of Court, the. Library of Congress and local record depositories. Use them but keep them in the proper perspective.

When faced with the vast number of secondary materials published and republished, you may conclude: "I'll never live long enough!" It is not suggested that you try to cover each and every one of the secondary sources described above. You would never live long enough. Through wise use of the guides and indexes prepared for your use and by confining yourself to *those which apply to your pedigree,* you can survey the materials already compiled on your pedigree ancestors in a short amount of time.

Archives

Records produced by a society on its own members, by virtue of the authority it exercises over them, are called archives.[12] They are searched during the *preliminary survey only if members of the family have been directly affiliated with the organization.*

Membership records. Every organization keeps some record of each member and his standing in the group. The amount of detail is up to the recording clerk. It may be just a list of members' names or it may contain information on parentage, birth, place of residence, movements from one area to another, special achievements and date of death or removal from the group. Life sketches of officers and members are usually preserved in manuscript form. Disciplinary proceedings can be especially interesting and valuable.

Administrative Records. Every institutional organization maintains administrative records which can contribute to the genealogical picture. Record is kept of all donations and expenditures. Charitable, insurance and scholarship funds used to educate children of members, to pay hospital and funeral expenses, to enable refugee members to migrate from one country to another and to relocate persons displaced by war, famine, plague or other disaster are carefully noted.

Archival records produced and preserved by institutional jurisdictions have much to offer the genealogist whose ancestors were members of such groups, but random searches in these records can be wasted, though interesting, effort during the *preliminary survey*.

Procedure

* Examine data from home jurisdiction searches for clues that indicate which institutional jurisdictions your family has been connected with. Military records, membership cards or certificates, financial records, uniforms and bulletins are prime items which lead to these organizations. Be careful not to overlook anything that is pertinent.

* List those institutional jurisdictions to which reference has been made on your survey outline. Always include those societies in or near the locality where your ancestors resided.

* Check the following list of directories to determine the addresses of those societies pertinent to your pedigree, the method you must use to search them (personal visit, correspondence, field researcher) and any restrictions or fees involved.

> American Library Association. *American Library Directory*. Chicago: American Library Association. 1968-69.

> Dunlap, L. W. *American Historical Societies, 1790-1860*. Madison, Wisc.: Privately Printed, 1944.

> Harcup, Sara E. *Historical, Archaeological and Kindred Societies in the British Isles: A List*. Rev. ed., London: Institute of Historical Research, 1968.

> Silvestro, Clement M. and Davis, Sally Ann. *Directory of Historical Societies and Agencies in the United States and Canada*. Nashville: American Association for State and Local History, 1965.

> Thoms, Robert C., *et. al. Encyclopedia of Associations*. 6th ed. Detroit: Gale Research Co., 1970.

> "U. S. Library Survey, Table III," *Handbook for Genealogical Correspondence*. Salt Lake City: Bookcraft, 1963. Over 600 libraries, historical societies, archives, and ethnic societies were contacted by the Cache Genealogical Library to determine the extent of genealogical records and services available through correspondence.

Whitehill, Walter M. *Independent Historical Societies.* Boston: Athaenum, 1962.

World Conference on Records. *Meet the . . . Hereditary and Lineage Societies.* Papers Presented at the World Conference on Records. Salt Lake City: Genealogical Society, 1969.

The World of Learning. Annual survey of the major libraries, archives, historical societies, museums and publishers throughout the world.

Some societies permit only members to use their facilities. If you are not a member, use the services of a field researcher who is.

* Contact those institutions applicable to your pedigree. If the organization is a local one, a personal visit is in order. Always utilize the facilities in your own immediate vicinity, if they pertain to the pedigree, before seeking information from jurisdictions in other areas. If the institution is some distance away you will have to conduct your searches through correspondence with the organization itself or hire a field researcher to make the searches for you. Whatever method you use, your work should be carefully planned *before* you begin.

* Check the published guides and indexes described under each source above. These will help you locate pedigrees, histories and other materials which apply to your ancestors quickly and efficiently. They have been prepared for your use, consult them.

* When the point of diminishing returns is reached — when too much time and effort is required for too little gain in data — stop hunting for elusive secondary materials in institutional jurisdictions and proceed to the pre-search analysis preparatory to research in original documents.

* A word of caution. Most of the libraries of institutional jurisdictions have large numbers of research source materials. DURING THE PRELIMINARY SURVEY ONLY SURVEY SOURCES SHOULD BE CONSULTED. Note the existence of research collections, their location and other important reference data about them so they can be searched at the proper time. If note is not made at the time they are discovered, memory will forget in which library they are to be found and searches will have to be made to determine that information. Be systematic in your work to avoid wasted time, effort and money.

CALENDAR
(COPYRIGHT 1972, GENEALOGICAL COPY SERVICE)

ENC. NO.	S NO.	DATE OF SEARCH	SOURCE: Description, Condition, Unusual Circumstances, How Searched.	JURISDICTION OR LOCALITY	PERIOD OF TIME	SURNAME OR NAME	RE-SULT
22	31	18 May 1970	Tinkling Spring: Headwater of Freedom by Howard M. Wilson, published by the Tinkling Spring and Hermitage Presbyterian Churches, Augusta County, Va. 1954. Copy in Genealogical Society, Salt Lake City. Call # 975.5 B4 Well documented. Gives locations of records used. Appendixes contain many documents.	Augusta County Va.	1752-1952	Johnson Kennedy Berry Eakle	ws ws ws mil

Emphasis has been placed upon American and English institutions in this chapter. Similar facilities can be found in almost every area of the world. They are available for the use of the researcher who is thorough enough to locate them.

STEP TWO: PRE-SEARCH ANALYSIS

CHAPTER SIX

STEP TWO: PRE-SEARCH ANALYSIS — EVALUATION OF SURVEY FINDINGS

The preliminary survey (step one), we have determined, must be performed for every pedigree ancestor preparatory to undertaking new research. This is done to prevent duplication of research effort and, more important, to provide a solid foundation for further research. Most surveys will uncover large quantities of genealogical information in home jurisdictions and those institutional jurisdictions pertinent to your pedigree ancestors. If your research base is to be sound, you must meticulously review these survey findings in order to develop a systematic research program. Imperfections in the survey, if they exist, must be found and corrected; unsolved survey problems will be magnified during subsequent research. This comprehensive review we call *pre-search analysis*. It consists of three procedures:

1. Evaluation of survey findings
2. Definition of research objectives
3. Completion of the research outline

Evaluation of Survey Findings

The survey outline, prepared at the beginning of home jurisdiction searches, should be compared with the calendar.

* Ask the following questions:

1. Were all existing survey sources pertinent to the family consulted?

2. Do I have, or have I examined the raw data used to compile every worksheet?

3. Did I compare the ràw data with the extracts to ensure that there was no editing or change of meaning?

4. Do I have a calendar entry for every source consulted

and a description of its condition whether or not it yielded information?

5. Do I possess all of the data essential to the compilation of complete and correct family group records for at least three or four generations?

If you can answer yes to each of these questions, you are ready to evaluate your findings.

Source Materials

Evaluation of source materials includes critical appraisal of the sources themselves, the data they yield and the evidence they provide. But you must recognize the differences between source, data and evidence and how these differences are distinguished. Each is evaluated separately before it can be related to the others. The words used to describe the kinds of source materials used by genealogists can be confusing unless such distinctions are recognized.

Sources are divided into two categories, primary and secondary, depending upon the circumstances under which they were compiled. But these designations do not always apply to each bit of evidence which the sources supply. Primary source materials may contain second-hand observations or opinions and yet they still retain their primary character. Secondary sources may contain primary material because of the circumstances under which they were compiled. Both kinds of sources are consulted in the preliminary survey and both will be discussed in detail in the paragraphs which follow.

Primary Sources. Is the testimony, oral or written, given by an eye-witness or mechanical device present at the event?[1] If the eye-witness was a participant or closely connected with the event which he reports, the credibility of his testimony is greater. If the eye-witness makes his report immediately or soon after the event, the reliability of his testimony is greater. Memory becomes more fallible as the gap between event and report widens.

The purpose of the creator is an important consideration. Some primary sources are the by-products of man's everyday duties and interests; some are produced with posterity in mind. Table Three shows this distinction.

Table Three.

Consciously Transmitted (Left for Posterity)	Unconsciously Transmitted (By-Products of Man's Life)
Written: Sacred writings, Chronicles, Narratives, Literature, Histories, Travelogues, Diaries, Memoirs, Inscriptions, Regnal Lists.	Written: Public Documents, Business Archives, Private Papers, Ecclesiastical Documents, Newspapers.
Oral: Ballads, Anecdotes, Tradition, Folklore, Interviews, Mythology, Recordings.	Oral: Language (in written form), Wiretaps, Dictaphone tapes
Objects: Paintings, Mosaics, Architecture, Public Works, Sculpture, Monuments, Effigies, Films.	Objects: Tools, Machinery, Ancient Remains, Coins, Clothing, Buildings, Household Utensils, Boundaries, Institutions.

Adapted from John M. Vincent, *Historical Research* (New York: Henry Holt and Co., 1911. Reprinted, 1929), 18.

Secondary Sources. If the account is given by a non-eye-witness it is second-hand. It is based upon what the reporter has heard or read, not upon what he has seen himself. *The greater the time lapse* between the secondary source and the events about which it tells, *the greater the reliability* of the evidence. Distortions from vested interests, pressure groups and lack of perspective decrease in proportion to the gap between the event and the report permitting greater objectivity. More eyewitness accounts are available for comparison and the interpretations of other non-eyewitness reporters provide background essential to a full understanding of the event. If the account reports the primary source upon which it is based, with accuracy and discernment, greater is its credibility. Secondary sources are equivalent to hearsay evidence in a court of law, but they are always admissable in genealogy if pertinent to the pedigree.[2] Explanations and interpretations of history, commentaries on events, biographies, pedigrees and genealogies, magazines and periodicals and family and local histories are considered to be secondary sources. They are second-hand accounts of the people and events they describe.

Original Sources. Is the account the earliest recording of a piece of information? Is it unpublished, uncopied, untranslated, just as it issued from the hands of its creators? Knowledge of originality helps to determine whether the source is first or second-hand. Evidence concerning a single event may be derived from several independent, but original sources. The birth of an ancestor can be recorded on a birth certificate, in the family Bible, on the church register, in the minister's daybook, on a passport, in a census enumeration and on an apprenticeship certificate. Each is an original record, the first recording of the event in that kind of document and each helps to substantiate and corroborate the details of that event.

Copied Sources. Is the account an extract, an abstract, a transcript or a photocopy of the original? *Extracts* are short, brief quotations from original documents. Omissions are indicated by three dots (. . .). No attempt is made to copy the original in its entirety but significant portions are reproduced verbatim. *Abstracts* contain the essential information from an original document — names, dates, places, relationships, clues and other pertinent data copied exactly as they appear in the record. *Transcripts* are verbatim copies of the original. The punctuation, dates and spelling used by the scribe are copied exactly. Errors are reproduced without change. Any editorial comments are indicated in brackets [ ] or footnotes. Some editors, however, supplement the transcription with interpretations and documents to create a more complete picture of the event described. The transcription and the supplementary materials are usually clearly separated and labeled. Extracts, abstracts and transcripts too often contain errors, omissions, unannotated editorial comments and inadequate indexes. If they appear in print, they may be issued in limited editions which are soon out of print.

Microfilm, microcard, microfiche, xerography, Verifax and photographs are photocopy reproductions of the original. They are the most reliable copies which can be obtained, but photography, even when sharp and clear, can create distortions which are not present in the original. Manuscript (handwritten) editorial comments, additions and changes; ink of differing shades and colors; changes made after the original was compiled; crossed out words or pencil notations in margins and between the lines, easily detected on the original, do not reproduce. Ink bleeding on one side often makes the reverse side of the page illegible on a photocopy; while careful study, the use of a magnifying glass and proper light will provide a fairly accurate reading from the original. Scratches from continued use make microfilm illegible. Type of paper, watermarks, chain marks and other signs of age, the very evidence required for dating manuscripts, are not visible. Gatherings of pages and stubs of missing leaves, evidence of the completeness of the record, are obliterated.[3]

Yet there are special advantages which copied records provide. They are more accessible, easier to preserve and often contain indexes. They may be translated from the original Latin, Greek or other difficult language. In a printed copy handwriting is no problem, authenticity has usually been determined and footnotes and other critical apparatus contribute to its evaluation. Ancient records, restricted because of their bad state of decay, are readily usuable in printed form. Infra-red photography can bring out words that are beyond recognition in the original where handwriting is faded, erased or crossed out. Original or copy — each form has its strengths and weaknesses which must be considered in any evaluation of sources.

Judging the Accuracy of Primary Sources

Primary sources are evaluated in terms of their authenticity as records and their credibility as evidence. Establishing that a document is an authentic record does not guarantee that it tells the truth, but questionable authenticity creates doubt in the ability of the sources to tell the truth. Questioning is the essential factor in this process. Facts never speak for themselves, they must be asked to comment.[4]

Is the Record Authentic?[5] Who created the record? A record by an official agency — government body, church or business firm — is considered authentic if it is found among the archives of that agency in a bona fide record depository, if it is a by-product of official activities, if it is free from erasures, deletions, additions or other changes. Testimony is considered to be authentic if it is given by an eye-witness who was physically present at the event, near enough to observe clearly, sound of sight, hearing, and mind, possessing an adequate memory and capable of reporting what was seen or heard. Documents of questionable authenticity should be subjected to thorough analysis. Diplomatics — the critical examination of documents in terms of paper, signature or seal, writing style, word usage and date — and paleography — the study of handwriting — will help. These techniques can determine quite accurately whether a document is real or forged.[6]

Dating. Dating manuscripts is an important art, usually reserved only for ancient writings, but which should be applied to modern ones as well. If the document bears a date, consider factors which could cause unintentional errors in dating. The scribe may write the wrong date at the beginning of a new year or a new month by mistake, he may copy his original source incorrectly or he may miscount a date given in Roman or Arabic numerals.[7] If the document lacks a date consider the kind of writing materials used: records written on stone, on lead, on pottery, on wood, on cloth, on wax, on clay tablets, on sheets of metal, on papyrus sheets, on vellum and parchment (differing grades of finished hide from cattle, sheep and goats) and on paper. The periods of time when each type was used varies along with its ability to survive. The quality of the material depends upon date and manufacturer. Is there a watermark? Do chain marks, wire lines show? Weave and composition of paper are also identifying marks. A careful study of these will usually lead to the date of writing. The document is usually written not more than five to eight years after the watermark date, allowing for the time the paper remained at the manufacturer's warehouse, at the stationer's and on the purchaser's desk before being used. Vellum manuscripts were so valuable, before the time of printing, that they were frequently chained or wired to the writing desk in the library. The marks made by these bindings can be used to determine the date of the manuscripts.[8] What kind of ink was used? Carbon ink was predominant for writing until about 300 A.D. when iron-gall replaced it; it came back into general use about the sixteenth century. Carbon ink rides on the surface of the document. It is dark brown or black in color and after a long time, it tends to flake and peel off, leaving a readable image on the surface. Iron-gall ink, light or medium brown in color, was used widely during the Middle Ages because it bit into the fibers of vellum and parchment, the principal writing materials of that period. It could be colored with dyes for use in illuminating manuscripts. Aniline dye inks became general after 1860 and are the most commonly used today.

Handwriting. Handwriting styles (calligraphy), like writing materials and ink, are developed for different periods of time and different cultural or national backgrounds. By identifying the script used, it is possible to place documents in the proper period of time and cultural origin. Distinction can also be made between specific, individual handwritings, especially after signatures became common in the sixteenth century. Since handwritings can change with age, physical condition, circumstances of writing and extensive use, it may take many documents for comparison before conclusions can be considered valid. The study of handwriting is a special skill which the genealogist can develop or he can consult an experienced calligrapher.[9] Before signatures became common, seals of wax, lead or gold were used to authenticate documents. Rulers, civil and ecclesiastical officials and private individuals had their own distinctive seals. By studying color, size, shape, impression, contents and attachment to the documents in question, authenticity and date can be determined.

Style and Contents. The arrangement of the words in the document, the use of abbreviations, the order and phrases in which words appear, the way in which the dates, names and titles of parties and witnesses are listed and the language used, help to validate the document. Spelling, grammar and punctuation are also important considerations. Are allusions made in the document to contemporary events? Do you know the whereabouts of the writer or compiler, persons mentioned in the document or recipient of the document? Date these and you can place the document in proper sequence.

Binding and Gathering. Was the binding made to fit that book or manuscript? Was it taken from another volume and used again? Are wormholes in the text in the same alignment with the binding? Note such items on the binding as ornamentation, stamps, clasps, ties and binder's marks. These are marks of identification and can be used to authenticate and date manuscripts or printed volumes. Study the gatherings, the ways in which the pages are stitched together. If pages are inserted or missing, the leaves on either side of the stitching will be uneven. Do the water marks or chain marks match on all of the leaves? Are the vellum pages arranged so that hair side matches hair side and flesh matches flesh or are they misarranged? If the volume is made of paper, do the leaves match or are there differences of color, weave or material content? Misarranged gatherings or ill-fitting bindings are indicative of changes made after the original volume was compiled. It may have been re-bound because the original binding was in need of repairs, it also may have been re-bound to disguise parts missing as a result of deliberate tampering.[10]

Visible Signs of Tampering. Words crossed out, use of different colors of ink, several styles of handwriting, erasures or additions may be signals of tampering. It is true that these occur in a normal written work but they also indicate unofficial changes. To erase writing from parchment was a difficult process. It could be done only by rubbing vigorously with pumice or scraping with a knife. It resulted in such damage to the original that it was easily detected. It was, therefore, easier to make a new document than to change an old one. The advent of paper led to changes on the original. Where writing has been erased or crossed out, the earlier writing can often be read with ultra violet light or infra-red photography.

Is the Record Credible?[11] Records produce evidence to prove the conclusions reached in genealogy. That evidence which answers specific questions about the event is called *direct (demonstrable) evidence.* That which provides inferences or suggestions from which answers can be derived is *circumstantial (indirect) evidence.* The ideal situation would be to have direct answers to every question asked, but genealogy is not that simple. Genealogists often must rely upon a preponderance of circumstantial evidence to prove that ancestral relationships are probable. Genealogists are dependent upon preserved records. Unless all the records have survived, probability is all that can be achieved. If you have carefully searched all surviving records, systematically organized your data, carefully evaluated it and shown that your conclusions are more likely than any other alternative, you can be satisfied.

Source materials provide individual items of information which constitute evidence or proof for genealogical events. First are the facts stated about the event itself — the date, where it took place, who was present, what happened. Second are the inferences, conclusions, interpretations or judgments concerning the relationship between the facts, and personal opinions often identical to inferences, but not always based on facts. Each item in the source should be evaluated in such a way that facts, inferences and opinions are carefully distinguished and considered separately. Too often facts and inferences are used as if they are one and the same. Errors result. Examine the entire source, line by line, questioning carefully each fact, each inference and each opinion. Nothing should be taken for granted. Consider the following questions:

Observation. Is it possible to see it like it is? Did the witness see what there was to see? Was he a trained observer? Was he located in the right place to see clearly? Was the event of such a nature that it could be observed? Did he have the physical ability to see clearly? Did he possess the proper historical, political, economic, sociological, genealogical knowledge to observe accurately? Was the witness looking through "spectacles" of bias? Did he see only what he wanted to see? Did he see only what his own frame of reference permitted him to see? Patriotism, desire for fame, religious belief — these can color the viewpoint of any witness and make it difficult to see it like it is.

Description. Is it possible to tell it like it is? Did the witness use analogy or imagery to describe what he saw? Did he depend upon others to communicate what he saw — translations into another language or writing down an oral report? Is his report based on his own knowledge of the event or merely on what he heard another say? Does the real meaning of his account differ from the literal meaning?

Was the statement made in good faith? Did the witness have reason to falsify or distort the information? In letters, biographies, diaries or memoirs intended for posterity, the person may describe himself and his motives as he wishes them to appear rather than as they actually are. The fewer the people expected to see the source, the more naked the contents will be. Letters or diaries intended for publication are less real than the secret diary, written in code or shorthand, intended only for the person diligent enough to decipher it. Personal financial gain, vain glory and local pride, personal satisfaction and desire to obtain or keep property are all motives for distortion. Statements not connected directly with the vested interest, however, are usually accurate. Evidence which is prejudicial against a witness and which would otherwise prove damaging to him, his family, his social position or his business is usually credible. Deathbed statements are valid. A man facing his Maker tries to make his peace with the world he expects to leave. Confessions or accounts of past sins, however, have been notoriously used to gain political or ecclesiastical preferment, business positions and social acceptance. These should be carefully examined for distortions before they are accepted. For example, a Congressman, seeking re-election was suddenly faced with his past — a military career which was non-existent. On nation-wide television he told the truth. He lost the election, as he knew he would, but it was preferable to make the announcement of fraud himself than to have it aired by others. His testimony, prejudicial in the extreme, can be believed. The testimony given in the memoirs of a member of Hitler's Nazi regime was published to gain political favor and social acceptance. The European edition is somewhat different from the American version because of the audience to which it is directed. Both editions and their motives should be carefully evaluated before conclusions are drawn.

Was the witness under pressure to distort his testimony? The lower the tension associated with an event and the more freedom a witness has to report, the greater is his credibility. Was he influenced by public opinion? Speeches and sermons designed to influence others are often embellished with exaggerations or false information to accomplish the desired effect. Government documents which pertain to non-political questions are accurate and excellent sources, but where they are politically oriented deliberate misstatements appear. The desire to appear in a favorable light before others leads to the same distortions. Is there evidence of literary formulas or conventional forms of expression which can distort the truth? Is there clear evidence that facts or data have been omitted? Are there gaps in the records? Do other documents make cross-references or illusions to data not included? Why? Sometimes documents are lost, sometimes they are destroyed or withheld for what they contain.

Dissemination. Is the event or testimony recorded soon after it occurred? How many copies were made? Before photocopy facilities were readily available, several copies of a government document were made by hand or typewritten — one for each of the parties involved, one for local government authorities, one for the national government body, one for legal counsel and perhaps other copies. These are subject to errors in copying, important omissions, interpretations and editing, all of which affect reliability. Were copies made by official scribes employed for the purpose, by other historians, genealogists or researchers desiring copies, by printing or by photocopy? Was the original a rough draft, changed and altered before the final copy was made? Do both exist for comparison? If the records were printed, is the printed copy based on the original? How many steps removed from the original is it? Were copies collated and compared with each other and with the original before the printed version was made? Did the publisher produce a quality printed work? Are there numerous typographical errors but no correction page? Are there obvious omissions or garbled passages?

If the work was edited, what editorial policy guided its preparation? If a group or society sponsored the project as part of a series of edited works, consult the introduction to the volume or to the first volume in the series. If these do not contain editorial policies check to scc if the society has published a separate guide to editing source materials. The American Historical Association (Washington, D. C.), Institute of Historical Research (London), American Association for State and Local History (Nashville, Tenn.), National Archives (Washington, D. C.), Historical Manuscripts Commission (London) and the British Records Association (London) all have standard editorial policies.[12]

Comprehension. Is it possible to understand it like it is? Each researcher has his own frame of reference, his own bias, his own "spectacles" through which he views the past. Too many genealogists view their ancestors in terms of the world in which they live not the world in which their ancestors resided. Documents must be placed within their own historical context to be understood and properly evaluated. You should be familiar with the social and political system in which the documents were produced. The creator of the document assumed that persons using it had the same basic understanding of life which he himself had, and he did not add items and information which were common knowledge. You should know the customs and traditions of the people sufficiently to read the document with the system of values they had. Be extremely careful to avoid reading into earlier documents, customs, ethical practices and conceptions which are not there. Avoid interpreting sources in terms of the moral code or way of life with which you are acquainted. For example, an ancestor's illegitimate birth may have been a source of social inconvenience and economic disadvantage but it was rarely a case of moral chastisement. In a society where only the oldest son could inherit the family estate, younger sons entered the Church or became soldiers and civil servants. They often did not marry because they lacked the social standing or the economic resources to support a family.

Corroboration. Is the evidence corroborated or supported by evidence from other sources? Corroborative evidence must come from other sources which are entirely independent to prove the reality of events or testimony. Official testimony, oral or written, should be compared with unofficial testimony whenever possible, for neither one is sufficient alone. Direct, competent, independent witnesses who report the same central fact and other casual matters can be accepted when they agree. Absence of contradiction or the "argument from silence," is an indirect way to corroborate evidence but it has certain problems. How well known was the event? Was it a matter of common knowledge? Did contemporaries have a chance to contradict or was the event unknown to them? If it is an obscure event, others probably omitted it because it was unknown or they considered it too unimportant to notice. *Their silence does not mean corroboration!* If it was spectacular in nature, lack of corroboration would make the document suspect.

Does evidence from two or more sources agree independently? Each conclusion, to be valid, should be supported by two or more reliable witnesses. If two sources contain identical errors they may be dependent upon each other or derived from a common source. If they contradict each other, one or both may be confirming a falsehood not supporting a fact. Sometimes testimony from only one witness can be found. In this case, the evidence must conform to known facts, be in the proper time sequence and have general credibility. Any conclusion based on testimony from one witness only must be so described and labeled.

Probability. Is the evidence probable? Does it coincide with known facts about dates, people and events? Does it fit patterns of human behaviour and physical abilities? Are there inconsistencies in the same source? There is no such thing as the perfect witness; every observer includes some fact and some fancy. But the more consistent the witness is and the more reserved his conclusions are, the greater is the credibility of his testimony. Truth rests on a chain of probabilities and such testimony is always more probable.

When judging the accuracy of primary sources give consideration both to the *authenticity of the record* and to the *credibility of the evidence* which it provides.

Judging the Accuracy of Secondary Sources

Evaluation of secondary sources is one of the most important steps in genealogical research. It is accomplished by questioning each source carefully. Secondary sources in genealogy are valuable in direct proportion to the primary sources used to compile them and the way in which the author approached his evidence. They are too valuable to overlook because of their uncertain reliability and too prone to error to accept at face value. Some genealogists still believe that if it is written down or printed it has to be true — no one would dare to print a falsehood. John Norden, a sixteenth century local historian, held a similar notion. He lived in a time of transition from rigid belief in tradition to dependence upon personal observation and documentary evidence. His contemporaries challenged the ancient tradition concerning the founding of Britain. John Norden considered the challenge as a threat to the very integrity of history itself. He declared:

> If the historie of Brute be but a fable, as some of late have by coniectures endevored to prove. . . what proof can ther be, of the truth of any historye? Which were longe contynued by manuscripts which were not, neyther coulde they be so generall as since the arte of Printing: and therefore in the beginning more casuall. And if this historie be false in the beginning, the succeeding partes can not be true. And who can tell when the true historie of Brytaine began? And of whome or whence it took its name?[13]

To Norden, only one answer was possible: History could not lie.

Yet written history often does lie! Some authors perpetuate errors intentionally to gain their own ends; others do so unknowingly because they have compromised their research in some way.

The following guidelines will help you in determining the accuracy
of the secondary materials you have searched.

Author and Method. Careful scrutiny of the author and his
purpose for compiling his work is called external criticism. Who
is the author? Does he give his name? Does he use a pseudonym
or pen-name? Is the work anonymous? Why? Is the title page lost
or did the author leave his name off to avoid detection? Authors
often omitted names during periods of political unrest when to
be identified would lead to censure or even imprisonment. They
omitted names to avoid social criticism when publication by
gentlemen was frowned upon. Some authors used initials, their
own or letters picked at random from the alphabet. William
Camden, a sixteenth century local historian, used "M" "N"
(Willia*m* Camde*n*) for some of his works. Some authors published their works in a foreign country and smuggled the finished
product into their own country for sale and distribution. During
certain periods of time, it was customary and quite common to
use pen-names. Women used pseudonyms as a disguise of sex
to avoid social criticism. John Collier, who humorously criticized
John Whitaker's *History of Manchester,* used the pen-name of
"Tim Bobbin" and the pseudonym "Muscipula Senior" for his
critical works.[14]

To determine authorship, follow these steps:

* Check the work itself. Read the preface, dedication, introduction, and other preliminary pages carefully. Watch for the
  same letters beginning each chapter, each section or each
  paragraph. Watch for individual letters which are in bold face
  type at intervals throughout the text. These, if present, are
  usually the author's initials. The whole name may be spelled
  out when the letters are placed side by side.

* Watch for illusions to the author and his life in the text itself.
  Watch also for references to other works he might have written.
  Authors usually cannot refrain from making an illusion or
  two to their other labors. By a careful reading of *The Descrip-
  tion of Somerset* written by Thomas Gerard of Trent (d. 1634),
  E.H. Bates was able to identify him as the real author of the
  History of Dorset, long attributed to John Coker.[15]

* Look for signatures on pages other than the title page. Visita-

tion pedigrees were signed by the head of the family or the one who gave the information about the family. Seals and book plates used on manuscripts can also be used to determine authorship.

* Watch for references to authorship in contemporay histories and modern studies. As you read other secondary materials and bibliographies note any references to authorship — supposed or real — of works pertinent to your pedigree. Write them down for future use so they are not forgotten.

* Check reference works in which identities have already been established by other scholars. Consult copyright files or licenses to print. A manuscript cannot be licensed for printing or copyrighted anonymously. The author or publisher is given in the records. The copyright files in the Library of Congress are well indexed and easy to consult. The records of the Stationers Company in London, which was responsible for licensing English books for printing, have been published and can be found in most research libraries.[16]

Reputation. Is the author an established authority of wide experience? Is he known for correct, careful work or does he sacrifice accuracy to save time, money or patronage? If he has been proved wrong in certain things, it does not mean that all of his work is wrong but it makes careful analysis necessary.

Background. To what social class does the author belong? Is he a nobleman, a yeoman or an artisan? Is he a parish minister or a bishop? How does he view the members of other social classes? Is he a local resident of the area about which he writes? Roy Brook, the author of *The Story of Huddersfield* (1968), is a native of Huddersfield. He attended the schools of the town; he walked the streets of the city, ate in its inns, heard services in its churches and attended burials in its cemeteries. It is possible that he might be less objective than someone who was not so closely tied to the city, but his personal knowledge of the places and people he writes about make his work more credible. Sir Robert Atkyns (d. 1711), a member of the landed gentry of Gloucestershire, confined his *History of Gloucestershire* to the members of his own social class. John Nordon (d. 1625), an itinerant surveyor, in his *Speculi Britannia Pars (View of Britain),* described the occupations of yeomen, tin miners and others of his class with much greater interest and feeling than he did the homes and country seats of the gentry and nobility.

Objectivity. Does the author try to be objective? True objectivity is almost impossible to achieve — the period of time in which one writes, the personal biases or viewpoint from which the subject is approached prevent it — but the author should try to be objective. Does he praise or blame his ancestors for the things they have done? He can show affection, respect and pride for his ancestors but he should not give undue praise — "they can do no wrong." He should avoid conclusions dictated by emotion or by his own moral values. He should judge events within the context of the time in which they occurred.

Purpose. Why did the author compile the work? His motive will determine the approach to the subject, the sources used and the questions asked of the evidence. Why did he write?

To make connections across the sea?
To fulfill a commission to write?
To obtain a profit?
To conform to the market — what is saleable?
To feel satisfaction in the doing?
To fulfill requirements for a graduate degree?
To satisfy curiosity?
To defend the family against attack by others?
To satisfy a true desire to know?
To prove his descent to be as good as anyone else's?
To retain, inherit or regain land or honor?
To assume a coat of arms?
To receive exemption from taxation?
To join a hereditary society?
To prove descent from the Gods or Adam?
To provide answers for history, medicine, genetics, demography, sociology or other discipline?

Source and Contents. A careful study of the secondary source itself and its contents is vital to proper evaluation. It is called internal criticism.[17] Study the volume: preface, dedication, introduction, summary or conclusion, bibliography and footnotes. These should always be read first for the author's approach, special methods he used to collect data, the sources he used, how he evaluated his data and the conclusions he reached. In older works, the title of the work will give much of this material in an abbreviated form. Consider the title to Richard Izacke's *History of Exeter* published in 1723.

> Remarkable Antiquities of the City of Exeter. Giving an Account of the Laws and Customs of the Place, the Offices, Court of Judicature, Gates, Wells, Rivers, Churches and Immunities: The Titles and Privileges of the several Incorporations; with their distinct Coats of Arms Engrav'd on Copper Plates. Together with a Catalogue of all the Bishops, Mayors and Sheriffs, from the Year 1049. Originally collected by Richard Izacke, Esq.; the present Chamberlain. To which is now added, A Correct Map of the said City, together with the Guildhall and Conduit.

The title serves the purpose of a table of contents and a guide to the author's identity. The title of the 1768 edition of Philip Morant's *History of Essex* gives a full account of the sources consulted — a bibliography.

> The History and Antiquities of the County of Essex. Compiled from the best and most ancient Historians; From Domesday-Book, Inquisitions Post Mortem, and other the most valuable Records and MSS., &c. Particularly from the Collections of the late Rev. Mr. Holman, and Mr. Samuel Dale; including those of Mr. Richard Symonds, Mr. Thomas and Mr. Nicholas Jekyll, the Rev. Mr. John Ouseley, Mr. Humfrey Wanley (who furnished Materials out of the Harleian Library), and the great Improvements of the late most accurate Mr. John Booth. The whole digested, improved, perfected, and brought down to the present Time by Philip Morant, M.A. Rector of St. Mary's Colchester, &c., and Fellow of the Society of Antiquaries. Illustrated with Copper Plates.

Original. Is the version to which you have access the original? A printed transcription of the original? A manuscript copy of the original? An extract? Many pedigrees, histories and biographies circulated in manuscript for several years and were copied several times. When the work was published, it was too often edited from a second-hand ·copy, not the original. Some times, the original could no longer be found and several copies were collated to make the printed version. Sometimes material was omitted from the printed version which was included in the original or added to printed versions when it was not in the original. Errors in copying, editing, important omissions in extracts, interpolation and interpretations added by the editor without indication — all of these can be present in a secondary work and affect its reliability. If the work was edited what editorial policy guided its preparation?

Audience. Who is the work intended for? Family members? Subscribers? Scholars? General public? The standards of excellence demanded by each of these groups is different and will often dictate the kind of information included and the accuracy of the evidence and conclusions. If illegitimacy is resented by the family, the history intended only for them will often hide or disguise the fact. Check the list of subscribers which appears among the preliminary pages of the volume. This will indicate the audience for which the volume is intended. If the subscribers are wealthy landed gentlemen (which is often the case) they may resent anything included which would cause them to lose face or show them in a bad light. They may refuse to pay for publication of the work. Works written for scholars are expected to have evidence which is clearly presented and carefully documented. Works written for the general public often omit footnotes, bibliography and other scholarly material in order to keep the price low and the appeal wide. Gossip and scandal are included to increase interest.

Publication. Is the work published by a well-known publisher who must safeguard his reputation and who will not issue a shoddy book? Is the work published in a pirate edition? Many manuscripts were copied and circulated widely before publication. Too often some enterprising publisher took his copy and rushed it into print in his own name. Then the author would issue his official version and a legal battle ensued. But claim to authorship may be disputed for years. Anthony Wood's *History and Antiquities of the University of Oxford* was written originally in English but Dr. Fell, of the University, paid two students to translate it into Latin and then he published it in 1674. Fell changed, omitted and added at will. A good English version based on Wood's original manuscript did not appear until 1792-96 when it was edited by John Gutch. Privately printed works may be excellent but they are more subject to error because they are not impelled to place prominence on facts. They have no need to sell a publisher on the merits of the work. They are often intended for a limited audience and the need for accuracy is considered less important.

Sources. What sources did the author use? Did he use original documents? Primary sources? Personal observation? Interview? Printed histories? Manuscript collections written by another pasted together to make a continuous narrative? Even good books can perpetuate errors if they rely on unverified material. The county histories published during the latter part of the nineteenth century in the United States often contained "filler" which was used in every history in the state with a few details added to make it apply to specific counties. These details were supplied by anonymous local agents. In using them as a source, the "filler" must be distinguished from actual facts by comparing several histories.

Plagiarism was called imitation a few generations ago and considered the highest form of praise. Once an author had changed, revised, beautified, corrected and added his own contributions to the work, it was his own. By the seventeenth century, writers were beginning to resent borrowing, lifting and rehashing of their material, but they, legally, could do little. This is the basic principle of the copyright law even today. Acknowledgement, however, was not considered necessary then but must be made today to avoid infringement of another's legal rights. Some early genealogists and historians scrupulously acknowledged their sources of information, some indicated none. To condemn the latter as plagiarists is to impose our own time upon an earlier one.

Collection of Data. How did the author collect his data? Did he personally view tombstones and monument inscriptions, documents in attics, basements and musty muniment rooms? Did he base his work on secondary materials only? Did he employ others to collect the data and send it to him? Did he use copies, microfilm or other photocopies of original documents? In 1954, Dr. Howard M. Wilson compiled the *Tinkling Spring: Headwater of Freedom,* a study of the Presbyterian Church and her people, in Augusta County Virginia, 1752-1952. He used original documents, microfilm and photostats of originals, pertinent secondary sources, newspapers, doctoral dissertations, maps and monumental inscriptions. He personally viewed and extracted the data from them. Student ministers were employed to handle his ministerial duties to free him for the undertaking. His book reflects his extensive and careful collection of data.

Length. How long is the work? What period of time does it cover? Material based on first-hand observation, like a description or survey of the present state of a town or local area is likely to be a fairly accurate description of conditions at the time. Material dealing with events and people of the past are frequently second-hand and more subject to error. If it is a short pedigree, three or four generations, it is more likely to be accurate than if it is long and covers several generations.

To assess the accuracy of secondary sources, it is often helpful to consider the opinions of both contemporary and modern historians and genealogists. They are not infallible but they can illuminate things which you might otherwise miss.

* Read a review of the source in a reputable historical or genealogical journal. The reviewer chosen usually has a good understanding of the subject, experience in that field and nothing to gain by giving praise or criticism unjustly. The majority of journals which publish book reviews began publication in the nineteenth century but some date from the seventeenth. If the work is a local history, check the journals of societies which pertain to that locality or are published there. If it is a biography or family history, check journals of the locality where the family lived. If it deals with a subject — business firm or farmed estate — check a journal which deals with that subject.

Each bound volume of periodicals and journals contains an index. In addition, a cumulative index is usually prepared every ten to twenty-five years and published as a separate volume or as a supplement to the current volume. Check the cumulative indexes for the book in question. If cumulative indexes are lacking or do not include book reviews, check the issues published within the first three years following the date of publication of the work itself. Remember that many older volumes — histories, biographies and other secondary studies — are being reprinted and reviews of these reprints can be located in current publications.

If the work was published or reprinted since 1905 check:

Book Review Digest, 1965 to date
Cumulative Book Review Digest, 1905 to date
Index to Book Reviews in the Humanities, 1960 to date

The following reviews from the 1967 volume of the *Canadian Historical Review* and the 1773 volume of *Gentleman's Magazine* are typical:

> *Toronto of Old.* By Henry Scadding. Abridged and edited by F. H. Armstrong. Toronto: Oxford University Press. 1966. Pp. xxxiv, 396, map, illus. $7.50.

> *The Settlement of Huron County.* By James Scott. Toronto: Ryerson Press. 1966. Pp. xvi, 328, illus. $5.00.

> Almost a century separates the first publication of Scadding (1873) and Scott's work on Huron County, Ontario. Unfortunately, we can report no improvement in local history writing over this period. Quite the contrary. Scadding remains a classic, vital, informative, graceful. The abridgment has reduced *Toronto of Old,* to the rambles along Toronto's main streets . . . And it has been strengthened by Mr. Armstrong's many informative footnotes. The editor has also appended a sixteen page introduction, sketching the background of the work . . . Used as a reference work it is still the best history of early Toronto. Scadding's judgments are always cool and suprisingly detached for a contemporary . . . With unfailing accuracy, with scholarly use of documents, and above all with the informed insight of a contemporary gentleman, he presents the full panorama of the young city.

> Scott's book is a total contrast. Like Scadding, it cannot be read at a single sitting, but in this case, it is because of sheer dullness. The writing is clumsy, the approach parochial; none of Scadding's grace is to be found here. Hasty judgments and sloppy errors mar it. And unlike Scadding, it has been badly edited . . .

> In the rather arid field of Canadian local history, one looks back on a classic like Scadding with both admiration and relief. Its reprinting is a major event. One

could only wish the Ryerson Press had shown as much imagination. How much more useful it would have been to have reissued one of the durable classics of local history, rather than adding *The Settlement of Huron County* to the dreary catalogue of forgettable books.

Michael S. Cross.

30. The Ancient and present State of the City of Oxford. Chiefly collected by Mr. Anthony a Wood; with Additions by the Rev. Sir John Peshall, Bart. 4to. pp. 408. Rivington.

"This work is chiefly the result" (as the editor quaintly expressed it) "of Mr. Anthony à Wood, in his MSS No. 8491, in Bib. Bodl." and "the account of the music-room, and its institution is the effect of the ingenious and very worthy Professor, Dr. William Hayes." It contains the history of the foundation of this city, its antiquity, situation, suburbs, division by wards, walls, castle, fairs, religious houses, abbey of St. Frideswade, churches, as well those destroyed at the present, with their monumental inscriptions, mayors, members of parliament, and, in short, a profusion of elaborate materials, collected by that very industrious but rude artificer, Wood , and not much polished or well digested by this Reverend Baronet, though a son of His. From the small specimen we have given of his style, little elegance or ornament can be expected. To antiquarians, however, the work may be useful, and to such, therefore we recommend it. One remarkable and very modern occurrence, in the annals of this city, Sir Jn. Peshall, however, has omitted, viz. the humiliation and offerings of the mayor and his brethren in St. Stephen's Chapel, and their pilgrimage to a certain castle not unlike Bocardo, in the year 1768, see Vol xxxviii. pp. 91, 122. Our author's descriptive talents may be collected from the following sentence: "Oxford is better seen than described. The magnificent colleges, and other most noble edifices, standing in and giving an air of grandeur to the streets, the many delightful walks, elegant gardens, rich chapels, grand libraries, the beauty of the meadows and rivers that on every side delight the eye, the sweetness of the air, the learning and frequent public display of it, and the politeness of the place, the harmony and order of discipline, not to mention the great number of strangers that continually visit us, and express their satisfaction, conspire to render it the delight and ornament of the kingdom, not to say of the world."

A new map of the city and views of All Saints, St. Mary's, and St. Giles's churches, are inserted.

* Consult an annotated bibliography. Some bibliographies contain brief evaluations of the work: sources used, approach or bias of the author, important items omitted, errors and other things of value in assessing a particular volume. The following annotated reference from Edward Cox's valuable *Guide to the Literature of Travel, Volume III* (1949), shows the value of such comments.

> 1746. Seacombe, John. Memoirs containing a Genealogical and Historical Account of the House of Stanley, from the Conquest to the Death of James, Earl of Derby, in 1735, with a full description of the Isle of Man, etc. 4to. Liverpool.
>
> This ill printed, ill spelt, ill written, confused book seems partly taken out of Bishop Rutter's MSS who was tutor to Lord Strange and chaplain in the family at the siege of Latham House, of which he wrote an account. — Gough, 610.

* Watch for assessments of historians or genealogists who have used the work in question. Was it consulted by contemporary scholars? Is it still considered accurate by today's standards? Some histories compiled centuries ago were widely used by contemporaries for evidence and are still basic works today. Sir William Dugdale's *Antiquities of Warwickshire* (1656) and John Stow's *Survey of London* (1598) are such studies. Anthony a Wood's biographical dictionary of Oxford alumni is the starting point for information on any writer or bishop who attended Oxford University to 1691. Its accuracy and reliability are recognized today.[18]

Articles which review and evaluate the work of others are to be found in the periodicals and publications of institutional jurisdictions. Consult the indexes and guides listed above (pages 80-81) for references to these. Histories and biographies based upon or containing critical comments on secondary materials can be located by checking bibliographies of histories and theses prepared by other scholars. (see pages 74-79).

Philip Morant's *History of Essex* is an interesting case study in how scholarly opinions change concerning the reliability of a secondary source. It was based on a series of manuscript collections and unpublished histories dating from the early seventeenth century. Consider the following manuscript pedigree.[19]

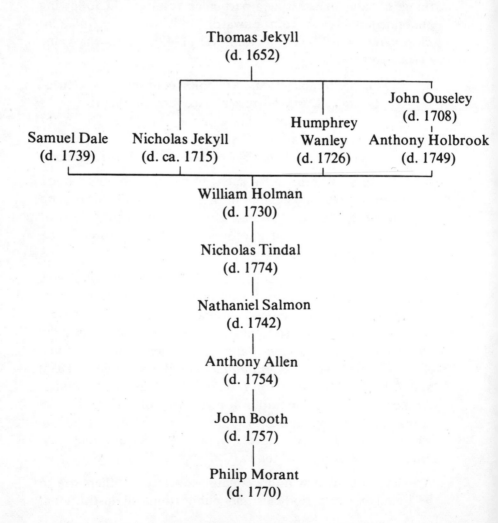

Thomas Jekyll started the collection of material in public records and private evidences (property records). From him the manuscripts descended in part to his grandson Nicholas and to his friend John Ouseley. Each of these men added notes of their own. William Holman obtained both sections of the collection with additional materials for the history of the county contributed by Samuel Dale and Humphrey Wanley. He arranged the extracts made by the previous owners under parish headings and added many things of his own. Philip Morant finally received the collection after four more local historians had made their contributions to it. He revised, rearranged the whole and published the first complete *History of Essex* in numbers — issued in sections serially each month — in 1763-64. It was republished as a unit in two volumes in 1768 and reprinted in 1816. These editions indicate its popularity and acceptance by contemporaries.

In 1835, Thomas Wright, while writing his own *History of Essex* followed Morant's account, for the most part, but added corrections and new matter based upon his own personal observation. Some thirty years later, H. W. King stated:

> It will have been noticed that the few wills from which I have already printed extracts have corrected many errors of Morant. Others, of which I have either copies or abstracts, rectify many more. The errors in date, and the confusion of persons are, in fact, more frequent than I could have anticipated, while his genealogies are often defective and inaccurate. This is becoming daily more apparent by my own limited researches, and the more extended investigations of others. Every Essex historian who has succeeded him has implicitly followed his text, and consequently repeated his errors; but no one has hitherto supplied his omissions.[20]

What appeared to be a credible, well compiled history was shown to have many errors on closer examination and comparison with other data. This does not mean that it should not be consulted. As part of the survey, this work, if pertinent to the pedigree, should be used because it contains a treatment of each individual parish in the county not covered by subsequent historians. It should be compared with other data collected, however, and evaluated carefully in terms of the other criteria listed in this section before basing research on its conclusions.

Both primary and secondary sources have strengths and weaknesses. Documents, however authentic and credible, give only a small segment of the whole picture. Religious records present the religious view, economic documents the economic picture. The researcher must examine all surviving documents which are pertinent to his pedigree and use them together. In this way, the weaknesses and strengths of each group help to balance the other.

Procedure

* Lay your work pedigree chart out in front of you. Pull all the worksheets pertaining to the ancestors on your chart and organize them alphabetically by head of household. Arrange chronologically where two or more bear the same given name.

* Begin with the worksheets for your own family group. All survey searches, like the pedigree, begin with the present generation — YOU — and move back in time. To begin with your 2d great-grandfather is a compromise in genealogy which will create stonewalls on your pedigree. Such walls will not be removed until you return to this point. Each generation supplies information vital to the identity of later generations. To omit yourself and your family makes it most difficult, if not impossible, to identify accurately later generations. The preliminary survey, if performed properly, should yield sufficient data to document your records from your own family unit back in time for at least three or four generations of pedigree ancestors. Sometimes the circumstances of life — emigration, orphan experiences, adoption, war, fire or other conditions — prevent you from reaching this goal, but generally, it is possible to go at least this far. Research usually begins with your 2d great grandfather and his generation. If this goal has not been met, you should carefully re-examine the preliminary survey. Chances are you have not systematically exhausted all survey jurisdictions and sources.

* Spread out the worksheets which apply to your own family

unit. If your notes have been taken on family group worksheets as recommended, the otherwise toilsome task of
assembling the data is now reduced to a mechanical process.

* Take a blank worksheet to serve as a summary sheet and
begin with the husband's line. Examine the data entered on
this line on each worksheet in front of you. Do they all a-
gree? If so, enter the husband's name on the summary sheet.
If there is any discrepancy of spelling or of name, resolve the
conflict. Evaluate the data in a good, better, best fashion. On
the back of the summary sheet, write a brief explanation of
your choice and why. Write the same comments on the worksheets in question.

* Examine the birth line of the husband's section. Compare for
argument, enter the unanimous conclusion of the worksheets
on the summary sheet or resolve any discrepancies and describe the action on the back of the summary sheet and on
the worksheets involved. Follow this same procedure for
each line on the family group sheet. When all lines are completed, clip the summary sheet to the worksheets on which it
is based.

* Fill out a permanent family group record from the summary
sheet. Type the information on a good grade of paper (25 to
50% rag content) or handwrite it legibly in permanent black
ink. Place your name and the names of your mother and
father on the permanent pedigree chart.[21]

* File the completed case history in a safe place. The case history will contain all of the worksheets, the summary sheet
and the explanatory notes for value judgments and conclusions which went into that permanent family group record.
The pertinent survey outline may also be included. This case
history will justify your actions to future generations. Files
which contain information pertaining to living persons
should be up-dated anytime new events occur — births, marriages, deaths. If they are documented immediately the file
will always be current if you are removed from research for
any reason.

* Turn next to your grandparents, perform the same examination of your survey findings. If you are satisfied with this
family unit, fill out a complete, correct family group record

for them, place their names on the permanent pedigree chart and file the completed case history. Follow this procedure for each family unit on each pedigree line. The first family on each line, where you detect any question as to completeness or correctness or where there is insufficient evidence to support valid conclusions, must become the starting point for research.

Many people have the mistaken idea that if information is written on a family group sheet, it must be true. If that data has been compiled by a loved one it is even more natural to think that they would compile only accurate records. Still others entertain the belief that, to prove complete and correct that which has been done in the past, each item on the family group sheet must be separately checked for accuracy. Neither extreme is acceptable. While it is true that you must prove or disprove survey findings, to check individual items proves only that the information was copied correctly. For example: a family group record is compiled from four sources. If you check out each of those four sources, you will only establish whether the data was copied accurately from those sources, not necessarily that the family is complete and put together accurately. Many sources exist which will yield information on your ancestors if you will but use them. If you only search four of them your chances of having a complete record are poor at best. It takes two sources to make an argument and a third may corroborate one or the other but still not establish the validity of either. If the preliminary survey is performed thoroughly and systematically, you will collect all of the data, evidence and conclusions which others have collected or compiled on your pedigree ancestors. By comparing the data carefully you can determine which families are complete and correct on the basis of the research performed by others. The first family about whom you have a question or where there is a lack of proper evidence to support the records, becomes the starting point for research.

If you keep your records systematically and accurately, your work — the survey findings for those who follow you — will withstand such careful scrutiny and can be built upon rather than re-done. Your posterity will bless you for the legacy you have provided.

CHAPTER SEVEN
PRE-SEARCH ANALYSIS: RESEARCH OBJECTIVES

The second phase of the *pre-search analysis* is the definition of research objectives. There are two types: ultimate objectives which are expressed as pedigree ancestors and their families and immediate objectives which are the searches necessary to prove them.

Ultimate Objectives

The family units which you identified as incomplete or incorrect on each pedigree line, during the evaluation of the survey, are by definition an ultimate objective. These are the families for which research will be undertaken. These are the families around which all search procedures will be planned and performed.

* First, outline what you know, about each ultimate objective family. Reduce your survey findings to basic essentials from which you can prepare a research plan. A mechanical device which proves very helpful in this reduction process is an identify graph. It provides a skeleton upon which you can correlate all of the relevant data for each ultimate objective.

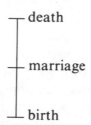

Take a plain sheet of paper. Down the left-hand margin, draw the graph. Then list chronologically, beginning with death data, each characteristic of identity you have. These data should not be confined to names, dates, places and relationships only. Occupation, religion, nationality, social affiliation, personal activities, physical characteristics, profession and military service are also of value in establishing individual identities.

* Place the name of each objective on a separate graph. Enter each event, the date, the locality (town or parish, county, state or country) and the source from which the data were obtained. The graph becomes a ready reference for all significant information in the life of an ultimate objective. You can see clearly *when* people were *where;* likewise, you can see at a glance the periods of time they are *lost* to you.

* Next, divide the pedigree into geographic segments. Place the graphs for each husband and wife side by side and compare them for dates and places of residence.

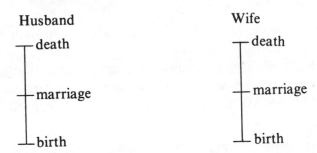

During the survey, you were involved with the complete pedigree. Now the identity graphs are used to separate the pedigree into convenient geographic segments 1) to group ultimate objectives together to prevent duplication of effort and 2) to organize notekeeping systems for more efficient handling. Though related these two aspects are not identical.

Ultimate objectives are grouped together, for research purposes, as long as they have basic jurisdictions (township, parish, county) in common. In this way they become unit problems rather than individual ones. Economy demands this mode of operation. Extracting data pertinent to all families known to have been in the same jurisdiction will save successive trips through the same records. It is expensive and time-consuming to search the same records twice, for the same period of time. By handling all families as a unit, resources will be conserved and accomplishments will be greater.

Notekeeping, too, should be divided. Begin a new calendar,

a new enclosure (document) file and a new alphabetical work-sheet file (see Chapter Two). Consolidate pedigree lines which are known to have common origins in a general geographic area. Residents of Texas and residents of Wisconsin, in 1875, may have lived together as children in central Kentucky in 1850. There is wisdom in keeping these together until you determine their origins.

Thomas Andrew Young

Andrew Finnegan Young
b. 10 Oct 1801
w. Augusta Co. Va.
m. 23 Nov 1825
d. 1 Aug 1866
w. Ross Co, Ohio

James Young
b. abt 1779
w. Ireland
m.
d.
w. Augusta Co, Va.

Margaret Kennedy
b. abt 1780
w. Virginia
d. Feb 1857
w. Augusta Co, Va.

Andrew Kennedy
b. abt 1750
w. Augusta Co, Va.

Margaret
b. abt 1754
w. Augusta Co, Va.

Mary Campbell
b. 17 July 1804
w. Hartford, Conn.
d. May 1836
w. Ross Co, Ohio

Michael Campbell
of Hartford, Conn.

Martha
of Hartford, Conn.

If this were your pedigree, two separate unit problems would be represented:

#1 The Youngs, Kennedys and Finnegans should be kept together. Their jurisdictions differ at this period of time, but the surnames and migrational patterns suggest that all three families are Irish in origin.

#2 The Campbells in Connecticut.

Which unit is handled first? What criteria are used to establish priority? Why? Work should begin with the ultimate objective families which are the most recent. Strive to get all pedigree lines back to the same period of time. Then if migrational trends bring two seemingly unrelated lines into the same original locality, it will be possible to search for them together and prevent costly duplication.

Immediate Objectives

Immediate objectives are always defined in terms of searches to be performed and not in terms of the missing data they supply. Marriage dates or places of death are not considered objectives but merely missing information for which searches are made. Immediate objectives are classified into three types:

1. General searches performed in basic jurisdictions.

2. Particular searches performed to complete research in other jurisdictions.

3. Particular searches performed to define or clarify general search dimensions.

General searches are defined as comprehensive searches performed *only in basic jurisdictions* where ultimate objective families have lived. Their purpose is to answer as many genealogical questions concerning the family as possible. Some genealogists expend the major portion of their resources making selective searches only — a will, a marriage certificate, an extracted court record. Such searches are costly. Seldom do they accomplish the ultimate objective. A general search, however, will use these sources and many more at a reduced overall cost to realize the objective.

Particular searches are defined as selective searches performed in other jurisdictions where ultimate objective families resided. Their purpose is to solve specific questions about the family. It is impractical, if not impossible, to conduct a general search on a state or national basis. Relying upon references obtained during general searches, you can effectively perform particular searches in these jurisdictions. Selective searches are also used to clarify general search dimensions (period of time, basic jurisdiction, surnames, and sources) which cannot be completely defined on the basis of survey data alone. The following diagram compares general and particular searches. Each will be discussed in greater detail in succeeding chapters.

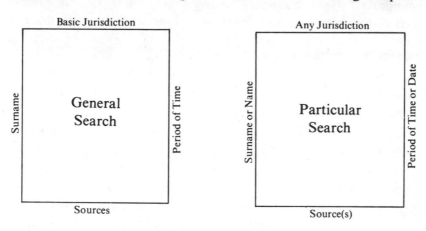

Research Axioms

The order in which the immediate objectives (searches) are performed is governed by seven fundamental rules or axioms. These axioms will impose system, eliminate haphazard methods and prevent wasted resources. Whenever a search ends against the proverbial *brick wall*, it is usually because one or more of these rules has been broken. Their proper application will destroy the barriers and reduce discouragement.

THE GENEALOGICAL RESEARCHER IS DEPENDENT UPON PRESERVED RECORDS. If you run out of records, your work is terminated. Do not spend time searching for something that does not exist.

RECORDS ARE PRODUCTS OF MAN'S ACTIVITIES IN SOCIETY (SOCIAL JURISDICTIONS). Records are produced by units of authority which we call jurisdictions. Records are the basis of authority; without them a jurisdiction can exert little control over the people. Parishes, towns, cities, counties, states and churches are some of the jurisdictions which influence the lives and activities of men.

RESEARCH MUST BE JURISDICTIONALLY ORIENTED. If you approach research properly, you must do it through the jurisdictions which produce the records upon which research is dependent. A thorough study of the jurisdiction should be made *before* the records are searched. When was the jurisdiction formed? What are its physical boundaries? Have boundary changes occurred? Has it always carried the same name? What functions and services does it provide? What special laws govern its duties? What restrictions does it have? What records were produced? Which of these still exist today? Where are they located? How is access best obtained? These items are essential knowledge if you are to search the jurisdiction effectively.

IT IS NECESSARY TO SEARCH ALL OF THE EXISTING RECORDS PRODUCED BY ALL JURISDICTIONS HAVING AUTHORITY OVER ANCESTORAL FAMILIES. You must search *all existing records* produced by every jurisdiction having authority over your ancestors, regardless of where they are currently deposited. Too many genealogists, amateur and professional, confine themselves to certain records. Vital statistics, censuses, probates and church records are the ones most often searched. If these sources do not exist, they are unable to continue their search. Yet, these four categories are only a small percentage of the total records which have survived the ravages of time and civilization. Determine what else was produced and proceed to search them all.[1]

When can you say that a family group is complete and correct? The most you can say is, "It is as complete and correct as existing source materials permit me to compile it." A young man became upset when a family group sheet he had compiled on his own father and mother was challenged. A short time later, his mother confided that in the back yard was buried a little brother of whom he knew nothing. The parents felt the death was a punishment for something they had done and they had never mentioned or recorded the event. Could he have compiled a complete record? This incident emphasizes the need to search all sources pertinent to the pedigree. Anytime you do less, you are making a research compromise. The final record is only as good as the research behind it. To compromise on which records to search, is to compromise on research.

Failure to search every jurisdiction in which an ancestor lived is another compromise. If an obituary notice states that an ancestor was born in Denmark, do not rush immediately to the place of birth, completely overlooking his life as a boy and young married man in New York and his death in Arizona. To obtain the data necessary to identify him in Denmark, retrace his steps, examining the records in all the jurisdictions through which he passed. It makes no difference how many jurisdictions a man lived in from birth to death, all should be searched. It makes no difference where the records are located if they are accessible they should be searched.

WHEN SEARCHING THE RECORDS OF A BASIC JURISDICTION, EXTRACT ALL OF THE DATA IN ALL OF THE RECORDS INVOLVING PEDIGREE SURNAMES FOR A DEFINED PERIOD OF TIME. The basic jurisdiction has the most influence over men's lives. It may be the county, the city, the township or some extra-legal body in the United States. It may be the borough, the civil parish, the monastery, the manor or a special jurisdiction called a peculiar in England. It differs for each period of time and locality involved. A careful study should be made *before research is begun* to determine the basic jurisdiction. Once pedigree families are identified in a basic jurisdiction and the period of time is defined, extract every entry involving your pedigree surnames from all of the records. You cannot afford to be selective, to make particular searches in a basic jurisdiction.

This same rule holds true for searches in the United States, Germany, Sweden, Ireland, Russia or Australia — even countries where surnames are derived from occupations, localities or patronymics. All Jones entries, all de Warrenne entries, all Jensen entries, all MacGrady entries should be extracted from the records of the basic jurisdiction. Family groups are compiled on the basis of comparison and unless all claimants for family membership are available for analysis you cannot compare

124

accurately.[2] It becomes apparent after a researcher has used source materials for a short length of time that if there is one man with a particular name, there are usually two or more. To extract only one or two of them is a compromise in research. To go through a set of records saying, "This John Jones is my relative, this William Jones is not my relative, this Patrick Jones is my relative . . ." is similar to plucking the daisy: "Is he or is he not?" If you knew enough about the family to be selective, you would have no need for research. Take all of the Joneses and assemble them in families to determine which are yours and which are not.

WORK FROM THE KNOWN TO THE UNKNOWN. This is a fundamental law yet it is the one most often broken. You must depend upon what you know to take you to the unknown. Unless there is reason to believe that the family was in a jurisdiction or locality, do not spend time and money searching there for them. Always begin with the most recent generation and move back in time. For each ultimate objective family study events dealing with the deaths of the persons and move backwards through their lives. Never search for birth data first. Begin with the jurisdiction in which the family unit lived last and check every jurisdiction through which it passed until the beginning of the family unit is reached — the marriage of the parents. Research should be outlined on the basis of known fact. Work with data which are known and project from this base to learn new facts.

ANY PARTICULAR SEARCH UNDERTAKEN PRIOR TO THE COMPLETION OF A GENERAL SEARCH MUST HAVE AS ITS OBJECTIVE, ONE OR MORE OF THE DIMENSIONS OF THE GENERAL SEARCH.

Do not write for a marriage certificate, an extract of a will, or any other kind of document in basic jurisdiction sources before performing a general search unless the objective is to define the dimensions (basic jurisdiction, surnames, period of time or sources) of that search. This axiom will save time and money. To perform research properly, you must eventually search all documents. For the same amount of money needed to procure one marriage certificate, you can hire a searcher to search and extract the data from ten.

Success in genealogy depends upon adherence to these axioms. Violation of any one will create problems detrimental to research success.

Only one immediate objective will be solved at a time. The choice of which is first is dictated by the needs of the ultimate objectives. Selections can be determined from the Flow Chart of Research Analysis. Questions are presented in ovals; immediate objectives appear in rectangles. Define the ultimate objective then begin with the first question, answering it yes or no. Follow the appropriate arrow. The first rectangle you encounter is your first immediate objective. Complete it, analyze it and proceed on following the flow of the diagram, based upon yes or no answers. A researcher's expertise can be measured by his ability to correctly answer the questions posed by the chart. You can get yourself into all kinds of difficulties by prematurely answering yes to one of these queries. A *yes* answer affirms willingness to invest time and resources for immediate searches, and a willingness to build all future work upon that *yes* judgment.

FLOW CHART OF RESEARCH ANALYSIS

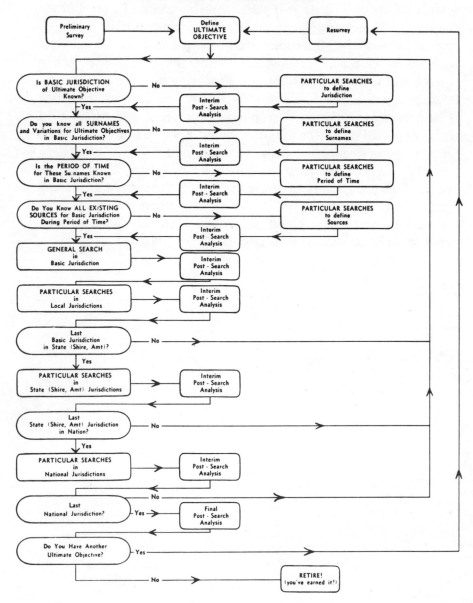

CHAPTER EIGHT
PRE-SEARCH ANALYSIS:
GENERAL SEARCH DIMENSIONS,
GENERAL SEARCH OUTLINE

Every genealogical puzzle is solved through searches and every search, no matter how insignificant it may seem, should be methodically planned before its execution. You should know what to do and how to go about doing it. Entirely too much research time is wasted because of inadequate preparation. The final phase of the *pre-search analysis* is the preparation of a complete and systematic work plan. This plan is called a research outline. It defines and organizes the dimensions of each immediate objective (search).

Basic Jurisdiction

Success in a general search is directly proportionate to the care taken to define each search dimension completely. Guesswork is always costly, both in time and money. The first dimension of a general search is the *basic jurisdiction*; indeed, general searches are performed only in *basic jurisdictions*. This is the unit within society exercising the most control over man — the jurisdiction which records his land transactions, probates his will, settles his legal disputes, collects his taxes — that sphere of authority with which he deals most frequently during his life. In the records of the *basic jurisdiction* lies the greatest possibility of identifying pedigree ancestors. These records also contain the information necessary to plan searches in subordinate (local) and higher (state and national) jurisdictions. Normally, the preliminary survey will identify the first *basic jurisdiction* where research is to be performed. If it does not, particular searches must be made to identify it (see page 146 below).

History. History and genealogy are inseparably interwoven; it is out of history that genealogy emerges. An exhaustive study of the *basic jurisdiction* whether it be a county in western America or a parish in Denmark, must be undertaken *before* research is begun.

* Commit yourself to the first three axioms or rules of research:

    1. Genealogists are dependent upon preserved records.

    2. Records are produced by jurisdictions.

    3. Research must be jurisdictionally oriented.

* Study the jurisdiction. Understand the institutions which existed; these created the records which you must search. Evaluation of these records and the evidence they contain is based upon knowledge of the creating authority and its purpose. Avoid superficiality; settle for nothing less than a complete study of the history, geography, social and economic background and political orientation. The notion that you can learn the jurisdiction from the sources is poor procedure.

You should consider the prominent influences that have a bearing upon the lives and movements of people: Why did they move? Where did they come from? Who did they come with? Where did they go when they left? The only way to trace families on the move is to understand their reasons for moving. A study of the locality where your ancestors resided will provide the answers to these questions.

Soil productivity and marketing possibilities. If farming was the occupation of an ancestor, he was dependent upon fertile soil to raise crops and livestock. Consider tobacco growing in early Virginia: farmers did not truly understand the value of fertilization or crop rotation. Tobacco leaches nutrients from the soil after three or four years and the soil will not support growth. With plenty of frontier, tobacco farmers moved onto new land. Men dependent upon marketing facilities to support a family drove herds of cattle across two or three states in each drive. The pastures looked greener and frequently led to family migrations.

National land policies. Land policies played a significant part in American migrational movements. At one time, land was the most marketable resource of value which the country had and the government devised many policies to realize profits therefrom. Such things as bounty land, lotteries, preemption rights, donation claims and homesteads were stimuli to movement.

Occupations. If your ancestor was a weaver living where the mill closed down two or three years after he married and started raising his family, he is not likely to be found in the parish registers. Where did he go for employment? Instead of searching blindly in the surrounding parishes in ever widening circles, draw a straight line to the nearest mill where a weaver could obtain work and search the registers there.

Industrial development. Prior to industrialization people were often born, married and died within a 20-mile area. As coal mines opened up and textile and steel mills came into existence, people were drawn from the farms into industry-centered urban settlements. Cities which were once small villages expanded into population centers almost overnight. Such areas, because of inadequate sanitation and crowded circumstances became natural breeding places for epidemics and unemployment. It has been estimated that during the early 1700's, one-fourth of the working population of England was drifting from place to place seeking work.

Wars. Wars cause migrations. They were regular occurrences in Europe. Armies trampled across the land persecuting the losers and plundering the neutrals. If an ancestor disappeared from a jurisdiction at the time of a military incursion, history will tell you what happened to him. He may have emigrated. He may have circulated around and settled 30 to 40 miles away where things were less chaotic. He may have just drifted until he could return and rebuild his life.

Religion. The struggles between religious groups have been responsible for major migrations, deaths and wars. Know the religious history of your locality and the influences religion had upon family customs. Religion also stimulated changes in the keeping of records.

Other important considerations include modes of travel, educational opportunities, voting qualifications and economic changes. Study local social customs: naming of children, marrying and remarrying, local festivals and folklore. Determine the demographic characteristics of the population: growth or decrease in the number of people in the area, average size of families, changes in ages at marriage and proportion of children in each family who married. Know the churches and fraternal organizations which the area supported. This knowledge is fundamental to understanding the records produced and their contents.

* Begin your study in general histories at the national level and move in descending order to the state or shire, county or parish, town or village. The national government usually dictated the structure of other jurisdictions within its territory and national histories provide a general picture in which to place local history and geography.

* Choose recent books on the subject first, then read some selected histories written near the time when your ancestors lived. Concentrate on the social, economic and institutional aspects of historical development. Use political changes as a skeleton on which to hang other information.

* Check the bibliographies listed on pages 74-79 for histories pertinent to your ancestry. If they are unavailable in your local library, obtain them on interlibrary loan or through out-of-print book services (see pages 196-98). You can also consult your local university for histories currently used as texts.

* Write the local library in the areas where your ancestors lived. Librarians frequently prepare lists of works recommended for the history of their area which can be used as a guide. The researcher who is knowledgeable in the historical background of his subject is ready to find and utilize source materials to advantage.[1]

* Study changes in place-names. Such information is essential if records are to be located. A good place to begin is a gazeteer. It will often list old or long forgotten names. Maps are useful but smaller places are not always shown. State and national statutes list official name changes. Be aware, however, that all name changes are not official, that is, legally recognized. Some are the result of local nicknames which replace the official designation. For these, contact older residents of the community: the retired postmaster or mortician, local reference librarians or land surveyors.[2]

* Know changes in boundary lines. Records are produced by jurisdictions; if you are to locate the records you must define past and present boundaries. Counties and states have come into and gone out of existence. Old towns have become ghost towns and new ones have risen. Boundary lines have changed in name as well as size due to laws and land acquisitions. Such dynamics will always be a part of society. Give special attention to ancestors who lived close to a jurisdictional boundary; they are apt to appear in the records of both sides. To determine boundary changes, check indexes to state and national statutes under the current name and follow the cross-references. Collections of American state statutes and English laws can be used at any law library.[3]

* Become well enough acquainted with the locality that you could discourse for thirty minutes, without notes, and keep your audience interested. Such familiarity will prevent mis-interpretation of records and equip you to perform successful research.

Geography. The influence of environment upon man is a significant feature in his movements and actions.

* Obtain a good geography of your basic jurisdiction and care-fully study those portions which describe natural resources, mineral deposits, climate, water supply, wildlife, forests, soil deposits and elevation. Incompability with the geo-graphic area stimulated migrational movements, creating a constant flow of people into and out of an area.

Maps. Maps can be a most valuable research aid. Several types are available. *Topographical maps* are drawn to a large scale and show elevations, positions of streams, lakes, roads, cities and towns. Current county maps, available from the state highway department, are topographical maps. They show every cemetery, every church, every school, every stream and creek in the county. Phillimore's in Sussex, England is reprinting the large-scale county maps of England originally drawn in the eighteenth century. *Political maps* emphasize political bounda-ries: counties, townships,. cities and other civil divisions. Several states have prepared genealogical descent maps of county or town boundaries showing each series of changes. Check with the state or local historical society, state archives or library or the state highway department for references and copies. *Communication maps* include highways, railroads, airlines and navigation routes. *City maps* detail streets, wards and subdivisions within the city, major business establishments, principal churches and governmental buildings. City administrative offices usually can provide these upon request. *Cadastral maps* show the quantity, value and ownership of real estate, sometimes even the names of current landowners. These are usually prepared for tax purposes, scaled 25 miles to the inch. Official tax maps are available in county assessors offices. County atlases published in the late nineteenth century are cadastral maps and can be found in most local libraries. *Historical maps* include dates and places of historic events. The "Walking Purchase Map" of early Pennsylvania and the centennial maps celebrating Civil War battles are examples.[4]

* Obtain two maps: one of the locality at the time your ancestors lived in the area and a current one. They should be large scale (1 to 2½ inches to the mile) and detailed enough to show small villages and hamlets, churches and cemeteries.[5] Write the New York Public Library or the Library of Congress for contemporary American maps and the British Museum for English ones. If they do not have the map you want, contact local libraries, historical societies, record offices or university libraries in the areas where your ancestors resided. Current maps for America are available through state highway departments or the U.S. Geodetic Survey (offices in each state capital and Washington, D.C.) and for England through the Ordnance Survey of Great Britain (Southampton).[6]

* Pinpoint the geographical location of your ancestors on the map. Become familiar with the neighboring towns and other places represented. Note geographic relationships between towns and other civil divisions. Determine what topographical features (rivers, mountains, lakes, swamps and canyons) had a bearing upon the habits and movements of the people living in that area. Note the present location of boundaries between states, counties, townships and ecclesiastical divisions.

Too many genealogists think the only things of importance are those which fit on a family group form. When you so restrict yourself, your chances of finding migrating ancestors are slim.

You must know your jurisdiction *before* you begin research in genealogical records.

Surnames

This dimension of the general search is the most neglected of all. Occasionally a researcher will get away with negligence in search after search; however, brick walls are made of misconstrued names. To define this dimension consider the following criteria:

All surnames. Extract all entries involving pedigree *surnames* when searching in a basic jurisdiction. Do not be selective. Selectivity leads to repeat searches. If the preliminary survey is thorough, you will have a number of *surnames* to take into your general searches. Supposing you have the names Jordan, Anderson, Hardin, Hill and Cooper. As you search the basic jurisdiction, you take *every piece* of information on *every person* bearing those *surnames* for a defined period of time. A tremendous task? An unreasonable one? Can you put together a complete family if you do not have all those who are family members? Could you possibly reconstruct the family on the basis of saying: "This John Jordan belongs to my family and this Henry Jordan does not?" Unless you have all of the Jordans you cannot accurately compare one family with another. If you knew enough to be selective, you could move further up the pedigree to begin.

Many argue that with such *surnames* as Jones, Smith and Johnson a general search procedure is impractical. Actually, it is the best argument for the general search. The more there are, the harder it is to tell them apart. Adhere strictly to Axiom 5 or settle for incorrect pedigrees and missing links.

If the ultimate objective has a middle or given name, which could be the surname of his mother or grandmother, take it along in the search. It is still the custom to give the first son the maiden *surname* of his mother as a middle or given name. For example: John *Baker* Eakle. If there are Bakers in the records, extract them. When the search has been completed a new *surname* may be identified and the pedigree may be extended. If it proves to be a false assumption, the loss in time is negligible.

Spelling Variations. It is a good idea to use phonetics —

write and pronounce aloud — all of the possible spellings that *surnames* could have. Train your eyes to look for all. Consider this list: Coyner, Coiner, Koiner, Koyner, Keinadt, Keiner, Chiner, Coynet, Koynat, Chyma, Coynart, Koinadt, Kainadt, Kiner, Keynot, Konnaught, Keinart, Keinot, Koynalt, Koinath, Conna, Kyner, Keinort. To avoid missing any pertinent entry pronounce all names silently to yourself as you search. The eyes can become conditioned to spot only those names for which they are looking, completely disregarding all other names and words on the page. This valuable efficiency can be disastrous! A classic example is the misspelling of the name Cox. One lady went through a census six times and could not find the name. Her eye was looking for an X and she overlooked all names without an X. The seventh time, following the advice to pronounce each name in the record, she found COCHS. Always copy the name as it appears in the record; do not change spellings. If you think it should be spelled differently, put your interpretation in brackets to indicate that it is you, not the source, talking.

Spelling is a comparatively new discipline; a few decades ago the spelling of a name was based upon the way the listener heard it pronounced. Foreign names were subject to English translations, dialects created changes and it becomes a matter of trying to second guess the clerk (who was probably an Irishman listening to a German) diligently writing what he thought he heard.

Phonetic transliterations can cause a great deal of trouble. A good example is the mix-up of Miltons and Meltons (later proved to be two separate families). The families knew which was which, but the clerks recording their documents did not distinguish between them. They mixed the Miltons into the Meltons and the Meltons into the Miltons. The only wise research procedure was to take both of the surnames — Miltons and Meltons. Once they were all extracted, it became possible to separate the two families. As it turned out, had only the Meltons been extracted, one document in ten would have been lost — mixed in with the Miltons.

Period of Time

The *period of time* is the biggest trouble spot in research. It is not an easy dimension to define properly. It takes some work.

One way out is to start the general search with the earliest records and proceed down to the present time, or to begin at the present time and work back. As each new maiden surname is discovered, however, you will have to go back again through the same records to obtain data concerning that new name. If each pedigree line produces one new surname about every 30 years, this method could prove extremely time consuming. Another solution frequently used, is to approximate birth and death dates from some known event and search the period between the two dates. Such mathematical formulas are misleading. In establishing the *period of time* for a general search it is essential to define, not guess at, this dimension. The following criteria can serve as a guide:

How long were the children of the ultimate objectives in the basic jurisdiction? Each person in the basic jurisdiction who bears the same surname as the ultimate objective family and who could be a child in that family should be followed to his grave. Such children are essential to complete the family unit. If one of them died unmarried, his probate will usually name all of his brothers and sisters with their children, many of whom may be scattered throughout the country. These ultimate objective children will either die and be buried in the basic jurisdiction or will have moved away. At the conclusion of the general search, you should know which. If they have moved to other jurisdictions, rely on the records in the basic jurisdiction to provide clues as to where they went. The eventuality that ancestors will, in their old age, join their children and be living in their homes at death should not be over looked. Only by following these migrant children, will you locate the parents in their old age.

The information you seek is that data needed to complete the family group of the ultimate objective: father, mother and children. Identification of each of the grandchildren with their spouses and families is not necessary to accomplish that objective. When the members of the generation, comparable to that of the ultimate objective children die out, the general search can be terminated.

When did the surname first appear in the basic jurisdiction? Avoid defining too short a search, even when you have evidence that your ultimate objective family stayed in a basic jurisdiction only a brief time. For example, Ancestor X and his wife lived in St. Mary's parish only two years and had no children there. This you know from his diary. Many people would consider it foolish to search at all, but if you do, certainly no more than three or four years. What could you possibly hope to find? But, can you accurately judge the *period of time* for a surname search by the activities of one family? People rarely moved in lone families. Prior to the twentieth century, migrations were group oriented, not individual movements. Daniel Boone took his brothers, sisters, aunts, uncles, cousins and neighbors; the whole family left North Carolina together. Your ancestors were social people too. Married men with families rarely moved at all unless some single relative pioneered the area first. Then he would entice his relatives to join him where the grass was greener, the soil richer and the money more plentiful. Watch for the surname itself, not just the ultimate objective family.

Let us consider an element in the general search approach unmentioned thus far: a general search should lay the foundation for the next generation — the father and mother of the ultimate objectives. While you perform a general search on the present ultimate objectives, you accumulate information on earlier generations. You will prove pedigree connections with brothers, sisters, uncles and aunts. Ultimate objectives cannot be identified without them. If the general search does not provide three generations: 1) children of the ultimate objectives, 2) the ultimate objectives themselves and 3) the fathers and mothers of the ultimate objectives, then you are far from extending the pedigree. A general search, therefore, should never be made for less than a generation (about 25 or 30 years). Give yourself the opportunity of finding parents and grandparents, brothers and sisters, uncles and aunts. Here are the foundations for future ultimate objectives.

Never extend the period of time beyond the possible date of marriage of parents of the ultimate objectives. If the surname appears early in the formation of the jurisdiction and remains there until the present day, or if there are missing maiden surnames on the pedigree, begin the search at the earliest time you would expect to identify new surnames — the marriage of the parents of the ultimate objectives. Each pedigree line produces another name and another line about every 30 years. The appearance of these new surnames makes it impractical to extend the search earlier than the expected date of marriage. A search extended beyond that time results in less control over searches, less precise definition of dimensions, greater possibility of error and more complicated analysis. Some overlap is unavoidable; keep it to a minimum by searching one generation at a time, adding new surnames as you go.

When was the basic jurisdiction formed? During the preliminary survey and through particular searches prior to the general search, you will make a thorough study of the basic jurisdiction where your ancestors lived. You should know the date of formation of that jurisdiction. There is little point in searching before the parish or county came into existence. There were no records and to consider the parent jurisdiction at this point is premature. That requires another general search, with a completely new set of dimensions. Make a careful study of your problem, evaluate it in terms of these criteria, base your definitions upon *those which are applicable* and with experience, you will do an expert job.

Each of these dimensions usually requires a series of particular searches to establish 1) that the family actually did live in the locality, 2) the spelling variations of the names and 3) the specific terminal dates of the period of time to be searched. The procedure for these particular searches is discussed in Chapter Nine below.

Sources

The fourth general search dimension, *sources*, should be as carefully defined as the basic jurisdiction, the surnames and the period of time. The thoroughness of the general search, indeed, whether or not it is a general search, depends upon how completely *all existing sources* created by the jurisdiction, which are pertinent to the pedigree, are listed and searched. Compiling such a comprehensive list requires effort.

Your list of *sources* should be started during the preliminary survey. Family histories, biographies, and other secondary works often indicate source materials used in their compilation. The libraries of institutional jurisdictions (genealogical societies, historical societies, etc.) usually contain primary sources and special collections. Make note of these *sources*, where they are located, the periods of time they cover and other pertinent details (see sample calendar entry immediately following). A series of particular searches can fill in any gaps which exist. The end result of this list is the research outline.

CALENDAR
(COPYRIGHT 1972, GENEALOGICAL COPY SERVICE)

ENC. NO.	S NO.	DATE OF SEARCH	SOURCE: Description, Condition, Unusual Circumstances, How Searched.	JURISDICTION OR LOCALITY	PERIOD OF TIME	SURNAME OR NAME	RE-SULT
22	31	18 May 1970	Tinkling Spring: Head water of Freedom by Howard M. Wilson, published by the Tinkling Spring and Hermitage Presbyterian Churches, Augusta County, Va. 1954. Copy in Genealogical Society Library, Salt Lake City. Call number: 975.5 B4 Well documented. Appendixes contain many transcribed documents.	Augusta County, Va.	1732- 1958	Johnson Kennedy Berry	WS WS WS
			NOTE: Manuscripts (176 pieces) on Zachariah Johnston are located in the Va. State Library, Richmond. Will get copies of them.				

Research Outline

If research is to be accomplished with a minimum expenditure of time and money, each general search must be carefully planned in advance. This plan is called the research outline. It summarizes the dimensions which have been defined above and organizes source materials in the order they should be searched.

* List your search dimensions on a research outline. A plain or ruled sheet of paper can be used or you can obtain additional copies of the examples in this book.[7]

* Enter the immediate objective — general search — at the top. Then indicate the basic jurisdiction, the surnames to be extracted and the period of time of the search.

* Gather data on sources and their locations during the preliminary survey. As you read family histories, biographies and local studies for genealogical data and general background, check the footnotes, bibliographies and appendices — the author's sources of information — for those which may pertain to your future research. While searching institutional jurisdictions pertaining to your ancestry, you will learn of other record categories and special collections preserved in each repository. Note their locations, the period of time they cover and any limitations on their use on the research outline at the time you discover them. Be sure to include non-documentary materials.[8] In this way much of your work defining the source dimension will already be finished.

* Check the guides and research aids discussed in Appendix Three for those sources for which you have no references or locations. Use guides available in libraries in your own vicinity first. If they are not available locally, obtain them through interlibrary loan or purchase them through your local book store or out-of-print book service (described on pages 196-98 below).

* Add any sources which may have been omitted to your outline. Each source you search should lead to at least one more; add these as you discover them so they too can be searched.

* Preserve the research outline for use during the post-search analysis. The data extracted from each source will be placed directly on worksheets; reports from field researchers and copies of documents and letters will be numbered in sequence, punched and filed in the enclosure files; and a complete description of each source, together with a blow-by-blow account of the circumstances of each search will be entered on the calendar. In this way, you, the re-

searcher, will have double control of sources and searches. Your posterity can carry on without undue loss of momentum if something should happen to you.

The research outline which follows contains a list of the records which could be produced by the basic jurisdiction. Blank spaces are left for you to add any others you may discover. Although the records are designated by English (American) titles, most countries of the world have equivalent jurisdictions with identical or similar types of records. You must still determine which of these sources are in existence today, where they are located and how they can be obtained. This carefully prepared outline of planned searches is based upon unemotional analysis. The only "ifs" between you and success are the existence of sources with pertinent information (an if over which you have no control) and sufficient knowledge in the use of these sources (an if determined by experience and practical application).

RESEARCH OUTLINE

(Copyright 1972, Genealogical Copy Service)

Immediate Objective: GENERAL SEARCH

Basic Jurisdiction: (County, Town, Independent City, City-County, Parish, Manor or equivalent).

_____

All Surnames: _____

_____

_____

_____

Period of Time: _____

DEPOSITORY	ADDRESS	METHOD OF SEARCH (Personal, Researcher, Loan, Correspondence, Copy)	REMARKS (Fees Restrictions)

Sources: This is a guide to the sources which *could have been produced* only. Compare with a current bibliography or guide to record holdings of the jurisdiction and check (___) those items still extant for your period of time. Circle each check (ⓧ) as you search that record. Some jurisdictions will have separate books for each source, others will record all of them in one volume or roll. Although the records are designated by English (American) titles, most countries of the world have identical or similar types of records.

A. CENSUS RECORDS:

U.S. Federal Censuses

___Indexes
___1790 ___1860
___1800 ___1870
___1810 ___1880
___1820 ___1900
___1830 ___1910
___1840 ___1920
___1850 ___1930

___Population Schedules
___1790 ___1840
___1800 ___1850
___1810 ___1860
___1820 ___1870
___1830 ___1880

___Restricted
___1900 ___1920
___1910 ___

___Slave Schedules
___1850 ___1860

___Mortality Schedules
___1850 ___1870
___1860 ___1880

___Veterans' Schedules
___1840, Revolutionary War
___1890, Union Army and Survivors

___Agriculture Schedules
___1840 ___1870
___1850 ___1880
___1860

___Religious Schedules
___1890 ___1926

___1906 ___1936
___1916 ___

___Industrial Schedules
___1850 ___1870
___1860 ___1880

___Mining Schedules
___ ___
___ ___

State Census Records
___
___
___
___
___

Territorial Censuses
___
___
___
___

Local Census Records
___Constable's Census
___
___
___

Other
___Military
___District Constable
___

B. PROPERTY RECORDS (Basic Sources):

LAND RECORDS:

Original Title Documents
___Entries
___Warrants
___Surveys
___Plats
___Patents (Grants)
___Proprietors Records
___Lotteries
___Homesteads

Title Conveyances
___Indexes
___Grantor
___Grantee
___Deeds
___Quit Claim
___Will
___Gift
___Tax
___Sheriff
___Warrantee
___Trust
___Lease

___Release
___Register of Title
___

Mortgages
___Real Estate
___Chattel
___Personal Property
___Uncancelled
___Liens
___Tax Liens
___Private Deeds of Trust

Miscellaneous Land Records
___Mining Claims
___Plat Books
___Bills of Sale
___Sale of School Lands
___Sale of Railroad Lands
___Sale of Swamp Lands
___Abstracts of Title
___Title Insurance
___Purchase Certificate
___Conditional Sales
___Charters
___Unrecorded Deeds

_____Quit Rents
_____Dower Release
_____Acknowlegement
_____Marriage Contract
_____Marriage Settlement
_____Contracts
_____Agreements
_____Mineral Rights
_____Power of Attorney
_____Confiscated Lands
_____Condemned Land
_____Water Rights
_____Maps
_____Town Minutes
_____Council Minutes
_____Farm Names
_____Exemptions
_____Claims Clubs Files
_____
_____

Court-Related Land Records

_____Escheat Proceedings
_____Decrees
_____Dower Rights
_____Courtesy Rights
_____Judgments
_____Processioning Lists
_____Boundary Reports
_____Land Commissions
_____Boundary Changes
_____Perambulations
_____
_____
_____

Other

_____
_____
_____

PROBATE RECORDS:

Court Records

_____Estate Docket
_____Guardianship Docket
_____Claims Docket
_____Minutes
_____Orders
_____Decrees
_____Judgments
_____Executions
_____Appeals

Petitions

_____Letters Testamentary
_____Administration
_____Guardianship
_____Appointment or Change
    of Guardian
_____Redress for Misuse or
    Waste of Property
_____Determine Heirs
_____Renunciation

Wills

_____Written
_____Nuncapative
_____Holographic
_____Codicils

Bonds

_____Administrator
_____Executor
_____Guardian

_____Appraiser
_____Trustee

Inventories

_____Real Estate
_____Personal Property
_____Guardians
_____Conservators
_____Partnership
_____Minors Estates
_____Appraisals
_____Appraisers Warrants
_____Reports

Publications

_____Announcement
_____Notice to Heirs
_____Notice of Sales
_____Notice to Creditors

Accounts

_____Administrator
_____Executor
_____Guardian
_____Trustee
_____Conservator

Divisions

_____Commission Reports
_____Settlements
_____Decrees
_____Dower Rights
_____Courtesy Rights
_____Awards
_____Private Disbursement
_____Ledgers

Releases

_____Executor
_____Administrator
_____Trustee
_____Guardian
_____Heirs

Claims

_____Registers
_____Accounts
_____Appeals

Miscellaneous

_____Unrecorded Wills
_____Widows Allowances
_____Orders to Find Heirs
_____Sales Documents
_____Marriage Settlements
_____Waivers
_____Changes of Name
_____Legitimation

Other

_____Memoranda
_____
_____
_____
_____
_____

COURT RECORDS:

Indexes

_____Plaintiff
_____Defendant
_____General

_____Cross Indexes
_____Parties
_____Actions

Dockets

_____Civil
_____Criminal
_____Equity
_____Trial
_____Petition
_____New Actions
_____Argument
_____Judgment
_____Summons
_____Estate
_____Orphans
_____Reference
_____Stet
_____Claims
_____Insolvents
_____Bankruptcy
_____Divorce
_____Imparlance
_____Prosecution
_____Special Proceedings
_____Subpoena
_____Costs
_____Lunacy
_____Adoption
_____Execution
_____Appeals
_____Appearance

Case Files

_____Civil
_____Criminal
_____Equity
_____Chancery
_____Estate
_____Divorce
_____Claims
_____Insolvents
_____Bankruptcy
_____Adoption
_____Assize Rolls

Bonds

_____Government Officials
_____Court Officials
_____Trustees
_____Prisoners
_____Apprentices
_____Masters

Court Actions

_____Presentments
_____Subpoenas
_____Petitions
_____Writs
_____Warrants
_____Summons
_____Promissory Notes
_____Depositions
_____Minutes
_____Actions
_____Orders
_____Decrees
_____Bills of Cost
_____Draft Minutes
_____Copy Minutes
_____Examinations
_____Cases Removed
_____Pleadings
_____Allegations
_____Interventions

_____Arbitration Reports
_____Pleas
_____Inquisitions
_____Complaints
_____Recognizances
_____Intentions to Appeal
_____Appeals
_____Fines
_____Precepts
_____Enrollments
_____Precedents
_____

Judgments

_____Judgments
_____Judgments Satisfied
_____Short Judgments
_____Equity Judgments
_____Abstracts
_____Final Concords
_____Verdicts
_____Opinions
_____Decisions
_____

Executions

_____Executions
_____Stays of Execution
_____Foreclosures
_____Attachments
_____Distraints
_____Property Sales
_____
_____

Miscellaneous Records

_____Indictments
_____Lists of Attorneys
_____Oaths of Allegiance
_____Documents
_____Exhibits
_____Court Taxes
_____Prisoners Petitions
_____Sacrament Certificates
_____Formularies
_____Attendance Lists
_____List of Constables
_____Gamekeeper Depositions
_____List of Gamekeepers
_____Fines and Forfeitures
_____Certificates
_____Declarations
_____Commissions of Officials
_____Roll of Societies
_____Register of Papists
_____Papist Estates
_____Sequestrations
_____Divorce
_____Alimony
_____Legitimation of Children
_____Bastardy Papers
_____Child Custody
_____Adoption
_____Coroner Files
_____County Attorney Files
_____Miners Court Files
_____Vigilance Committees
_____Committees of Safety
_____Committees of Correspondence
_____Witness Books
_____Memorials
_____Loose Papers
_____Name Changes
_____Aliases

___Child Support
___Convictions
___Habitual Criminals
___Drug Users
___Insanity Cases
___Printed Court Records
___Inquisitions of Lunacy
___
___
___

Other

___
___
___
___
___

COURT RELATED RECORDS

Sheriff (Police) Records

___Constables Returns
___Warrants
___Writs
___Habitual Criminals
___Arrest Registers
___Fingerprint Files
___"Mug" Files
___Dockets
___Deed Books
___Lien Records
___Accounts
___Daybook
___Daily Report
___Morning Report
___Offense Report
___Investigation Report
___Criminal History Files
___Property Received
___Booking Record
___Fee Lists
___
___

Jail Records

___Register of Prisoners
___Daybook
___Work Register
___Medical Register
___Roll of Prisoners
___U.S. Prisoners
___Prisoners of War
___Inventories of
   Belongings
___Transfers
___County Farm Books
___
___
___

Jury Records

___Grand Jury
___Petit Jury
___Coroner Jury
___Minutes
___List of Jurors

Vital Records

___Birth Register
___Birth Certificate
___Stillbirth
___Death Register
___Death Certificate
___Coroners Files

___Case Books
___Attendance Records
___Pay Lists
___Discharges
___Jury Tickets
___
___

Lawyers Records

___Daybook
___Account Book
___Correspondence
___Briefs
___Depositions
___Documentary Exhibits
___Trial Transcripts
___Case Files
___Register of Cases
___
___

Naturalization

___Intention
___Petition
___Oath of Allegiance
___Certificate
___Change of Name
___Interview
___Witness Affadavit
___Minutes
___
___

Constable Records

___Accounts
___Register of Servants
___Presentments
___Indictments
___Writs
___Warrants
___Hue and Cry
___Distraint List
___Watch and Ward
___Slave Patrol
___Daybook
___Arrest Register
___Crime Returns
___List of Papists
___Rate List
___Petty Sessions Journal
___Precepts
___Orders
___
___
___

Gamekeeper Files

___Writs
___Warrants
___Game Certificates
___Gamebooks
___Registers
___
___
___

___Physicians Files
___

Marriage Records

___Intentions
___Banns
___Publications

Manorial Records

___Subsidy Rolls
___Muniment Rolls
___Hundred Rolls
___Leet Rolls
___Leaseholds
___Heritable Copyholds
___Copyholds
___Freeholds of Inheritance
___Customary Freeholds
___Fine Arbitrary
___Fine Certain
___Heriots
___Alienation Rolls
___Quit Rents
___Yearly Rents
___Oath of Fealty
___Court Attendance Rolls
___Reliefs
___Acknowledgments
___Stewards Accounts
___Enrollments
___Purchase Deeds
___Distraints
___Powers of Attorney
___Mortgages
___Sales Contracts
___Maps
___Plats
___Surveys
___Land Divisions

MISCELLANEOUS PROPERTY RECORDS:

Slavery Records

___Manumissions
___Freedom Certificates
___Petitions
___Register of Slaves
___Register of Free Negroes
___Bills of Sale
___
___
___

Tax Records

___Poll Tax
___Personal Property
___Real Estate
___School
___Poor Rate
___Highway
___Inventory
___Cattle
___Oxen
___Maimed Soldier
___Prisoner
___War
___Window
___Hearth
___Militia
___Carriage
___Servant
___Hairpowder

___Stamp
___Gun
___Plate
___Inheritance
___Franchise
___Income
___Sales
___Merchant
___Uninhabited Homes
___Arms
___Tithe Registers
___Tithe Commutations
___Discoveries
___Faculty Lists
___Lists of Freemen
___Lists of Freeholders
___Rate Lists
___Valuations
___Minors Valuations
___Assessors Lists
___Exemptions
___Delinquents
___Abatements
___Abstracts
___Redemptions
___Forfeitures
___Tax Liens
___Tax Sales
___Federal Tax Liens
___Collectors Bonds
___Appeals
___Board of Review
___Minutes

Indentures

___Servants
___Apprentices
___
___

Animal Registration

___Bull
___Ram
___Marks
___Brands
___Estrays
___Stallion
___
___

Maps

___Plats
___Road Surveys
___County Atlases
___Election Districts
___Militia Districts
___Plans
___
___

Other

___
___
___

C. NON-PROPERTY RECORDS (Supplementary Sources):

___Consent Affadavits
___Applications
___Health Records
___Bonds
___Contracts
___Settlements
___Licenses
___Bonds

___Registers
___Returns
___Waivers
___Secret Marriages
___Annulments
___Negro Cohabitations
___
___

Militia Records

___ Pay Rolls
___ Muster Rolls
___ Size Rolls
___ Appointment of Officers
___ Delinquents
___ Court Martial Minutes
___ Court Martial Files
___ List of Males over 16
___ Slave Patrol Reports
___ Watch Reports
___ Discharges
___ Pensions
___ Selective Service
___ Resolutions
___ Subscriptions
___ Exemptions
___ Train Bands
___ Levy Register
___ Widows Support
___ Widows Burials
___ Veterans Burials
___ Application for Burial
___ Survivors Burials
___ Logbooks
___ Commissions
___ Deportations
___ Instructions
___ Oaths
___ List of Arms
___ Letters
___ Orders
___ Beacon Lists
___ Accounts
___ Bounties
___ Pension Applications
___ Pension Warrants

___

School Records

___ Tax Lists
___ Censuses
___ School Board Minutes
___ Teacher Lists
___ Accounts
___ Teacher Health
    Certificates

___
___
___

Poor Relief Records

___ Warning Out Records
___ Permit to Settle
___ Permit to Visit
___ Removal Orders
___ Travel Permit
___ Settlement Certificate
___ Passport
___ Character Certificate
___ Security Bonds
___ Bastardy Bonds
___ Tax Exemptions
___ Registers of Unmarried
    Persons
___ Orphan Register
___ Orphan Recognizances
___ Laborer Certificates
___ Deportation Records
___ Reports of Public Inns
___ Reports of Boarding
    Houses
___ Almshouse Bonds
___ Pensions

___ Overseers of the Poor

___ Minutes
___ Orders
___ Accounts
___ Reports
___ Medical Registers
___ Medical Reports

___ Poorhouse Records

___ Rolls
___ Registers
___ Journals
___ Diaries
___ Daybooks
___ Letterbooks
___ Work Reports
___ Placing Out Records
___ Apprenticeships

___

Public Welfare

___ Case Histories
___ Unemployment
___ Accounts
___ Correspondence
___ Probation List
___ Probation Files
___ Parole Register
___ Welfare Rolls
___ WPA Assignments
___ Termination of
    Employment
___ Delinquent Children
___ Adoptions
___ Reports

___
___

Board of Health

___ Minutes
___ Letterbooks
___ Autopsies
___ Medical Registers
___ Infirmary Registers
___ Workhouse Registers
___ Vaccinations
___ Immunizations
___ Doctor Lists
___ Midwife Registers
___ Nurse Registers
___ Nurse Reports
___ Case Histories
___ Quarantine Register

___

Voting (Election) Records

___ Register of Voters
___ Register of Intended
    Voters
___ Voter Lists
___ Register of Freemen
___ Lists of Freeholders
___ List of Rejected Voters
___ Campaign Expenses
___ Nomination Petitions
___ Election Indentures
___ Intent to Become a Citizen
___ Temporary Removals
___ Poll Books
___ Poll Tax
___ Oaths of Allegiance
___ Oaths of Office

___ Loyalty Oaths
___ Loyal Addresses
___ Freemen Oaths
___ Freemen Admissions
___ Returns
___ Proclamations
___ Absentee Ballots
___ Bonds of Officials
___ Contested Elections
___ Protests

___
___
___

Licenses and Permits

___ Professional
___ Physicians
___ Dentists
___ Veterinary
___ Peddlar
___ Midwife
___ Architect
___ Building
___ Business
___ Animal
___ Occupation
___ Burial
___ Vehicle
___ Entertainment
___ Public Inn
___ Clerical
___ Church
___ Expirations
___ Firearms
___ Deadly Weapons
___ Osteopaths
___ Enbalmers
___ Nurses
___ Chiropedists
___ Chiropractors
___ Alehouses
___ Slaughterhouses
___ Peddlers
___ Friendly Societies
___ Alcoholic Beverages
___ Rest Homes

___
___

Bounties

___ Indian Scalps
___ Animal
___ Prisoners of War

___
___
___

Corporation Records

___ Corporations
___ Articles of Incorporation
___ Partnerships
___ Church
___ Dissolutions
___ Charters
___ Business
___ Fraternal Groups
___ Social Clubs
___ Business under Assumed
    Name
___ Extinct Corporations
___ Friendly Societies

___
___
___

Council (Commission) Records

___ Minutes
___ Proceedings
___ Daybooks
___ Letterbooks
___ Court Records
___ Orders
___ Accounts
___ Proclamations
___ Reports
___ Petitions
___ Payrolls

___
___

Road Records

___ Petitions
___ Minutes
___ Condemned Land
___ Plats
___ Supervisors Reports
___ Appointment of Road
    Officials
___ Surveys
___ Work Reports
___ Prisoner Details
___ Repairs
___ Compensations
___ Valuations

___

Miscellaneous

___ Local History Files
___ 4-H Club Files
___ Notary Public
___ Agricultural Records
___ Publications
___ Loan Records
___ Fenceviewers Records
___ Protocol Books
___ Stonemason Marks
___ Trade Marks
___ Appointments of Officials
___ Appointments of Justices
    of Peace

___
___

Other

___
___
___
___
___

CHAPTER NINE

PRE-SEARCH ANALYSIS:
PARTICULAR SEARCH DIMENSIONS,
PARTICULAR SEARCH OUTLINES

A *particular search* is any selective search in which the dimensions are dependent upon the immediate objective of the search and the circumstances under which the search is to be performed. In one jurisdiction all surnames may be extracted for a definite date from only one source. In another, only one individual name will be sought in several sources for a defined period of time.

You should carefully define your problem before you set out to solve it. You should know precisely what you need and how to go about finding it. "What is my immediate objective? Why do I need to perform a *particular search?*" Then, as with the general search, define the dimensions of that search: jurisdiction or locality, surname or name, period of time or date and source(s). Because these dimensions are variable and are determined by the objective of the search, increased emphasis is placed upon the need for wise definition. THINK SYSTEM NOT SOURCE! The system will dictate the sources to use. Do not risk frustration and waste of resources by guessing at these dimensions.

Particular searches are justified for two reasons only:

1. The definition or further clarification of the dimensions of a general search.

2. The completion of research in jurisdictions subordinate (local) or higher (state and national) than the basic jurisdiction, after the completion of a general search.

Defining General Search Dimensions

The first immediate objectives of any research program should be general searches in those basic jurisdictions where you know your ultimate objective families lived. Before you can actually proceed with a general search, however, you must completely define its dimensions. Rarely will survey findings alone provide enough data to accomplish this; a series of well planned *particular searches* is needed.

Basic Jurisdiction. The findings of the survey will usually provide at least one possible basic jurisdiction where your ultimate objective families resided but you must prove that your people were actually there. If the survey does not identify a basic jurisdiction at all, it becomes your first immediate objective to identify it (see Flow Chart on page 140 above). In America, the basic jurisdiction can be defined by making selective searches into census schedules, indexes to land records, indexes to probate files, indexes to court cases or annual tax lists. If the basic jurisdiction is unknown, check records indexed on a state or national basis.[1] In England, the basic jurisdiction can often be defined by consulting census schedules, marriage indexes, printed parish registers (Anglican and Nonconformist) and Bishop's transcripts. If the basic jurisdiction is unknown, consult vital registration records (after 1837) located at Somerset House or other records indexed on a country-wide or shire basis. Other sources suitable to such *particular searches* will be learned as you study source materials for each country.[2]

Surnames. Before a general search is performed, it is essential to determine actual spelling variations and language translations for each surname included in the search. Frequently, the same *particular search* used to define the basic jurisdiction will reveal spelling peculiarities.

Period of Time. A carefully defined period of time will make each research objective easier to solve and less expensive. Once you know that an ultimate objective actually lived in the basic jurisdiction and what variations of the surnames appear, determine what period of time you must search the jurisdiction to complete the general search. Start at a specific date when you know your ancestors were present in a locality and search both ways — prior to and after that specific date — until you have defined the dimension in accordance with the criteria set forth on pages 134-37 above. *Never use mathematical formulas* *for general searches.* General search periods of time must be defined precisely.

Sources. Each *particular search* undertaken to define a general search dimension is a specific search in a specific source. To accomplish the objectives for which the search is made, first the sources which could provide the needed information are listed. Then the list is rearranged in the order which will answer the objective with the least amount of money and effort. If the fact may be available in any one of six sources, search first the one most easily obtainable that is most likely to produce results. If it fails to yield the data sought, search the next most promising, and so on. Following each search, evaluate the results to determine whether or not the needed data was obtained. Once the objective is filled, move to the next immediate objective.

Research Outline

The following example is suggested as a format for planning *particular searches* to define general search dimensions.

RESEARCH OUTLINE

Immediate Objective: _____

Jurisdiction: _____

Surnames or Names: _____

_____

_____

_____

_____

Specific Date: _____

Source	Name and Address of Depository	Method of Search	Remarks

* State your immediate objective on the top line of a research outline. A plain or ruled sheet of paper may be used. Then, list the basic jurisdiction and the surnames of your ultimate objective families as your survey findings list them. Include all the possible spellings which those names could assume.

* Add a specific date when you know your ancestors resided in that basic jurisdiction. This date will be used to search both directions — prior to and after the date, until the period of time is defined. Consider especially those who could be children of ultimate objectives, the date when your surnames first appear in the records, the possible marriage date of those who could be parents of the ultimate objectives and the date when the basic jurisdiction was formed.

* List the sources produced by the basic jurisdiction which could prove that 1) your ultimate objectives actually lived there, 2) the surname spellings by which they were identified and 3) the length of time they resided in that jurisdiction. Then rearrange the sources listed in the order which you will search them — the order which will solve the objective with the least expense and effort.

RESEARCH OUTLINE

Immediate Objective: _To define Basic Jurisdiction, Surnames, Period of Time for General Search_

Jurisdiction: _Augusta County, Virginia_

Surnames or Names: _Young, Yong, Yun, Ung, Un, Jong, Junge Finnegan, Fynigin, Feniken, Fenigan, Phinegan, Phynican, Vinegan Kennedy, Kenaday, Cannaday, Ceneday, Chindy_

Specific Date: _22 Feb 1857_

Source	Name and Address of Depository	Method of Search	Remarks
Census	Genealogical Society, Salt Lake City, Ut.	Personal	Microfilm Copy
Land Index	Genealogical Society, Salt Lake City, Ut.	Personal	Index to 1921 Records to 1860
Probate Index	Genealogical Society, Salt Lake City, Ut.	Personal	
Tax Lists	Virginia State Library, Richmond, Va.	Researcher	

* Search the most likely source first and evaluate your findings. If the objectives are solved, move to the next immediate objective. If not, search the next source listed, and so
on.

* Make every *particular search* in a basic jurisdiction, undertaken to define general search dimensions, contribute to the
eventual completion of that general search. For example,
you search a census to prove that your ancestors actually
lived in a locality at a given time. If they are listed, extract
all of the data involving those surnames from the record
while you are at it. If you search a land index to discover
possible spellings of surnames and you find your ancestors
listed, extract all pertinent entries while you have the record.
As you carry out the general search you will not need to
search that census record or land index again. Economy
requires this. It would be waste to pay unnecessarily for the
same records twice.

Searching Other Jurisdictions

After the completion of general searches, research must
be carried into those jurisdictions exercising authority
subordinate or higher than the basic jurisdiction. There are
great quantities of records available outside the basic jurisdiction but it can be expensive to obtain data from them without general search results on which to base such searches.
The general search should disclose references and clues
necessary for the planning of these searches. Why search
every church, cemetery and school in a county 20 miles
square for a family known to have lived "somewhere in the
county" when you could perform a general search first to
locate the precise section of the county where they lived.
Using this information, churches and cemeteries nearby
can be checked quickly for data they may possess. Perform
the general search first, then outline the dimensions of
searches into other jurisdictions toward which you have been
directed.

Subordinate (Local) Jurisdictions. Generally, when you
perform the finish work in local jurisdictions following a
general search, the surnames and the period of time remain

exactly the same as they were defined for the general search. All entries involving all surnames, for the period of time are extracted from all of the existing sources produced by that local jurisdiction. The following research outline lists these local jurisdictions and their records. You should fill in the pertinent blanks and search those subordinate authorities toward which your survey and general searches have directed you.

RESEARCH OUTLINE

(Copyright 1972, Genealogical Copy Service)

Immediate Objective: SEARCH OF SUBORDINATE (LOCAL) JURISDICTIONS

All Surnames: _____

_____

_____

_____

Period of Time: _____

MUNICIPAL JURISDICTIONS (Village, City, Town)	LOCATION OR ADDRESS	METHOD OF SEARCH (Personal, Researcher, Loan, Correspondence, Copy)	REMARKS (Fees Restrictions)

Sources: This is a guide to the sources which *could have been produced*. Check (✓) those items still extant for your period of time, circle each check (✓) as you search that record. Sources of municipal jurisdictions are identical or similar to the non-property records of basic jurisdictions.

____Letterbooks
____Petitions
____Ordinances
____Decisions
____Accounts
____Disbursements
____Proclamations
____Charters
____Seals
____Reports
____Dockets
____Minutes
____Orders
____Bonds
____Judgments
____Distraints
____Executions

____ Police Records
____
____

Jail Records
____Constable Records
____ Justice Records
____Merchant Court
____ Pied Powder Court
____ Mayor Court
____ Police Court
____ City Court
____ Municipal Court
____ Justice Court
____Husting Court
____ Burgess Rolls
____ Freemen Records

____Assessors Rolls
____Firewarden Accounts
____Firemen Discharges
____Watch
____Local History Files
____Publications
____Directories
____
____

____Censuses
____Inventories
____Births
____Deaths
____Marriages
____ Medical Registers
____ Cemetery Records

____Trade Records
____Tax Records
____Fee Books
____Water Records
____Sewer Records
____Street Repairs
____Poor Relief Records
____Licenses and Permits
____Animal Registration
____Voting Records
____Bounties
____Plans
____Maps
____Fence Viewers Records

ECCLESIASTICAL JURISDICTIONS*	LOCATION OR ADDRESS	METHOD OF SEARCH (Personal, Researcher, Loan, Correspondence, Copy)	REMARKS (Fees, Restrictions)

*Branch, Congregation, Kirk, Consistory, Session, Meeting, Mission, Synagogue, Chapel, Ward, Parish, Stake, Diocese, District, Classis, Presbytery, Body, Circuit, Society, Synod, Archives, Assembly, Convention, Association, Conference. Parishes were also units of local civil government in England, Colonial America and several countries of Europe. See General Search Outline for those records.

Sources: Check (_✓_) those items still extant for your period of time. Circle each check (_✓_) as you search that record.

Sacramental Records
___Birthright
___Birth
___Christening
___Baptism
___Blessing
___Circumcision
___Confirmation
___Ordination
___Dispensation
___Marriage
___Banns
___Sacramental Certificates
___Divorce
___Annulment
___Dissolution of Marriage
___Permission to Marry
___Intentions
___Death
___Burial
___Burial in Woollen
___Touching for King's Evil
___Penances

Membership Records
___Lists
___Admissions
___Catalogs
___Removals
___Transfers
___Excommunications
___Sufferings
___Suicides
___Manumissions
___Disownments
___Disfellowships
___Terminations
___Catechisms
___Catechumens
___Catalogs
___Disciplinary Proceedings
___Choir Diaries
___Youth Associations
___Womens Associations

Cemetery and Memorial
___Sexton
___Monuments
___Tombstones
___Plots
___Memorials
___Misericords
___Brasses
___Stained Glass Windows
___Monetary Contributions

Administrative Records
___Minutes
___Diaries
___Journals
___Vestry Books
___Churchwardens Accounts
___Donations
___Convocation Papers
___Glebe Leases
___Collection Lists
___List of Parish Officials
___Bell Ringing List
___Bastardy Papers
___Bills
___List of Paupers
___Returns of Papists
___Act Books
___Emigration Papers
___Valuation Lists
___Appointments
___Altered Appointments
___Property Deeds
___Bishop's Transcripts
___Contributions
___Subscribers
___Disbursements
___Contracts
___Tithe Records
___Repairs
___Poor Relief
___Pew Rents
___Pew Assignments
___Tax Rolls
___Rates
___Processioning Lists
___Church Court Minutes
___Maps

___Surveys
___Photographs
___Committee Reports
___Church Books
___List of Delegates
___Censuses
___Glebe Terriers
___Charity Accounts
___Loan Fund

Ministerial Records
___Ministerial Rolls
___Pastoral Registers
___Daybooks
___Accountbooks
___Diaries
___Correspondence
___Military Chaplain Registers
___Presentations
___Beneficies
___Pluralities
___Institution Bonds
___Consecrations
___Inductions
___Licenses
___Nominations
___Testimonials
___Character Vouchers
___Ministers Dependents
___Visitations
___Personal Papers
___Sermons
___Associations
___Directories
___Yearbooks
___Insurance Fund
___
___
___

Mission Records
(Indian and Heathen)
___Reports
___Correspondence
___Bulletins
___Travel Lists
___Accounts
___Contributions

___Personal Papers
___Committee Minutes
___Committee Journals
___Committee Diaries
___Medical Reports
___Memorials
___Subscription Lists
___Maps
___Anti-Opium Reports
___Tracts

Collections
___Indexes
___Newspapers
___Correspondence
___Histories
___Biographies
___Bulletins
___Historical Magazines
___Yearbooks
___Directories
___Dedication Programs
___Commemorative Programs
___
___

Institutional Records
___Schools
___Universities
___Charities
___Divinity Schools
___Convents
___Hospitals
___Seminaries
___Libraries
___Historical Societies
___Mission Societies
___
___

Other

EMPLOYMENT JURISDICTIONS	LOCATION OR ADDRESS	METHOD OF SEARCH (Personal, Researcher, Loan, Correspondence, Copy)	REMARKS (Fees Restrictions)

Sources: Check (✓) those items still extant for your period of time. Circle each check (Ⓥ) as you search that record.

Freemen Records
___ Lists
___ Petitions
___ Applications
___ Admissions
___ Oaths
___ Certificates
___
___

Craft (Gild) Records
___ Membership Lists
___ Labor Contracts
___ Apprenticeship
___ Indentures
___ Releases
___ Journeymen
___ Masters
___ Yearbooks
___ Bulletins
___ Newspapers
___ Trademarks
___ Signs
___ Directories
___ Account Books
___ Insurance Registers

___ Charity Records
___
___

Employee Records
___ Personnel Applications
___ Examinations
___ Personnel Files
___ Payrolls
___ Salary Books
___ Interviews
___ Service Records
___ Sales Records
___ Promotions
___ Pension Files
___ Sick-leave Registers
___ Workmen's Compensation
___
___
___

Banking Records
___ Minutes
___ Stockholders Records
___ Trusts

___ Real Estate Files
___ Loans
___ Safe Deposits
___ Photographed Transactions
___ Dividends
___

Business Records
___ Minutes
___ Ledgers
___ Journals
___ Account Books
___ Day Books
___ Correspondence
___ Retail Credit Files
___ Sales Catalogues
___ Charge Accounts
___ Income Tax Files
___ Stockholders Records
___ Inventories
___ Invoice Books
___ Bonds
___ Deeds
___ Contracts
___ Photographs
___ Histories

___ Diaries
___ Partnership Agreements
___ Investment Records
___ Mortgages
___ Mill Books
___ Shop Books
___
___
___

Labor Union Records
___ Membership Records
___ Correspondence
___ Contracts
___ Salaried Officers
___ Applications
___ Pensions
___ Minutes
___ Negotiations
___ Histories
___ Publications
___ Job Register
___ Tramp Register
___ Tramp Certificates
___
___

PROFESSIONAL JURISDICTIONS*	LOCATION OR ADDRESS	METHOD OF SEARCH (Personal, Researcher, Loan, Correspondence, Copy)	REMARKS (Fees Restrictions)

*Doctor, Lawyer, Dentist, Apothecary, Midwife, Nurse, Mortician.

Sources: Check (✓) those items still extant for your period of time. Circle each check (Ⓥ) as you search that record.

Personal Records
___ Commonplace Books
___ Daybooks
___ Account Books
___ Journals
___ Diaries
___ Letterbooks
___ Registers of Cases
___ Correspondence
___ Case Files
___ Fee Books
___ Licenses
___ Apprenticeship Records
___ Bills
___ Malpractice Suits

___ Suits for Non-payment of Debts
___ Waste Book
___ Treatment Book

Fraternal and Professional Associations
___ Membership Files
___ Minutes
___ Accounts
___ Correspondence
___ Insurance Fund
___ Directories
___ Yearbooks
___ Publications

___ Histories
___ Charity Records
___ Scholarships
___ Fellowships
___
___
___

Mortuary Records
___ Daybooks
___ Ledgers
___ Account Books
___ Burial Registers
___ Funeral Programs

___ Funeral Cards
___ Obituaries
___ Death Certificates
___
___
___

Other

SOCIAL JURISDICTIONS*	LOCATION OR ADDRESS	METHOD OF SEARCH (Personal. Researcher. Loan. Correspondence. Copy)	REMARKS (Fees Restrictions)

*Justices of the Peace, Schools, Hospitals, Cemeteries, Insurance Companies, Newspapers.

Sources: Check (✓) those items still extant for your period of time. Circle each check (⦸) as you search that record.

Local Justice of the Peace
- ___ Civil Docket
- ___ Criminal Docket
- ___ Orders
- ___ Attachments
- ___ Judgments
- ___ Executions
- ___ Case Files
- ___ Daybooks
- ___ Accounts
- ___ Diaries
- ___ Memoirs
- ___ Warrants
- ___ Writs
- ___ Constables Returns
- ___ Marriages
- ___ Apprenticeships
- ___
- ___
- ___
- ___

School Records
- ___ Elementary
- ___ Secondary
- ___ Trade
- ___ Vocational
- ___ College
- ___ University
- ___ Registrar
- ___ Matriculation Lists
- ___ Attendance Lists
- ___ Examination Lists
- ___ Tuition Lists
- ___ Tutor Bills
- ___ Subscription Lists
- ___ Graduation Lists
- ___ Degree Lists
- ___ Report Cards
- ___ Pupil Lists
- ___ Teacher Lists
- ___ Alumni
- ___ Sorority
- ___ Fraternity
- ___ Social Unit
- ___ Honorary Society
- ___ Transcripts

- ___ Censuses
- ___ Tax Lists
- ___ Minutes of School Board
- ___ Reports
- ___ Account Books
- ___ Yearbooks
- ___ Directories
- ___ Newspapers
- ___ Diplomas
- ___ Awards
- ___ Lotteries
- ___
- ___

Hospitals
- ___ Military
- ___ Seamen
- ___ Public
- ___ Private
- ___ Infirmaries
- ___ Admissions
- ___ Patient Index
- ___ Diagnosis Index
- ___ Out-Patient Index
- ___ X-rays
- ___ Case Files
- ___ Out-Patient Files
- ___ Birth Register
- ___ Death Register
- ___ Accounts
- ___ Insurance Claims
- ___ Malpractice Suits
- ___ Histories
- ___ Discharges
- ___

Cemetery Records
- ___ Family
- ___ Private
- ___ Commercial
- ___ Public
- ___ Religious
- ___ National
- ___ Sexton
- ___ Family Bible
- ___ Tombstone
- ___ Monuments

- ___ Plots
- ___ Hatchments
- ___ Tablets
- ___ Memorials
- ___ Burial Permit
- ___ Grave Opening Order
- ___ Deeds
- ___ Monetary Contributions
- ___ Perpetual Care Fund
- ___ Plats
- ___ Maps
- ___
- ___

Insurance
- ___ Life
- ___ Marine
- ___ Fire
- ___ Automobile
- ___ Health
- ___ Accident
- ___ Dental
- ___ Obstetrical
- ___ Storm
- ___ Fidelity
- ___ Machinery
- ___ Burglary
- ___ Credit
- ___ Glass
- ___ Building and Loan
- ___ Vehicle
- ___ Policies
- ___ Contracts
- ___ Application Files
- ___ Policy Register Books
- ___ Account Books
- ___ Renewals
- ___ Premium Payments
- ___ Dividend Records
- ___ Minutes
- ___ Committee Records
- ___ Mortgage Records
- ___ Loans
- ___ Payrolls
- ___ Stockholders Records
- ___ Real Estate Files
- ___ Missing Heirs Files
- ___ Valuations

- ___ Investigators Reports
- ___ Admissions Register
- ___ Agent Licences
- ___ Powers of Attorney
- ___ Travel Permits
- ___ Claims
- ___ Medical Files
- ___ Maps
- ___
- ___

Newspapers
- ___ Indexes

- ___ **Announcements**
- ___ Birth
- ___ Death
- ___ Marriage
- ___ Divorce
- ___ Anniversary

- ___ **Legal Notices**
- ___ Probate
- ___ Auction
- ___ Divorce
- ___ Bankruptcy
- ___ Court Claims
- ___ Delinquent Taxes

- ___ **Columns**
- ___ Genealogical
- ___ Historical
- ___ Special Events
- ___ Stories
- ___ Obituary
- ___ Testimonials
- ___ Affadavits
- ___ Court Cases
- ___ Advertisements
- ___ News Items
- ___ Unclaimed Mail
- ___
- ___
- ___

HOME JURISDICTIONS*	LOCATION OR ADDRESS	METHOD OF SEARCH (Personal, Researcher, Loan, Correspondence, Copy)	REMARKS (Fees Restrictions)

*Family Friends, Associates, Neighbors, Distant Relatives, Old Timers, Descendants.

Sources: Check (✓) those items still extant for your period of time. Circle each check (✓) as you search that record.

Family Records
- ___ Family Bible
- ___ Family Traditions
- ___ Personal Knowledge
- ___ Legal Papers
- ___ Personal Papers
- ___
- ___
- ___

Farm Records
- ___ Accounts
- ___ Daybooks
- ___ Laborers Register
- ___ Cropping Book
- ___ Diaries
- ___ Memoranda

Estate Records (Plantations)
- ___ Accounts
- ___ Correspondence
- ___ Sale Books
- ___ Valuation Books
- ___ Inventories
- ___ Property Register
- ___ Diaries
- ___ Auctioneer Notebooks
- ___ Surveys
- ___ Plats

- ___ Estate Maps
- ___ Testimonials
- ___ Tenant Applications
- ___ Tenant Complaints
- ___ Arbitration Pleadings
- ___ Arbitration Awards
- ___ Tithe Records
- ___ Enclosures
- ___ Crop Books
- ___ Gamebooks
- ___ Pensions

INSTITUTIONAL JURISDICTIONS*	LOCATION OR ADDRESS	METHOD OF SEARCH (Personal, Researcher, Loan, Correspondence, Copy)	REMARKS (Fees Restrictions)

*Patriotic Societies, Ethnic and Minority Groups, Scientific Societies, Ecclesiastical Associations, Learned Societies, Fraternal Societies, Clubs and Lodges. These groups are called Friendly Societies in England.

Sources: Check (✓) those items still extant for your period of time. Circle each check (✓) as you search that record.

Membership Records
- ___ Lists
- ___ Enrollment Books
- ___ Admissions
- ___ Transfers
- ___ Removals
- ___ Terminations
- ___ Biographies
- ___ Bequests
- ___ Disciplinary Proceedings

Organization Records
- ___ Minutes
- ___ Histories
- ___ Donations
- ___ Disbursements
- ___ Accounts
- ___ Yearbooks
- ___ Bulletins
- ___ Newspapers
- ___ Directories

- ___ MSS Collections
- ___ Printed Collections
- ___ Personal Papers
- ___ Oral History Files
- ___ Correspondence
- ___ Alumni
- ___ Printed Transactions
- ___ Memorials
- ___ Charitable Funds
- ___ Insurance Funds

Other
- ___
- ___
- ___
- ___

SHIPPING (PORT) JURISDICTIONS	LOCATION OR ADDRESS	METHOD OF SEARCH (Personal. Researcher. Loan. Correspondence. Copy)	REMARKS (Fees Restrictions)

Sources: Check (✓) those items still extant for your period of time. Circle each check (ⓥ) as you search that record.

Customs Records
___Ship Lists
___Enrollments
___Enrollment Bonds
___Registers
___Licenses
___Clearance Records
___Masters Oaths
___Arrivals
___Departures
___WPA Ship MSS
___Manifest Books
___

Ships Records
___Crew Lists
___Register of Seamen
___Passenger Lists
___Seamens Oaths
___Seamens Certificates
___Partnership Agreements
___Contracts
___Seamens Wage Suits
___Payrolls
___Wage Claims
___Letterbooks
___Logbooks

___Journals
___Insurance Policies
___Cargo Lists
___Bills of Lading
___Bills of Exchange
___Account Books
___

Immigrant Aid Societies
___Registers
___Membership Lists
___Minutes

___Petitions
___Account Books
___Contracts
___Correspondence
___Donations
___Loans
___Sick Benefits
___Scholarship Funds
___Applications
___Claims
___Repayment
___

Higher (State and National) Jurisdictions. The dimensions for searches in jurisdictions higher than the basic jurisdiction are dictated by the jurisdiction itself. References to these jurisdictions will be obtained from preceding general searches.

Surnames. *Be selective* and extract only those entries which are likely to be members of ultimate objective families. For these searches specific names will be necessary. Obviously, all the Smiths living in the United States are not related. You will need given names as well as surnames to identify your Smiths. Be sure to take into account all possible spellings of the surnames. If the given name is unusual, consider possible variations for it also.

Period of Time. You will need specific dates for searches in state and national records. Allow for possible error, however, by adding from 2 to 5 years on either side of the date and by searching a 5 to 11 year period. Many official record keepers search a 5-year period as a matter of routine, but not all of them do. Be sure you calculate and specify your needs accordingly. For example, if your ancestor could have applied for a Revolutionary War pension in 1838, add 5 years to each side of the date and search 1833-1843. In this way, if your date is not completely accurate you will still find the proper entry. If preceding general searches do not yield specific dates, the following table of mathematical formulas can be used to calculate them for these *particular searches.*[3]

PERIOD APPROXIMATION CHART*

Date Wanted	Known Information	Formula
Birth	Age at dated event	Subtract age from date Add 5 years to each side Search 11 year period
Birth	Marriage Date	Subtract 16 years from date Subtract 40 years from date Search period between dates
Birth	Birth or Christening of child: Female — only child	Subtract 16 years from date Subtract 50 years from date Search period between dates

Birth	Female — several children	Subtract 16 years from date
		    of first child
		Subtract 50 years from date
		    of last child
		Search period between dates

Birth	Male — only child	Subtract 16 years from date Subtract 70 years from date Search period between dates

Birth	Male — several children	Subtract 16 years from date
		    of first child
		Subtract 70 years from date
		    of last child
		Search period between dates

Marriage	Age at dated event	Calculate age 15 Add 25 years to date Search period between dates
Marriage	Birth or Christening of child: Only child	Subtract 34 years from date Add 1 year to date Search period between dates

Marriage	Several children	Subtract 34 years from date
		    of last child
		Add 1 year to date of first
		    child
		Search period between dates

Death		Calculate birth date
		Add 90 years
		Search period between date
		    last known alive and 90th
		    year

*Adapted from *Basic Course in Genealogy*, Vol. II by Derek Harland (Salt Lake City: Bookcraft, 1958), 104-117. (Reissued in 1963 as *Genealogical Research Standards*.)

Sources. In higher jurisdictions, those sources which "could have" data pertaining to your ultimate objectives will be searched. If any doubt arises in defining "could have," search them! For example, if you have no specific evidence that your ancestor fought in the Civil War but he was a young adult during that period of time, check the Civil War records for him. If you have no direct reference that your ancestor attended Harvard College, but he lived a few miles from the school, check the records.

The following research outlines list the records which could have been produced by state and national jurisdictions of the United States. You will have to determine their present location, how you will search them and if there are any restrictions on the records.[4]

RESEARCH OUTLINE

(Copyright 1972, Genealogical Copy Service)

Immediate Objective: SEARCH OF STATE (UNITED STATES) JURISDICTION

PEDIGREE NAMES: SPECIFIC DATES:

_____

_____

_____

_____

_____

_____

DEPOSITORY	LOCATION OR ADDRESS	METHOD OF SEARCH (Personal, Researcher, Loan, Correspondence, Copy)	REMARKS (Fees Restrictions)

Sources: This list is a guide to the documents *which could be found*. Compare it with a current bibliography or guide to the record holdings of the State Archives, State Library or State Historical Society where your ancestors lived. Check (____) those which pertain to your pedigree and circle the check mark (____) as each one is searched.

A. SPECIAL INDEXES

____Land Grants
____Military Pensions
____Military Grave Sites
____Newspapers
____Births
____Marriages

____Deaths
____Divorces
____Adoptions
____Name Changes
____Censuses
____Naturalizations

____Probates
____Cemeteries
____Post Offices
____County Histories
____Pedigrees
____Genealogies

____Entries
____Deeds
____Land Claims
____
____

B. PROPERTY RECORDS

Land Records

____Licenses to Purchase
____Permits to Settle
____Entry Books
____Entry Assignments
____Entry Takers Receipts
____Entry Takers Returns
____Entry Certificates
____Survey Certificates
____Surveys
____Plat Books
____Ejectment Plats
____Grants
____Patents
____Land Grant Lists
____Suspended Land Grants
____Proprietory Grants
____Homesteads
____otteries
____Proprietary Leases
____Manor Lease
____Lease Roll
____Copyhold Lease
____Crown Lease Book
____Land Divisions

____Deeds
____Ground Rents
____Quit Rent Rolls
____Debt Books
____Land Returns
____Tax Sales
____Tax Exemptions
____Tax Liens
____Tax Lists
____Tax Farms
____Chattel Bills of Sale
____Headright Claims
____Proof of Rights
____Transfer of Rights
____Donation Land Grants
____Immigration Contracts
____Lists of Indentured Servants
____Immigrant Land Allowances
____Surplus Land
____Deficiency of Land
____Indian Land
____Indian Deeds
____Proclamation Land
____Bounty Land
____Continental Line Land

____Land Speculations
____Condemned Land
____Confiscated Land
____Abandoned Land
____Land Memorials
____Railroad Land
____Swamp Land
____School Land
____Caveats
____Alienations
____Fines
____Distraints
____Instructions
____Queries
____Abstracts
____Insolvencies
____Accounts
____Arrears
____Disclaimers
____Petitions
____Complaints
____Inquests
____Escheats
____Fee Tails
____Entails

____Inquisitions
____Devises Lists
____Heir Lists
____Quit Claims
____Mortgages
____Balance Books
____Deceased Persons Deeds
____Invoice Books
____Outlawry Books
____Postage Books
____Duties on Carriages
____Fee Lists
____Mineral Rights
____Water Rights

Warrants

____Common
____Special
____Gift
____Grant
____Orders
____King's

Probate

___Petitions
___Bonds
___Inventories
___Wills
___Administrations
___Claims
___Advertisements
___Judgments
___Settlements
___Marriage Settlements
___Illegitimate Births
___Legitimations
___Name Changes
___Divorce
___Adoption
___Annulment
___Insanity
___Lunacy
___Guardianship
___Appeals
___
___
___

Court Records

___State Supreme Court
___Governor and Council
___State Assembly
___Errors and Appeals
   Probate Appeals
___Civil Appeals
___Criminal Appeals
___Prerogative Court
___Court of Delegates
___Admiralty
___Oyer and Terminer
___Gaol Delivery
___Assize
___Exchequer
___Chancery
___Claims
___Ordinary
___Surrogate
___Common Right
___Conference
___Circuit
___Indexes
___Dockets
___Minutes
___Orders
___Writs
___Precepts
___Petitions
___Judgments
___Decrees
___Verdicts

___Concords
___Escheats
___Printed Court Reports
___Bankruptcy Petitions
___Cause Books
___
___

Appeals

___Transcripts
___Briefs
___Exhibits
___Files
___Opinions

Jury Records

___Grand Jury
___Petit Jury
___Minutes
___List of Jurors
___Case Register
___Attendance Lists
___Pay Lists
___Discharges
___Presentments
___Tickets
___Papers
___

Attorney General Files

___Dockets
___Daybooks
___Writs
___Petitions
___Correspondence
___Case Files
___Accounts
___Briefs
___
___

Tax Records

___Tax Lists
___Tax Exemptions
___Tax Liens
___Tax Farms
___Tax Sales
___Income Tax
___Sales Tax
___Inheritance Tax
___Special Tax
___Property Tax
___Vehicle Tax
___Ad Valorem Tax

___Appeals
___Appraisals
___

Treasury Records

___Revenue Books
___Revenue Receipts
___Interest Books
___Foreclosures
___Bankruptcies
___Delinquent Accounts
___Public Loan Papers
___Property Loan Maps
___Veterans Loan Fund
___Consumer Credit Files
___Fines and Recoveries
___Bond Registers
___Bond Elections
___Board of Revenue
   Minutes
___Accounts
___Ledgers
___Audits
___Correspondence
___Claims
___
___

Surveyor General Records

___Reports
___Bonds
___Commissioners Reports
___Commissioners Accounts
___Commissioners Letters
___
___

Boundary Records

___Land Commission Reports
___Maps
___Surveys
___Changes
___Claims Files
___
___

Maps

___Surveyors
___Highway
___County Boundaries
___Demographic
___Election District
___Geodetic
___Manuscript

___Printed
___Town Plans
___Plats
___Plantations
___
___

State Police

___Drivers Licenses
___Criminal Identification Files
___Arrest Report
___Offense Report
___Motor Vehicle Accident
   Claims
___Liability Insurance
___Accident Reports
___Traffic Commission Reports
___Daily Report
___Officer's Daily Report
___List of Officers
___Personnel Files
___Promotion
___Correspondence
___
___
___

State Prisons

___Register of Prisoners
___Medical Register
___List of Personal Property
___Work Register
___Day Book
___Admissions
___Transfers
___Releases
___Death Register
___Probation Register
___Statement of Conduct
___Board of Examiners
___Parole Rolls
___Probation Rolls
___Investigation Reports
___List of Probationers
___List of Paroles
___Detention Homes
___Industrial Schools
___Juvenile Files
___Reform Schools
___
___
___

C. NON-PROPERTY RECORDS

Military Records

___French & Indian Wars
___Indian Battles
___Revolutionary War
___1812
___Mexican War
___Mexican Border Battles
___Civil War
___Spanish-American War
___Philippine Actions
___World War I
___World War II
___Korean War
___Vietnam
___Formosa

___Greece
___
___
___Militia Returns
___Troop Returns
___Muster Rolls
___Muster-in Rolls
___Muster-out Rolls
___Enlistments
___Enrollments
___Journals
___Logbooks
___Letter Books
___Morning Reports

___Pay Rolls
___Paymaster Rolls
___Expenses
___Vouchers
___Orders
___Accounts
___Orderly Books
___Training Rolls
___Indian Affairs
___Expeditionary Forces
___Frontier Scouting
___Prairie Logbooks
___Receipt Rolls
___Correspondence
___Annual Reports

___Military Loans
___Comptroller's Statements
___Quartermaster Rolls
___Ordnance Records
___Equipment Inventories
___Clothing Returns
___Discharges
___Missing Roster
___Dead Rolls
___Deceased Soldiers
___List of Recruits
___Casualty Lists
___Battle Reports
___Transfer Rolls
___List of Rejected Men

____Inventory of Effects
____Final Settlements
____Gallantry Reports
____Rolls of Honor
____Drill Rolls
____Induction Orders
____Desertions
____Service Affadavits
____Bounty Lands
____Bounty Receipts
____Warrants
____Surveys
____Land Warrant Returns
____Pensions
____Invalid Pensions
____Pension Claims

Pension Board

____Minutes
____Correspondence
____Examiners Reports
____Applications
____Survivor's Applications
____Proof of Service
____Military Claims
____Depositions
____Disabled Veterans
____Death Claims
____Claims Settlements
____Tax Exemptions
____War Claims
____Commissary Claims
____Confiscated Property
____Abandoned Property
____Exchange of Prisoners
____Slave Patrols
____Oaths of Allegiance
____Passports
____Certificates of
       Citizenship
____Prisoner Lists
____Invasion Records
____Grave Site Indexes
____Petitions for Pardon
____Debt Certificates
____Bill of Credit
____Substitutions
____Adjutant General's Report
____Recruiting Agents' Reports
____Recruiting Books
____Recruiting Accounts
____Recruiting Rolls
____Draft Records
____Enlistment Contracts
____National Guard
____Selective Service
____State Guard Rosters
____Military Code
____Home Guard Rolls

Courts Martial

____Minutes
____Depositions
____Trials of Regulations
____Courts of Inquiry
____Articles of War

Officers Records

____Commissions
____Lists
____Rosters
____Service Records
____Examinations
____Retired Officers
____Personal Papers

Military Academies

____Register of Cadets
____Register of Graduates
____Admissions
____Dismissals
____Day Books
____Medical Registers
____Clothing Accounts
____Appointments
____Nominations
____
____

Soldiers' Homes

____Minutes of Trustees
____Donations
____Reports
____Accounts
____Day Books
____Death Register
____Medical Register
____Visitors' Register
____List of Personal Effects

Hospitals

____Day Books
____Sick Reports
____Wounded Reports
____Morning Reports
____Medical Inspections
____Substitutes
____Death Registers
____Surgeon's Register
____Admissions
____Transfers

Naval Records

____List of Ships
____List of Officers
____List of Enlisted Men
____Accounts
____Inventories
____Muster Rolls
____Pay Rolls
____Open List Musters
____Substitutes
____Description Books
____Bounties
____Prize Money
____Prize Goods
____Service Files
____Wills
____Effects
____Dispatches
____Officer's Service Files
____Passing Certificates
____Certificates of Citizenship
____Naval Courts Martial
____Logbooks
____Ship Journals
____Wage Claims
____Seamen's Wage Suits
____Leave Register
____Sick Roster
____Wounded Lists
____Casualties
____Death Register

Naval Academies

____Register of Cadets
____Register of Graduates
____Admissions
____Dismissals
____Medical Registers
____Clothing Accounts
____Day Books

Seamen's Homes

____Registers
____Entry Books
____Pensions
____Wills
____Death Register
____Letters of Admissions
____Transfers
____List of Personal Effects
____
____

____Orphans' Homes
____Orphans' Schools
____Admission Papers
____Proof of Parentage
____Marriage Records
____Widow's Claims

Naturalizations (Before 1891)

____Petitions
____Denied Petitions
____Applications
____Customs House Books
____Register of Arrivals
____Head Tax Register
____Deported Aliens
____Alien Crew Lists
____Soldiers Naturalizations
____Clothing Rolls
____Sick Register
____Examiners Reports
____Criminal Record Files
____
____
____

Customs Records

____Greenwich Hospital Tax
____Out-letters
____In-letters
____Seizure of Smuggled Goods
____Shipping Warrants
____Salaries
____Officers Pensions
____Minutes
____Establishments
____Wage Records
____Ships Registers
____Wreck Depositions
____Order Entry Book
____Register of British Ships
____Residence Affadavits
____Oaths of Allegiance
____Ship Entry Books
____Muster Certificates
____Impressment Orders
____Impressment Warrants
____Naval Reservists
____Lighthouse Dues
____Quarantine Register
____Enrollments
____Enrollment Bonds
____Clearance Records
____Accounts
____Ledgers
____Impost Books
____Abstracts of Duties
____Bounty Lists
____Licenses
____Customs Farms
____Customs Patents
____Appointments of Collectors
____Surety Notes

____Bonds
____Oaths of Office
____Salary Lists
____Service Records
____Capacity Rolls
____Excise Tax
____Liquor Tax
____Excise Board Minutes

Shipping (Port) Records

____Ships Logbooks
____Journals
____Cargo Lists
____Bills of Lading
____Bills of Exchange
____Accounts
____Manifest Books
____Marine Insurance Policies
____Instructions
____Bottomry Bonds
____Charter-parties
____Bills of Sale
____Entry Papers
____Licenses to Carry Arms
____Wartime Contracts
____Letter Books
____Protection Passes
____Pension Contributions
____Pirate Ransom Forms
____List of Sea Officers
____Discription Books
____Seamen's Apprenticeship
       Certificates
____Crew Lists
____Register of Seamen
____Seamen's Oaths
____Seamen's Certificates
____Passports
____Seamen's Wage Suits
____Payrolls
____Wage Claims
____Passenger Lists
____
____
____

Ship-building Records

____Purchase Books
____Stock Books
____Wage Books
____Contracts
____Personnel Records
____
____
____

Canal Company Records

____Reports
____Petitions
____Minutes
____Proceedings
____Personnel Records
____Bills of Lading
____Newspaper Files
____Correspondence
____Survey Maps
____Passenger Lists
____Bonds

Governor's Records

____Register
____Correspondence

Reports
Accounts
Proclamations
Messages
Vetoes
Executive Orders
Minutes of Executive Council
Reports of State Agencies
Appointments
Removals
Resignations
Passports
Permits to Travel
Pardons
Paroles
Extraditions
Memorials
Claims
Petitions
Royal Commissions
Orders in Council
Royal Instructions
Bonds
Exclusive Grants
Confiscations

Marriage Records

Licenses
Bonds
Allegations
Returns
___

Committees of Safety

Minutes
Accounts
Correspondence
Militia Records
Court Files
Orders
Associator's Files
Confiscations
___

Council of Safety

Grants
Correspondence
Minutes
Accounts
Orders
___
___
___

State Employees

Civil Service
List of Freemen
List of Associates
Oaths of Office
Oaths of Allegiance
Appointments
Removals
Resignations
Bonds
Payrolls
Service Files
Pensions
Applications
Exams
___
___

General Assembly

Calendars
Indexes
Dockets
Proxy Books
Whip Lists
Oath Books
Correspondence
Letterbooks
Journals
Proceedings
Minutes
Debates
Ledgers
Expense Accounts
Certificates of Election
Election Frauds
Contested Elections
Governor's Messages
Vetoes
Reports of State Officials
Inquiries
Inquisitions
Investigations
Public Hearings
Oral Testimony
Sound Recordings
Document Exhibits
Conference Reports
Petitions
Memorials
Protest Books
Voting Polls
Resolutions
Slip Laws
Enrolled Bills
Bills
Vetoed Bills
Amendments
Statutes
Laws
Statutes at Large
Constitutional Amendments
Constitutions
Referendum
Recall
Initiative
Divorce
Incorporations
Rent Rolls
Tax Lists
Loose Papers

Committee Records

Minutes
Correspondence
Appointments
Reports
Hearings
Exhibits
___

Election Records

Nomination Petitions
Register of Delegates
Applications for Office
Declarations of Candidacy
Convention Petitions
Petitions
Certification of Nominees
Election Certificates
Contested Elections
Election Violations

Request for Recount
___
___
___

Health Department

Births
Marriages
Deaths
Immunizations
Special Clinics
Public Health Nurses
Hospital Licenses
Special Education
Adoptions
___
___

Welfare Records

Old Age Assistance
Dependent Children
Blind
Disabled
Unemployable
Unemployed
Child Welfare
Medical Care
Food Distribution
Adoption Agencies
Home for Unwed Mothers
Day Nursery Licenses
Crippled Children
Hospitals
Alcoholic Clinics
Drug Centers
Mental Health Centers
Tuberculosis Sanitorium
Training Schools
Industrial Schools
Indian Schools
___
___
___

Unemployment Insurance

Claims
Fraud Investigation Reports
___
___
___

Employment Agency

Personnel Lists
Job Lists
Day Employment Roster
___
___
___

Business Regulation

Business Licenses
Professional Licenses
Trades Licenses
Examinations
Applications
Certificates
Renewals
Business Permits
Brokers
Brokerage Firms
Contractors
Abstractors
Real Estate Agents
Apprenticeships

Inspection Records
___
___
___
___
___

Insurance Records

Correspondence
Agents Complaints
Field Investigations
Field Correspondence
Workmen's Compensation
Powers of Attorney
Court Summons
Policy Holders
Policy Holders Suits
Admissions Registers
Unlicensed Companies
Applications
Appointments
Cancellations
Employees Bonds
Firemen's Relief Bonds
Fire
Storm
Marine
Life
Health
Accident
Business
Fidelity
Building & Loan
Plate Glass
Liability
Machinery
Burglary
Credit
Livestock
Real Estate
Vehicle
___
___

Corporation Records

Articles of Incorporation
Extinct Corporations
Partnerships
Charters
Dissolutions
Trade Names
Trade Marks
Business Under
      Assumed Name
___
___

Turnpike (Highway) Records

Surveys
Board Minutes
Commission Elections
Inspection Reports
Correspondence
Road Petitions
Highway Lands
___
___
___

University Records

Account Books
Registrar
Matriculation Lists

____Examination Lists
____Tuition Lists
____Subscription Lists
____Graduation Lists
____Degree Lists
____Alumni
____Sorority
____Fraternity
____Social Unit
____Honorary Society
____Transcripts
____Reports
____Yearbooks
____Directories
____Newspapers
____Awards

School Board Records

____List of Free Schools
____Reports
____Letters
____Teacher Training Registers

____Transportation Records
____
____
____

Miscellaneous

____W.P.A. Inventories
____Loose Papers
____State Censuses
____Indian Treaties
____Indian Agreements
____

____**Local Records on Deposit**

____Town
____County
____Borough
____City
____School District
____Court District

____Business Firm
____Church
____Family
____Estate
____
____

Publications

____Newspapers
____Historical Journals
____Directories
____Yearbooks
____Bulletins
____Acquisitions
____Guides to Holdings
____Histories
____Biographies
____Atlases
____Record Collections
____Blue Books
____Official Manuals

Private Collections

____Letters
____Diaries
____Memoirs
____Journals
____Albums
____Biographies
____Account Books
____Speeches
____Sermons
____Household Accounts
____Legal Papers
____Commonplace Books
____Memorandum Books
____Newspaper Clippings
____
____
____

RESEARCH OUTLINE

(Copyright 1972, Genealogical Copy Service)

Immediate Objective: SEARCH OF NATIONAL (UNITED STATES) JURISDICTION

PEDIGREE NAMES: SPECIFIC DATES:

_____

_____

_____

_____

_____

_____

Sources: The non-current records of the United States Government are preserved in the National Archives in Washington, D.C. and in Federal Record Centers across the country. They have been classified, inventoried and described.

RECORD CREATING AGENCIES

Check (___) the agencies which pertain to your pedigree names listed above.

General

___Constitution
___Amendments
___Bill of Rights
___Statutes
___Executive Orders
___Proclamations
___Rules and Regulations of Federal Agencies
___Boundary Claims
___Boundary Commissions
___Arbitrations
___International Conferences
___International Commissions
___Treaties
___Indian Treaties
___Foreign Countries

Legislative Agencies

Senate

___Electoral Papers
___Impeachments
___Standing Committees
___Select Committees
___Presidential Messages
___Reports of Executive Agencies

House of Representatives

___Select Committees
___Standing Committees
___Hearings
___Exhibits
___Contested Elections
___Reports of Executive Agencies
___Records of the Clerk

Joint Committees

(Records sent to House of chairman at conclusion of committee work)

Miscellaneous

Expositions
Memorial Commissions
Army Pensions
Navy Pensions
Heirs Pensions
Contracts of the War Department
Government Printing Office

Judicial Agencies

___District Courts
___Court of Claims
___Circuit Courts
___Circuit Courts of Appeals
___Commerce Court
___Admiralty
___Administrative Office
___Supreme Court
___Copyrights
___Naturalizations

Presidential Agencies

___White House Office
___Committees
___Commissions
___Boards
___Unemployment Relief
___Foreign Trade
___Bureau of the Budget
___National Resources Planning Board
___CIA
___Government Reports

Department of State

___Continental Congress
___Diplomatic Records
___Consuls
___Passport Applications
___Appointments of Personnel
___Amnesty and Pardon
___Territories
___Copyright Registers

Department of Treasury

___Southern Claims Commission
___Bureau of the Customs
___Bureau of Public Debt
___Old Loan Office
___Public Accounts
___Customshouse Records
___Court Records of Confederacy
___Fish Bounty Papers
___Industrial Bounties
___U.S. Coast Guard
___Bureau of the Mint
___Internal Revenue
___Comptroller of Currency
___Insolvencies
___U.S. Secret Service
___Narcotics Control

___Foreign Funds Control
___Prize Money Records

Department of Defense

___Joint Chiefs of Staff
___Strategic Services
___Joint Boards
___Strategic Bombing Survey

Department of the Army

___Secretary of War
___Civilian Personnel
___Revolutionary War Records
___Chief of Ordnance
___Paymaster General
___Quartermaster General
___Chief of Finance
___Judge Advocate General
___Army Commands
___Inspector General
___Surgeon General
___Commissary General
___National Guard
___Headquarters of the Army
___Chief Signal Officer
___Chief of Engineers
___Adjutant General
___Commissary General of Prisoners
___Provost Marshal
___Bureau of Refugees, Freedmen, Abandoned Lands
___Panama Canal
___Military Government of Cuba
___Provisional Government of Cuba
___War Department General Staff
___Military Government of Veracruz
___Selective Service
___Chief of Arms
___Expeditionary Forces
___Army Service Forces
___War Department Claims Board
___Foreign Claims
___Chief of Chaplains
___Seized Enemy Records
___German
___Italian

Department of the Navy

___General Records
___Office of Naval Records
___Bureau of Yards and Docks
___U.S. Marine Corps
___Bureau of Ordnance
___Navy Personnel
___Hydrographic Office
___Medicine and Surgery
___District Shore Establishments
___Naval Observatory
___Judge Advocate General
___Chief of Naval Operations
___Bureau of Supplies
___Bureau of Aeronautics

Department of the Air Force

Department of Justice

___Federal Prisons
___Appointments of Judges
___Immigration and Naturalization
___U.S. Attorneys, Marshals
___Solicitor of the Treasury
___Pardon Attorney
___Court of Claims Section
___FBI
___War Risk Litigation
___Veterans Life Insurance Claims

Post Office Department

___Site Location Maps
___Postal Site Reports
___Appointments of Postmasters
___Espionage (1917-21)

Department of Interior

___National Park Service
___Bureau of Indian Affairs
___General Land Office
___Commissioner of Railroads
___Geological Survey
___Fish and Wildlife
___Territories, Inland Possessions
___Bureau of Mines
___Bureau of Reclamation
___War Minerals Relief
___Petroleum Administration
___National Bituminous Coal

___Bituminous Coal Division
___Railroad Surveys
___Wagon-road Surveys

Department of Agriculture

___Civilian Conservation Corps
___War Food Administration
___Agricultural and Industrial Chemistry
___Entomology and Plant Quarantine
___Plant Industry, Soils
___Forest Service
___Extension Stations
___Animal Industry
___Marketing Services
___Agricultural Economics
___Agricultural Engineering
___Foreign Agricultural Relations
___Dairy Industry
___Farm Credit
___Human Nutrition and Economics
___Commodity Exchange
___Soil Conservation
___Agricultural Adjustment
___Surplus Marketing

___Commodity Credit
___Farm Security Administration
___Rural Electrification
___Federal Crop Insurance
___Farmers Insurance

Department of Commerce

___U.S. Industrial Commission
___Bureau of Marine Inspection
___Bureau of Census
___Coast and Geodetic Survey
___Bureau of Standards
___Patent Office
___Weather Bureau
___Foreign and Domestic Commerce
___Public Roads
___Civil Aeronautics
___Inland Waterways

Department of Labor

___Labor Statistics
___Employment Service
___Women's Bureau
___Labor Standards
___Wage, Hour and Public Contracts

Federal Security Agency

___Public Health Service
___Office of Education
___Food and Drug Administration
___Children's Bureau
___Social Security
___National Youth

Federal Works Agency

___W.P.A.
___Public Works

General Services

___National Archives
___Public Buildings
___Federal Supplies

World War I Agencies

World War II Agencies

Department of Urban Development

Others

___U.S. Soldiers Home
___Smithsonian Institute
___Interstate Commerce Commission
___Veterans Administration
___Civil Service
___Federal Trade Commission
___National Academy of Sciences
___U.S. Maritime Commission
___Prison Industries
___Federal Reserve System
___Maritime Labor
___Civil Aeronautics
___Transportation Investigation
___Virgin Islands
___Spanish Government of Puerto Rico
___Confederate Records
___Law Observance and Enforcement
___Reconstruction Finance
___National Recovery
___Tennessee Valley Authority
___Securities and Exchange

GUIDES AND INVENTORIES

Consult the preliminary inventory, special list or guide to the records of those agencies which you checked (___) to determine the specific records produced, the dates they cover and their locations. Most of these can be consulted in research libraries near you. Copies can be obtained from the National Archives free or at nominal cost. Out-of-print copies are available on microfilm.

List of Record Groups in the National Archives and the Federal Records Centers. 1969. 39 pp.

Guide to the Records in the National Archives. 1948. 684 pp.

National Archives Accessions. 1940-1967. (Replaced by Prologue)

Guide to Genealogical Records in the National Archives. 1964. 145 pp.

Guide to Federal Archives Relating to the Civil War. 1962. 721 pp.

Guide to the Archives of the Government of the Confederate States of America. 1968. 536 pp.

Handbook of Federal World War Agencies and Their Records, 1917-21. 1943. 666 pp.

Federal Records of World War II. Vol. I: *Civilian Agencies.* 1950. 1073 pp.
Vol. II: *Military Agencies.* 1951. 1061 pp.

Prologue. Journal of the National Archives. 1969. In progress.

Preliminary Inventories. #1-171. In progress.

Special Lists. 1-22. In progress.

Copy the identifying information for each record you intend to search from the inventory or guide. Indicate its present location and the method you will use to search it. Many of the records are available on microfilm in research libraries, Federal Record Centers or they can be ordered direct from the Government Printing Office. Check (___) each record as you search it.

√	RECORD	NAME AND ADDRESS OF DEPOSITORY	METHOD OF SEARCH (Personal, Researcher, Loan, Correspondence, Copy)	REMARKS (Fees Restrictions)

\	RECORD	NAME AND ADDRESS OF DEPOSITORY	METHOD OF SEARCH (Personal, Researcher, Loan, Correspondence, Copy)	REMARKS (Fees Restrictions)

168

Any search, regardless of its objective or the jurisdiction involved, should be carefully planned. To violate this principle will lead to compromises for which you will have to account in later searches. Adherance to this rule will bring maximum success and accomplishment, subject only to the limitations of existing records themselves.

You are ready to perform outlined research:

Table Four.

Step	Jurisdiction	Names (Ultimate Objectives)	Search Procedure (Immediate Objectives)
Outlined Research: Systematic collection of information from primary and secondary research sources	**Basic:** Town Independent City Borough Manor Parish Mining District County City-county City-state	All surnames	General searches
	Local: Municipal Ecclesiastical Employment Professional Social Institutional	All surnames or pedigree ancestors	Particular searches
	Higher: District State Territory Province Colony Country	Pedigree ancestors	Particular searches

In the preceding four chapters, we have developed a logical procedure for pedigree analysis or problem definition. When these steps are followed, each in its turn, each thoroughly performed before the next is begun, genealogy is reduced, as much as possible, to an objective, mechanical process eliminating human subjectivity and associated error. The greatest trouble spot in genealogy — analysis and planning — is overcome. It is now possible to solve any genealogical research problem if that problem is soluble. This is as it must be if genealogical research is a science. There can be no room for aimless guessing or waste. There will always be missing documents and collections unavailable for searching. You should not spend your lifetime searching for those sources which do not exist or which cannot be searched. When your research outline is exhausted, the data collected should be evaluated and family units compiled. If closed collections, which may change the picture, become available, if new (previously unknown) sources are discovered, or if missing documents are found, the data from these must be obtained and then compared with that gathered before. Such is to be expected. But no genealogist should ever need to re-do your work if it is done in accordance with these principles. Let succeeding generations build upon your work, or your efforts are wasted.

STEP THREE: OUTLINED RESEARCH

CHAPTER TEN

STEP THREE: RESEARCH —
SYSTEMATIC COLLECTION OF RESEARCH DATA

Research is the systematic collection of data and evidence from primary and secondary research sources. To you, the student, who have diligently studied the preceding chapters, all of which are preparatory to research itself, it may seem unbelievable that the time to search documents has arrived. These preparatory steps through which you have come should have schooled you in the collection, evaluation and use of primary and secondary source materials. This experience will enable you to conduct research in a well-organized and professional manner. As original research progresses, these preliminary disciplines will pay off handsomely.

The background and knowledge of your ancestors, which you now possess, will enable you to recognize and identify them in subsequent searches. The only brick walls which you face at this point are limitations of the records themselves. Skill and ability are needed for the planning of searches and analysis of records. Anyone who can read and write can be trained to extract data. If the records are in a foreign language or written in a special hand, more training is necessary. But the real skill of a researcher lies in planning and analysis which precedes the searches in sources — areas in which you have become expert.

The discussion of each type of source created and its genealogical use is a complex study in itself and beyond the scope of this volume. You are referred to subsequent volumes in this series and the texts written by others which treat this aspect of genealogy.[1] This chapter will deal primarily with the procedures and techniques used in searching the records, whether you do the actual searching yourself or whether you enlist the aid of family members, records keepers or field researchers.

What is a Record?

A record is any book, manuscript, official paper, periodical, map or document, film, tape or photograph containing genealogical, biographical or historical information which provides evidence used as the basis of proof. Document, record and source are often used interchangeably to indicate any one of these. The record holdings of most repositories are divided into archives, manuscript collections and printed volumes. *Archives* consist of those documents produced as by-products of official or administrative duties. Personnel records are part of the archives of a business firm. *Manuscript collections and printed volumes* are records deliberately collected from other agencies, libraries or private individuals for preservation. They may include archival records created by the agency or library from which they were obtained but they are not produced by the repository where they are currently held. The personnel records of a business firm become manuscript collections in a local historical society. Printed volumes, in which manuscript notes and marginal additions are written, are usually classified as manuscripts.

To obtain the most information from any record — archive document, manuscript collection or printed volume — it is necessary to understand its essential parts:

Title Page: Usually the first printed page in the book, or the first written page of a manuscript is the title page. It contains the full name or title of the record, the author, compilor or editor, place of publication, publisher and usually the date of printing. On the back of this page appears the copyright date, if there is one, previous editions and dates of publication. This bibliographic data is absolutely necessary to identify properly each source consulted; it should be entered on the calendar as part of the description of the source.

Frontispiece: A photograph, picture, a map or old engraving that appears in the front of many old books is called the frontispiece. It is usually separated from the title page with onion skin paper. In very old books, the engraving ghosts itself on the onion skin.

List of Subscribers. These are the people who contributed toward publication and are purchasers of the book. Publication by subscription began in the sixteenth century and is still in use today.

Commendatory Verses. These are short poems praising

the record and the author's ability. They date from the sixteenth century and can be found in every kind of book — even textbooks and scientific treatises. Since 1800 the foreword or introduction written by a friend of the author or some influential person has replaced verses. In some countries they appear on the title page, but they can be found in any part of the book.

Preface. The purpose of the record is stated, usually by the author, in the preface. You should always read this *before* searching the record.

Table of Contents: Its function is to list and summarize each chapter or part of the book. It indicates the beginning page number of each chapter.

List of Maps or Illustrations: This is a listing of pages where they appear. It enables you to locate them quickly. Maps, graphs or illustrations may be scattered through the book or placed together in one spot.

Dedication. The dedication of a modern book consists of one or two lines only; the dedication of older works was lengthy. Dedications have been in use since antiquity. They are found at the beginning of the record, embedded in the text or part of the critical or editorial preface. There may be separate dedications for each chapter, print, illustration, coat of arms or other part of the document. They usually follow a pattern: a short statement of the purpose of the work, why it was compiled, praise for the patron who made it possible and gratitude or plea for his support and protection.

Introduction: The introduction interprets or explains the contents of the volume. This explanation should always be read before *searching* the record. It will enable you to search more efficiently and it will aid your analysis of the contents.

Text. The main part or body of the record is the text.

Margin or Foot-notes: These provide additional information for the reader. Margin notes are generally written by hand on the page of the text or between the lines. Foot-notes are indicated by an asterisk or numbered in small arabic numbers printed at the bottom of the page, at the end of each chapter or section or at the end of the record. They should always be read, because they indicate the sources from which the text is taken.

Appendix: Pertinent information on the subject, not part of the text, is included in the appendix. This material may provide evidence or proof to substantiate conclusions drawn by the author or it may lead you to additional sources.

Bibliography: The alphabetical listing of references — books, manuscripts or documents — used to compile the record or to furnish additional information on the subject covered is called the bibliography. It may be located at the end of each chapter, section or volume.

Addenda: This is a section containing material added after the text was printed. It is usually placed in the back of the book.

Glossary: The section which defines technical, little known or foreign words is called the glossary.

Indexes: These are alphabetical or chronological listings of material treated in the record. They may be divided into sections — names of persons, subjects, places — or all entries may be included in one master index. Location varies: The index is usually at the end of the volume but it may be found in the front, in the middle or scattered in several sections throughout the record.

Every record will not contain all of these parts, but several of them will be represented in each record you search. If you know what to look for you will not overlook something essential to your evaluation of the source or something pertinent to your pedigree.

When you search a record for the first time, examine all of its parts carefully. Do not begin with the text. Study the table of contents to get an overview of the organization of the record. Then read the preface, foreword, introduction and conclusion for the compiler's purpose, method and results. Examine the bibliography, footnotes and appendixes for documentation of evidence. Last of all, study the text. If you proceed in this way, your understanding of the text will be greater and your search will progress with greater ease and speed.

Finding Records in a Depository

The researcher is dependent upon record depositories for his source materials. Much emphasis, in the past, has been placed upon field work to collect data. The building of superhighways and turnpikes, dams and reservoirs, the expansion of city limits, the increased number of suburban developments, shopping centers and malls, the destructive effects of war and riots and a tremendous increase in population have all contributed to the destruction of topographical features, cemeteries, monuments and old buildings. Personal examination of places and buildings, where possible, is still profitable and provides the feel of an area at the time ancestors lived as no other method can. But to obtain the information from the old church or its graveyard, it is increasingly necessary to use written, secondary accounts or primary sources located in depositories. A knowledge of these facilities is essential to get the most out of their resources and this knowledge should be gained *before* research is undertaken. Your success in finding the right sources is in proportion to your knowledge of archive research.

Classification Systems. Libraries are organized to make it easy to find information quickly. The records are arranged on shelves, in files or cases, in numerical or alphabetical order, according to the classification system used. The majority of libraries use either Dewey-Decimal or Library of Congress classification. You should become generally acquainted with both these systems.[2]

Dewey-Decimal System:

000-099	General Works, Encyclopedias, Bibliographies
100-199	Philosophy, Ethics
200-299	Religion
300-399	Social Science, Education, Law
400-499	Linguistics
500-599	Pure Science: Chemistry, Mathematics
600-699	Applied Science: Business, Engineering
700-799	Fine Arts, Recreation
800-899	Literature
900-999	History, Geography, Genealogy, Archaeology
Biography:	Alphabetically under surname of subject
Fiction:	Alphabetically under surname of author

Library of Congress System:

A   General Works
B   Philosophy and Religion
C   History, Auxiliary Sciences
D   History, Topography
E, F America
G   Geography, Anthropology
H   Social Sciences
J   Political Science
K   Law
L   Education
M   Music
N   Fine Arts
P   Literature, Language
Q   Science
R   Medicine
S   Agriculture
T   Technology
U   Military Science
V   Naval Science
Z   Bibliography, Library
     Science

I, O, W, X, Y   reserved for
     future expansion

Card Catalog. The classification number of each record can be found by consulting the card catalog. It is the KEY to the library. It enables you to find records quickly and to use them intelligently. The catalog is not a bibliography; it is an index to what the library has, where to find it and how to use it.

The cards in the catalog are arranged alphabetically in drawers. At intervals are guide cards, which should be used as the guide words in a dictionary are used. They indicate where to begin looking in the tray. Every record usually has at least three cards in the catalog, so that you can locate it by looking under the author, the title or the subject.

CATALOG: *Key to the Library*

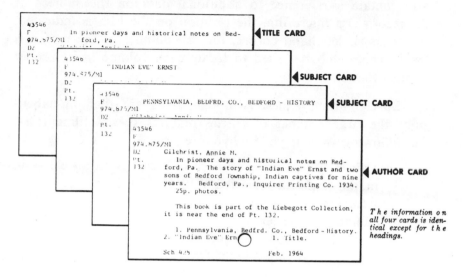

TITLE CARD
SUBJECT CARD
SUBJECT CARD
AUTHOR CARD

The information on all four cards is identical except for the headings.

ANALYSIS OF AUTHOR CARD *(above)*

Actual size of cards

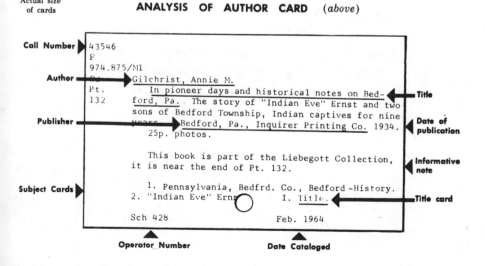

Call Number ▶ 43546
F
974.875/M1
Author ▶ Gilchrist, Annie M.
Pt.   In pioneer days and historical notes on Bed- ◀ Title
132   ford, Pa. The story of "Indian Eve" Ernst and two
sons of Bedford Township, Indian captives for nine
Publisher ▶ years. Bedford, Pa., Inquirer Printing Co. 1934. ◀ Date of publication
25p. photos.

This book is part of the Liebegott Collection, ◀ Informative note
it is near the end of Pt. 132.

Subject Cards ▶ 1. Pennsylvania, Bedfrd. Co., Bedford –History.
2. "Indian Eve" Erns◯ I. Title. ◀ Title card

Sch 428   Feb. 1964

▲ Operator Number   ▲ Date Cataloged

Every catalog card has complete bibliographic information about the record in question. It contains the number of pages, lists illustrations, maps and subjects within the volume. It may also contain a reference to additional data on the subject. If the record is a microfilm, the position on the film is indicated. In the upper left hand corner, the call number of the record is listed. This number is used to locate each volume in its proper number classification.

Special Filing Rules. Although cards are filed alphabetically, the large number of entries requires special filing rules. The following will help you find your records:

1. **Articles:** When the first work of a title is an article — a, an, the — it is disregarded in filing. This is true of articles in foreign languages also.
   Example: The genius
              Genius and Valor
              A genius in the family

2. **M' Mc:** Names beginning with M' and Mc are filed as though they were spelled Mac.
   Example: McCune
              MacCunn
              McCurdy

3. **Common Abbreviations:** Common abbreviations are arranged as though they were spelled out.
   Example: Dr. — Doctor
              Mr. — Mister

St. — Saint

U.S. — United States

4. **Author Cards Precede Subject Cards:** Author cards precede subject cards; works by an author are filed before works about him.

5. **Many Entries:** Several cards may be made out on one record or subject. Books containing information on the same subject may be listed under several different entries, all in different parts of the catalog. Think of all the possible entries that could be made for any given record.

Example: Court — History of British System

Great Britain — Court System

British Court System — History of

6. **Order of Entries under Same Word:** When the same word is used for several kinds of headings, they are filed in this order: person, subject, title, place.

Example: Maine, Sir Henry J. S. (person)

Maine, (Battleship) (subject)

Maine, Beautiful (title)

Maine, York Co. (place)

7. **Organizations as Authors:** An author may be an organization, a government, an institution or a society. The author card may be found under some such heading as the following:

Salt Lake City, Utah, Board of Health

New Jersey, Legislature

U. S. Navy Department

Great Britain. Census Office

8. **Pseudonyms:** Books are listed under the author's real name with a cross reference from his pseudonym if he has one.

Example: Twain, Mark, Pseud. see Clemens, Samuel Langhorne

9. **Societies and Institutions:** Publications of societies or institutions are filed under the name of the society or institution, not under the words Bulletin, Proceedings, Transactions, etc.

Example: Society of Colonial Wars, Report.

10. **Numerals:** Numerals are filed as if spelled out: 1 as one; 40,000 as forty thousand; 1918 — nineteen eighteen if a date, otherwise nineteen hundred eighteen.

11. **Word-by-Word Filing:** Cards are filed alphabetically under a word-by-word arrangement. Many dictionaries, periodical indexes and other reference books use a letter-by-letter arrangement. The difference between the two systems is quite significant and may be illustrated by the following two examples;

Example:	Word-by-word filing:	Letter-by-letter filing:
	New Jersey	Newark
	New York	New Jersey
	Newark	Newspapers
	Newspapers	Newton
	Newton	New York

Search time will be saved by knowing the author's full name and the correct title or subject of the book. You should orient yourself to think in terms of author and title rather than call number. The call number is just a means of locating the volume on the shelf; it does not locate it in the card catalog.[3] Learn to use the catalog properly. It is the KEY to the records in any library.

Libraries and record depositories usually have several divisions; not all of the records will be kept in the same department. There may be a business library, a medical library, a genealogical library and a map library within the main library or in a special room of its own. Each division may have its own personal card catalog or index. Most libraries and depositories also have special collections of source materials: family histories, maps, parish registers, personal papers of important local persons, etc. These are often removed from the main sequence of classification and listed separately. They may be housed in special rooms or buildings away from the main library. If this is the case, be sure to check the listings in these divisions as well as the main card catalog.

Reference Department. An important aid for research is the reference department of any library. Librarians will respond to brief, easy to answer requests: checking indexes for specific information (names, places or dates), acquainting you with library holdings, supplying bibliographical citations, recommending local searchers familiar with their records, helping to locate old maps, atlases or pictures of the locality, providing dates or specific information on local history and settlement. These items, which often take the average person a great deal of time to locate, reference librarians can supply quickly because they know exactly where to look.

Nothing will pay bigger dividends than learning to find and use efficiently the information preserved by libraries and other record depositories. Once these techniques have been mastered, it is possible to search successfully in any record depository.

Searching Research Sources

Research sources require special techniques in order to understand their use and their limitations. The following guidelines will aid you in this task.

* **Check a secondary study of the source first.** Wise use of sources and understanding of the data they contain is dependent upon knowledge of the historical context and background in which they were created. Contents and genealogical application are also important considerations. Other historians or genealogists may have studied the documents carefully and prepared a description of their contents to aid you in their use. These periodicals feature such studies on a regular basis.

  American Archivist (1938—)
  American Neptune (1941—)
  William and Mary Quarterly (1892—)
  Essex Institute Historical Collections (1859—)
  National Genealogical Society Quarterly (1912—)
  American Genealogist (1923—)
  New England Historical and Genealogical Register
     (1847—)
  American Association for State and Local History Bulletin (1941—)
  Library Trends (1952—)
  Library Quarterly (1931—)
  Special Libraries (1910—)

College and Research Libraries (1939—)
American Antiquarian Society Proceedings (1812—)
Archives (1949—)
Amateur Historian, Now Local Historian (1952—)
London University Institute of Historical Research Bulletin (1923—)
History (1916—)
Genealogists Magazine (1924—)
Library (1920—)
Society for Army Historical Research Journal (1921—)
Journal of the Society of Archivists (1959—)

Introductions to edited documents also contain thorough source studies. Genealogical manuals discuss records found in specific jurisdictions (see Bibliographies at the end of this volume) and bibliographies of record collections are often annotated to provide this information. Learn what data the records can be expected to yield and how to use them before you search sources but reserve full judgment until you have actually examined the records yourself.

* **Become proficient in the language in which the records are written.** Even if the language is English, try to understand the meanings of the words as they were *understood by the writer* not as they are used today. Table Five — words used by Geoffrey Chaucer in his *Canterbury Tales* and their modern English equivalents — will clarify this point.

Table Five.

Word	14th Century	Modern English
Boy	Rascal, knave	Male child
Careful	Full of care for someone else	Caution for oneself
Defend	Forbid	Protect
Crul	Curly	Cruel
Cunning	Ability	Sly
Doubt	Feat	Doubt
Geste	Tale, deed	Jest, joke
Gladly	Willingly	Happily
Harlot	Rascal, thief	Prostitute
Nyce	Ignorant, foolish	Nice
Science	Knowledge	Science
Unkouth	Unknown, strange	Without manners, training
Luxurie	Lust	Extravagance
Upryght	Lying on back	Morally correct
Vertu	Power	Moral practices
Gentle	Upper classes	Kind, considerate

To translate foreign words into English is not sufficient. Know the language well enough to think and evaluate in that language itself. Words are products of cultural background and unless you understand that background the nuances and subtleties of the language will escape you.

* **Know how to read sources.**

"The barrier of old script, the forbidding appearance of pages of unrecognizable, apparently meaningless writing is enough to stop any genealogical researcher. The skillful uniform writing of the trained clerk written on vellum with ox gall, which does not fade in a thousand years, can be read with some practice, but phrases written in variable handwriting of some scribes combined with faded and worn-off ink, or written on rotted or discolored or partly torn away pages, seriously aggravate the problem of reading. Tough and hopeless as the task may look, it will yield to practice, to good methods, good light, a good magnifying glass and other obtainable aids."[4]

Old documents become yellowed with age, the ink fades and the words are difficult to read. These tricks can facilitate searching: Learn how to use a magnifying glass. If you do not possess one of your own, most libraries have them. Using the regular side of the glass, it is possible to control sharpness and contrast between the writing and the paper. Experiment until you can read the words. Place a sheet of yellow, orange or green paper on the viewing surface. This will remove the glare, increase the contrast and make it easier to read. Magnifying the print is also helpful. Let your eyes do their work without undue strain. Frequently, look off into the distance, roll your eyes or close them tightly a number of times. This will rest them and allow you to read for longer periods of time.

A common problem is early handwriting. First, obtain a key to the handwriting or language which you are reading. If none is available, make one of your own. Study the formation of the letters and words. Note the way each clerk forms his letters so you can recognize similar letters in other parts of the record. Watch the following especially: M and W, E and O, U and V, F and S, N and R, L and T, A and O, and E and I. These are the ones usually mistaken for each other. Refer to the key often. Begin by reading the record where the writing seems to be clearest. Become familiar with the localities, the surnames and the given names that appear over and over in the records. Know the phrases, words and abbreviations used in each type of document. Knowledge of the probable contents will enable you to read them much faster. Finally, record these circumstances on your calendar. Too many genealogists are prone to skip over the hard to read passages, but this is a research compromise. Since you will need all the evidence the record contains; these passages are not to be ignored. They must be read.[5]

* **Know how to use indexes properly.** Indexes can save time by preventing fruitless searching for information buried somewhere in the volume, but you should depend on them only to the extent that they are complete. Carefully analyze the index and if you suspect it to be incomplete, take the time to search the entire record. Records that cover many years in several volumes usually have a master index as well

as separate volume indexes. Experience has shown that both should be checked; one often supplements the other. Be sure to watch for more than one index in each volume or indexes located at the beginning or in the middle of the record instead of at the end. When consulting the record for the first time, take a few minutes to find the indexes.

Indexes can be made as the documents are entered or after the record is completed. Both types have their problems. The index made as the documents are entered is usually not in alphabetical order. A's may be together but Anderson entries may precede those for Abbott. Some letters of the alphabet fill up more rapidly than others; clerks enter the overflow under such letters as Q and V, which are seldom filled. Examine the entire index if some of the letter areas are full. An index made after the record was compiled may be more correct. The compiler alphabetizes each entry and usually double-checks it for accuracy. Yet index entries for documents involving more than one person may include only one of the names. This is especially true of court records. It then becomes necessary to check the entire index to obtain references to both parties.

To determine if all entries have been indexed, randomly open the record and select four or five names, places or events listed on the pages before you. Check each one in the index. If they all appear, the index is usually complete. Such an index can be used. If any are missing, the index contains selected entries only. Search such volumes page by page.

If index entries do not coincide with the actual record, the original may have been rewritten, but not the index. For example, the record shows signs of age and wear. A clerk is commissioned to re-copy the entire record into a new book. As no two people write exactly the same, more or less pages are used in re-copying than in the original. Thus, the index entries do not correspond with the re-copied record. Take the record, note the index entries and determine how many pages it has taken the clerk to recopy each document. Then it should be possible to locate the right entries. If you can't figure out the paging in this manner, search the record page by page.

If the record has a reliable index, use it. If you suspect that it may be incomplete, search page by page even though it may be tedious and time-consuming.

* **Take proper care of records.** Few people know how to handle aged or rare documents, books and manuscripts. The things most libraries or archives suggest in the care and use of these records include:

1. The older and more rare a book is, the more careful you should be. It is a good idea to ask the librarian to assist you in finding the information that you seek.

2. Always examine the records on a flat surface. In some libraries, book racks or stands are provided to hold books upright for easier reading. This reduces strain on the binding.

3. Documents that are folded should be unfolded and re-folded *exactly* as they were originally folded.

4. Open old books with extreme care as the glue or sewing may be in bad condition. If you hear a cracking noise, call it to the attention of the librarian.

5. Do not fold the corners of the pages as they are usually brittle and tear easily. If it is necessary to mark your place ask the librarian for an accepted bookmark. Pencils, rulers or smaller books should never be used as bookmarks. They cause bindings to break.

6. Always avoid moistening the figures when turning the pages. Moisture causes deterioration of the record.

7. Be careful not to bend the back of a book unnecessarily. This too will cause the binding to crack.

8. Please refrain from marking, underlining or making corrections in any record. Remember that you are not the only one to use it and your data may be no more correct than that in the record. Most libraries have regular procedures for submitting corrections to source materials and secondary works. Some libraries have a book of corrections where these are placed and a small reference is made in the record in question directing the user to the corrections there.[6] Present the librarian

with a documented copy of any corrections you have and let her put them in the proper place. If the author or editor is still living, submit your documented corrections directly to him for inclusion in future editions. They can usually be reached through a letter addressed to the publisher.

9. Always find out if the library allows the use of pens *before* using them. Many libraries restrict the use of such writing materials.

10. Carry old or large books carefully, with a firm grip so there is no danger of dropping them.

11. Do not rest your hands or forearms upon the records. Nor is it wise to place your note paper over the book when taking notes. Before tracing a diagram or map, check with the librarian. Some libraries provide illuminated tracing tables, some libraries do not allow tracing at all.

12. Never turn the pages from the bottom or the top of the page; they are likely to tear. Turn from the corner or side.

13. Utilize the services of the librarian. Show a consideration for the records and she will be glad to help you.

If you use old records with care, they will be preserved for others to consult.

* **Know the limitations placed on sources** and cooperate with the record depository enforcing them. Limitations on the use of records are imposed for several reasons: The documents are brittle and easily marred. To subject them to continued use creates a physical hazard to the records themselves. People discussed or described in the records are still living and to permit widespread use of them would violate their rights of privacy. Examples are the twentieth century censuses. The donor of the collection may deposit records in a local archive with the stipulation that they not be released for use until a certain date or that their contents not be published for a specific period of time. Some libraries restrict their collections to the use of society members or graduate students who have exhausted secondary materials and are well exper-

190

ienced in research. Some libraries freeze collections for the use of one researcher at a time to protect his right to publish and to prevent duplication.[7] Cooperation in accepting such restrictions will lead to better cooperation from the archivist. Note such limitations on your calendar and if the records are made available at some future time, obtain access to them and complete your search.

* **Make thorough abstracts of the documents searched.** Learn what items are important for genealogical identification and carefully abstract that data at one time. It is costly and time consuming to re-search documents over and over because important information was overlooked or not abstracted.

An abstract should contain:

All names including neighbors, witnesses, clerks, bondsmen
All places
All dates
All relationships
All references to other documents
All property descriptions — land, personal property, chattels, shares
All considerations — money, affection, produce, exchanges, agreements, contracts
All signatures or marks exactly as they appear
All historical information that may serve as clues to other sources — occupation, religion, military service, nationality, membership in organizations, involvement in migrations, acts of God.
All biographical descriptions.

* **Proof read each abstract.** Each abstract made should be double-checked against the source, when it is made, to insure against copy errors. Be sure that dates and names are copied exactly with no change of spelling or meaning.

* **Know the value of printed primary sources.** Printed volumes of primary sources can be valuable for the genealogist if they are prepared accurately. Numerous volumes have been published. Some institutions have been especially formed to edit and publish specific categories of records. Examples include parish register societies, the Pipe Roll Society, the Monumental Brass Society, the Catholic Record Society and the Place-

Name Society. Periodicals contain extracts, abstracts, transcriptions and photocopies of documents and other source materials. Check the indexes and guides listed on pages 80-81 above. Many important series of records in the Public Record Office have been published in transcribed or calendared form: The Rolls Series (medieval chronicles and memorials), the Close Rolls, Patent Rolls, Feets of Fine, Inquisitions Post Mortem, Chancery Proceedings, Treasury Records, State Papers — Foreign, Domestic, and Colonial — Acts of the Privy Council and many others. Boyd's and Phillimore's Marriage Indexes are the products of private publication.

Printed sources can provide a fairly complete index to the original, giving volume and page references so the original can be quickly checked. This is especially valuable for court files which are rarely indexed in their original form. Frequently, original manuscripts are difficult to read due to the unfamiliar handwriting of the clerks, the abbreviations used, Latin and French terms and the fading ink of ages past. A well-trained, experienced editor can often make a better transcription than an untrained genealogist. Such a copy can be used as a guide to understand the words in each document and can save you hours pouring over hard to read documents. Printed sources can replace missing records which have been destroyed or otherwise lost. In spite of the varying quality which transcriptions possess, they often represent the only existing copies of many records and they must be used for what they contain.

* **Be willing to search for documents you need.** Seldom, if ever, will all the documents necessary to identify a pedigree ancestor be found in one place. There are several reasons. First, authority over an individual is splintered among numerous jurisdictions. Town, village, county, school district, tax district, state, nation, church and institution all exercise some control. Second, deposit of documents in central archives is difficult. Each jurisdiction is apt to guard its records jealously. Preservation of records is a third reason. Some categories survive intact, others in part, others not at all. Libraries ininterested in increasing their manuscript holdings in specific areas often purchase portions of a collection without concern

for the unity of that collection or the locality to which it applies. Descendants and other relatives carry manuscripts with them as they move from one area to another and they are subsequently deposited many miles from the original locality of the family. Sale, bequest, gift and loan contribute to scattering of sources as well.[8]

In this age of one-stop banking and one-stop shopping, where you can obtain all you need in one place, it is possible to think that all research can be done in one depository. *Never make the mistake of becoming a "one-stop" genealogist.*[9] Use local facilities first. If they lack what you need obtain it on loan or on microfilm from the depository which does.

* **Know how to locate lost manuscripts.** If the collection is a private one or a public one in private hands, check local libraries and historical societies to see if the records have been acquired by them. Check local histories and printed document collections to see if some of them have been transcribed and published. Pay a personal visit or send an agent to the original house where the creator of the records lived. Check the attic, garage, stable, locked muniment room, basement and closets for records. If the family has moved to another locality, trace the family and its descendants. If the creator or his family are no longer available, study his will or administration. Who got his papers? Trace married daughters and their families, and cousins of the family. Were they sold to a local book dealer or auctioneer? Trace the buyers. Did someone borrow the manuscript and forget to return it? Trace the borrower and his heirs.[10]

If public record officials report that "all of the records were burned," check anyway. Most of the time "all of the records" did not burn. Some categories were salvaged; others were reconstructed from originals in possession of property owners, local solicitors or lawyers, newspaper accounts, surviving indexes, appellate court records and other documents. If they have not been reconstructed, the researcher, himself, can often do so by checking records produced by other jurisdictions. Local archive units — town, county, city — were often given printed sets of state or national government publications, which are now non-existent. Complete sets can still be found in local archives or libraries. State statutes, military records and other government documents can be found in this way.[11]

It is extremely rare that all records created by all jurisdictions are destroyed. Some usually survive. Record clerks and other officials are often unaware of the records they have in their custody, especially non-current ones. Check attics, vaults, basements, stairways, elevator shafts, sub-basements, garages, storerooms and other out-of-the-way places in public buildings for records thought to be lost. Finally, realize that records may be destroyed due to neglect, disinterest or fear of their contents and abandon the search when no more leads are available.

Procedure

An essential consideration for performing research is the procedure followed — the actual mechanics of obtaining records or employing field researchers to obtain the data they contain for you. These suggestions are made to help you make the most of your time and resources.

Equipment

Plan each search carefully so that every minute spent in research yields the greatest return. Part of this planning includes the equipment you use. Since you use depositories to obtain information, there is little value in taking previously compiled family group sheets, calendars or enclosure files when you go to search records. This wastes time which could be better spent collecting new or additional information. You collect all pieces of the genealogical puzzle, then you analyze them comparing each piece with every other piece. This usually cannot be done efficiently at the library. The following items will permit about four hours of steady research.

1. **Clipboard or folder.** This will help to keep papers and worksheets together. Avoid large bags, sacks, attache cases or purses. To protect their valuable holdings, many libraries require that these be checked at the door.

2. **Pens and Pencils.** Have a good supply of pencils in case libraries do not permit the use of ink.

3. **Blank Worksheets.** Usually two hundred sheets (whether

you use cards, computer forms, family group sheets, or notebook pages to be torn out and filed separately) will suffice for four hours work.

4. **Research Outline.** The most essential item is the research outline for the current immediate objective on which you are working. If you carefully stick to the plan you have made, your time will be spent efficiently.

5. **Current Calendar Page.** As each search is made, enter it on the calendar, describing the source and the circumstances of the search.

Armed with these items, you will be equipped for efficient use of time. You will enjoy your work and librarians will be pleased to have you use their facilities.[12]

If You Search the Records Yourself

Always use local facilities first. It is possible to perform many searches in your own local public or branch library. Even if their holdings are small, they can provide the services to obtain what you want from the holdings of other depositories. Simply arrange your personal schedule and pay them a visit.

* When entering the library for the first time, go to the reference desk. Learn the location of the card catalog, the various departments, the hours and any special rules or regulations you will be required to keep. In general, get your bearings. Many depositories publish guides to their facilities which they present to new patrons and this guide will usually provide answers to these questions. You should be able to locate materials in any library by yourself without having to be waited on by the librarian. But if you have a question or if the records are in closed stacks, seek the help of those trained to aid you.

* If you have used the library before, go directly to the card catalog to determine what records are available and applicable to your research objective. Taking the research outline, which you planned *before you came to the library,* consult the catalog for those records you wish to search.

* Copy the necessary bibliographic information, including the call number of the record, from the cards to the current page

of your calendar. Include any special instructions, notations of maps, illustrations, indexes, or other references on the same subject which the card contains. It is usually wise to copy the pertinent data for all the records you need to search from the catalog at the same time. In this way, you can determine what is available to you. Leave a few lines after each entry to describe the record and its contents as you search it. You can use this listing to plan your library work at home. This will save time by not having to consult the catalog each time you visit the library. But periodically re-check the catalog to see if the library has added any new sources to its holdings, which may have direct bearing on your genealogical problems. Learn to identify all records by their authors and titles and do not depend upon the call number alone. It is for convenience in locating records. You should know who was responsible for the record. An author is not only a person; an institution, society or governmental unit may also be an author. If you perform research juris-dictionally, this will present little problem. You will study the jurisdiction first to determine who produced the records — who was responsible for the compilation — *before* you search the records.

* To obtain the records you want, take the call number, the title and author of the record and go to the proper area. If the stacks are open to the public, take the records from the shelves. If the stacks are not open, fill out a call slip and present it to the page or librarian. She will obtain the record for you. *Never copy the call number directly from the catalog to a call slip.* Once the slip is gone, you have no further record of that source. If information is copied first onto the calendar and then to a call slip, you will have the pertinent description from the catalog card on your calendar.

* Each time you take a book from the shelf, browse among the other books with similar call numbers or those located nearby in the same subject area. You will find additional records in this way which you may not discover in the card catalog because you are unaware under what heading they are filed.[13]

* Take the records to the designated areas and search through

them for pertinent data. Extract the data directly onto work-sheets and keep the details of the search on your calendar, including the condition of the source, a brief statement of the data found, the names involved and the results of the search. It is a waste of energy and a cause of error to copy genealogical information into a notebook and then recopy it onto worksheets at home.

* Recheck the extract made against the source while it is still in front of you. Correct any deviations from the source which you may have made and note on the worksheet that it has been rechecked.

* When you are through with the records, the library usually requests that you return them to specially designated areas for the attendants to replace upon the shelves.

* Upon your return home, file your worksheets alphabetically. If for some reason you do not intend to finish any search, a note should be made on the calendar with an explanation.

* Plan your next trip to the library by deciding what sources you will search and filling out any call slips. This will save time which, when you get to the library, can be spent in searching records.

If your local library lacks the records you need, you have several alternatives:

Use interlibrary Loan. No single library has all the materials needed for research. Through interlibrary loans, however, a local library can borrow records which it does not own from other libraries across the country or around the world. It is the most frequently used and least expensive way of obtaining books, microfilms, theses and even some manuscripts. Requests for loans must be handled through local libraries; patrons are not allowed to borrow books in their own behalf.

* Place your request through your local public librarian giving her the complete bibliographic data needed to identify the records you want. She will determine the nearest library which has the record and order it. You will be notified when the records arrive and you will be required to use them under whatever provisions the lending library stipulates. The only charge is usually the postage (book rates which are quite in-

expensive) to and from the home library. If you know the name and address of the library which has the record, give that information to the librarian also. This will speed up the loan. If the record does not circulate, the home librarian will obtain a cost estimate for microfilm or xerox copies. She can also arrange for copies to be made. If you are unable to locate the book you need, there are Bibliographic Centers to assist in locating and borrowing copies of individual titles.[14] Regional centers in Denver, Seattle and Philadelphia have union catalogues of books, microfilms, manuscripts and newspapers. Through these, copies of most books can be located within the region. If they cannot be found there, recourse is made to the Library of Congress. Its *National Union Catalogue* gives nationwide coverage of book titles held by American libraries. A *Union List of Serials, Union List of Microfilms* and *Union List of Newspapers* are also available. Copies can be found in most large libraries.[15] Similar centers are to be found in Canada, Great Britain, Germany and other countries. Interlibrary loans are not restricted to American records; records of other countries can be obtained in the same way.

The Out-of-Print Book Services. University Microfilms (Ann Arbor, Michigan) has a program whereby any out of print book — English or foreign — can be produced on demand as microfilm or xerox copies. Catalogs of those books already in their collection are available on request.

* For titles not presently in the collection, send author, title, publisher, original publication date and location of the original. If necessary, University Microfilms will obtain copyright clearance to reproduce the book. They will microfilm the book page by page and inspect the negative for accuracy. The patron receives a positive copy and the negative is added to their growing library. The entire service costs less than normal copy work. Xerox copies can be supplied at a higher cost. Several other publishing firms specialize in reprinting books which are no longer available. These include the Kraus Reprint Corporation (New York), Genealogical Publishing Company (Baltimore), AMS Press (New York), Gale Research Company (Detroit) and Burt Franklin (New York). They will supply catalogues on request. If the book you wish

is not yet available, place your request with them. If it has fairly broad application, they usually will consider reissuing it. Reprints, however, can be quite expensive.

Make a personal visit to the depository which has the resources you need. If your trip is well planned, in advance, it is quite frequently less expensive to visit the areas where your ancestors resided and search the records yourself than to hire a field researcher or have photocopies made. If your children are old enough, they will enjoy helping with the searches too. Use the money you would pay a researcher to have a nice vacation as a family and do the research yourself.

* If this is the alternative you take, *notify the record depository of your visit in advance.* Explain to the archivist or librarian the purpose of your visit and the records you plan to search, so he can assist you. Records are often housed in other buildings and must be brought to the archives for your use. Ask if there are any specific rules with which you must comply. Some depositories require letters of introduction or character references which you should take with you. A tape recorder and camera or other means of photographing documents and inscriptions are musts. They will save much time, and will produce transcripts or copies of records with much less error than copying by hand. Your own equipment will provide copies with less expense than using facilities of depositories you visit.

If You Assign the Work to Family Members

A researcher is one who is expert in the use of all sources, but it does not follow that only you are qualified to search them. Under careful supervision, anyone who can read and write and who is capable of following directions can extract the data needed. As family researcher, you are only obligated to insure that the pedigree is compiled properly. You need not personally do all the searching. At the next family meeting when someone securely says, "If there is anything I can do . . ." take him up on it. Provide worksheets, instructions on filling them out for the sources he is to extract and a list of searches from the research outline, with a due date.

This is a primary justification for the systematic, orderly

procedures we have suggested: analyze and control the work but train and assign others on a piece work basis to assist with time consuming searches.

If You Use Official Record Keepers and Archivists

Official record keepers can help, especially with particular searches to define the dimensions of jurisdiction, surname, period of time and sources. If this is the alternative you take, remember Axiom 7: ANY PARTICULAR SEARCH UNDERTAKEN PRIOR TO THE COMPLETION OF A GENERAL SEARCH, MUST HAVE AS ITS OBJECTIVE ONE OR MORE OF THE DIMENSIONS OF THE GENERAL SEARCH. This axiom will protect your pocketbook. You must search all the records anyway, during the course of your research, so don't dollar yourself to death. Never write for A DOCUMENT. Write for information to help you define and organize your searches. The fact that the information may be embodied in a document is coincidental.

* When writing to busy public record keepers and clergy, correspondence should be short and to the point. They will usually take the time to read only one page. The following rules may help you.

   1. Do not ask too much on one occasion. Think through your request carefully.

   2. Always indicate willingness to pay for time spent in your behalf, but work out the financial arrangements in advance. Never let them bill you. Be honest! Quite often a county clerk or a parish priest cannot foresee what he is going to get into. $5.00 of research may turn into $10.00 before he is through. They are usually honest enough to charge only the $5.00 quoted, but if they have incurred that much time, pay them the extra money. They will be more willing to help another time.

   3. Never ask a county official or minister to make a general search. Hire a researcher. It will be cheaper in the long run.

   4. Remember that the first three months of the year

are the busy months for tax offices, vital statistics offices and county clerks; so try not to write during those months. You may run the risk of receiving no reply.

5. Always state an about date and in or near a certain place. If you are too specific, the official may search only the date and place you list. Your dimensions may be incorrect; so allow a little leeway to obtain the right information.

6. If an agency sends you a form to fill out, transfer the information you want to the form and return it.

7. Never demand information. Remember the receiver of your letter is not compelled to answer it. You are seeking a favor.

8. Use the correct title of the official. Check the *Handbook of Genealogical Correspondence* for proper forms of address and salutation.

9. Never ask a record official to make photostat copies of a document or packet of documents without first giving you an estimate of the number involved and the total cost. Some packets contain almost one hundred papers of various sizes and photocopy costs vary from 4¢ to $3.50 per page!

If You Employ a Field Researcher

Much research will be done vicariously through a field researcher. When you have completed the preliminary survey, performed the pre-search analysis and finished your research outline the next thing is to locate the name and address of a person who will help you search those records to which you do not have direct access. It is not necessary for him to be a trained genealogist. For records in ancient script or foreign languages, special skills are needed, but many records can be extracted by anyone who can read and write.

* Contact the archivist or clerk in charge of the records which you want searched, and ask him to recommend someone who is acquainted with the records. If there is any one capable of doing the work, he will usually know and be able to re-

commend him. He may even be willing to do the work himself, for a fee. Some record depositories keep a list of researchers for just such inquiries.

* Check with the county librarian, university librarian, head of the history department of the university or the high school librarian. Ask them to recommend a history teacher or student majoring in history or interested in the locality whom you could hire to do part-time research in the area.

* Consult local historical societies or genealogical societies for a member who would be willing to do some research for you.

* Contact local lawyers and abstractors. These people are acquainted with the records and can usually do the searches in a minimum of time. This is especially true of court and land records. Their fees will be higher but it may prove less costly in the long run.

* If there is no one in the immediate area who can do a general search, import a researcher. Contact the state archivist to find out who is using the records. Sometimes you are farther ahead to import a researcher than to rely on a local person who is not interested.

* Check the genealogical periodicals which are full of advertisements for researchers. Avoid anyone who offers to do research by the name or the pedigree. Always hire by the hour and retain only those who do quality work.

* As a last resort, consult the Chamber of Commerce, local tourist information center or the postmaster in the town. They may know of someone who could help. Many towns have a local historian, some officially designated and some self-appointed to the task. One of these may help you.

* Be sure to work out financial arrangements in advance; never let them bill you. Ask for an itemized expense account. In this way you know where your money goes.

* Give a new researcher a trial run. Ask what his hourly rate is. Send enough money to cover 7½ to 8 hours to search and 2 to 2½ hours to compile the report. When you receive the report, analyze the work carefully. Does he follow instructions? Does he itemize expenses? Does he keep a record of

all searches whether or not they yield data? Does he engage in a minimum of evaluation while searching records? Does he consult you before striking out on his own? If he does a good job, ask for an estimate of how long it will take to complete the search and let him finish. If he does not, hire someone else.

There are a lot of people who purport to be researchers, when in reality all they want to do is make a fast buck! What other occupation can you pursue with no training, except knowing how to read and write, and still earn $2.50 to $10.00 per hour with a minimum of effort? There are a lot of well-trained researchers, with a good knowledge of source materials who will do their best to provide good service. When you find one, allow him some lee-way in research. Tell him what you want, but indicate that if circumstances dictate otherwise, to let you know. Tell him to watch for source materials you may not know of. Then pay for the service rendered.

* Itemize each record you want searched and the type of extract you want. Outline the search dimensions (surnames, period of time, jurisdiction and sources). Be sure the researcher understands you want an abstract of the historical and genealogical data and not a transcription of the whole document.[16] Specify historical as well as genealogical data or they will often omit valuable clues.

* Retain control of your research. A researcher may know more about the records, their locations and contents than you do but he can never know as much about your ancestors. Don't send your pedigree to him. Many researchers search only for the individuals on that chart and completely neglect other members of the family. Carefully plan the work you want done and have the researcher perform those searches which you cannot do yourself and submit the data to you for evaluation and compiling of family units.

* Ask the researcher to keep a careful calendar of all searches he makes. Send an example and the type of information you want. Explain that you want an accurate log of all searches, the condition of the sources and the result — whether or not anything was found.

* Do not let a researcher compromise your research. Most researchers are dollar conscious, trying to do as much as possible, in as short a time as possible to save you money. They might compromise standards just for a few dollars. Tell them to study indexes carefully before they rely upon them. If they have reason to believe them incomplete or faulty, ask to have them searched page by page. This may take longer, so tell them to give you an estimate of the cost for the extra time. Your finances are limited, but let them know you want standards kept high.

STEP FOUR: POST-SEARCH ANALYSIS

CHAPTER ELEVEN
STEP FOUR: POST-SEARCH ANALYSIS

Just as every action undertaken in research should be carefully planned, every search performed should be thoroughly evaluated. Step Four: *Post-Search Analysis* provides the techniques for this evaluation.

Interim Post-Search Analysis

Upon completion of any given immediate objective, an interim analysis should be performed to determine what progress has been made and what further steps are necessary.

* Compare the calendar with the research outline to see if all prescribed sources, as outlined, have been searched.

* Carefully examine the research data. Compare it with the information available at the beginning of the search. If the problem is solved, move on to the next immediate objective as outlined in the pre-search analysis. If the objective has not been reached, are there other sources which could be searched to complete it? If so, check those sources. If not, the problem should be re-defined through a new pre-search analysis. Refer to the Flow Chart on page 126. The small rectangles show where interim analyses are indicated.

Final Post-Search Analysis

When ultimate objective families have been traced from death, through marriage, back to the time of birth, accounting for every jurisdiction in which they have resided during their lifetime, a final *post-search analysis* is required.

* Compare the calendar with the research outline to be sure all prescribed searches have been made and all sources consulted.

* Lay your pedigree chart in front of you and pull the worksheets pertaining to the ultimate objectives and their families.

* Arrange the worksheets alphabetically, by head of household. Where more than one of the same name occurs, arrange chronologically. Research notes are already extracted on family group sheets and the task of assembling data becomes a mechanical process without serious regard for quantity.

* Lay out each worksheet which applies to the first ultimate objective family unit, jigsaw fashion, so each piece of data and its source is clearly seen. Take a summary sheet (blank worksheet) and go through the data line by line in the following manner: Start with line one — NAME OF HUS-BAND — consult all of the worksheets to see if they agree on what should go on that line. If they are in agreement, enter the name of the husband in the proper place. If there is a discrepancy, the data and the source from which it came must be evaluated and the discrepancy resolved. Take the calendar and check the source in question, analyze the condition and type of source. Then, if necessary, recheck the source in the enclosure file again to see if the information was copied correctly.

* Move to line two and proceed in the same manner. If you come to a line where you have no information at all, leave it and go on to the next. Proceed line by line. With all of the data on worksheets in front of you, you do not have to wade through stacks of notebooks, odd papers or under-lined items in the sources themselves to compile your family group. You merely compare each line as you go, in a mechanical way.

* After all of the lines on the sheet have been considered, look carefully at any gaps that occur. Compare the calendar with the research outline once more to see if you have overlooked any jurisdiction or sources that might supply the missing information. If you have, perform the searches and add the data to the sheet. If you have not, then you will have to get along without the information.

Family members are identified by names, dates, places and relationships. The most important identification, however, is that of *relationship*. Names, dates and places are merely identifying characteristics to prove the actuality or probability of relation-ship — wife to husband and children to parents. Too often, genealogists become so involved with the search for names and dates that they neglect the careful evaluation and proof of relationship of one family to another.[1]

A family unit is complete and correct if the husband and wife are proven to be, in fact, husband and wife and if the children are proven, with direct evidence or a preponderance of circumstantial evidence, to be, in fact, all the children which that couple had. The family unit is connected to the generation which preceeded it by the same kind of evidence. Rarely will research, beyond the first four generations back from the present, provide dates and places for every line on the family group sheet. Exact birth and death dates are not easy to find, especially in America or among the lower classes in European countries. These must often be approximated from known information concerning the family members.[2]

To prove parent-child relationship, follow these additional steps:

* Condense the data for each ultimate objective on a separate identity graph. Review Chapter Seven for procedure.

* Using the pedigree chart as a guide, compare connecting evidence common to each generation. To prove parent-child relationship, you must have events that took place in the life of the child between birth and marriage which are coincidental with events that took place in the life of the parents between marriage and death.

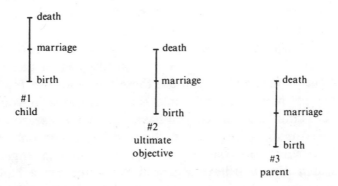

* Ask these questions of each generation:

    1. Does the evidence on ancestor #1 (child) between birth and marriage coincide with the evidence on ancestor #2 (ultimate objective — father) between marriage and death?

    2. Can any conflicting evidence be easily resolved?

    3. Does the evidence point directly to parent-child relationship?

    4. If not, is there enough circumstantial evidence to prove a parent-child relationship?

    If the answers to these questions are in the affirmative you have established a new pedigree ancestor — proven and verified — whose name may be placed upon your permanent pedigree chart.

* Complete the case history. Using the completed summary sheet as a guide, copy the data on a permanent family group sheet and place it in your book of remembrance or family record book. Take the worksheets from which the final sheet was prepared and clip them to the summary sheet. If you have made any value judgments during the analysis, make note of this in brackets [] on the worksheets in question and on the back of the summary sheet, so that others will know why you have compiled the family group as you have.

    The completed case history consists of worksheets containing all raw data identified with sources, value judgments in brackets and a narrative summary of how you formulated your evidence to establish the pedigree relationships. Pertinent identity graphs can also be included. All of these items are filed together for posterity. They, with the calendar, research outline and enclosure files, will justify you in generations to come. Your children can use these files and in a few minutes, see just how you formulated the conclusions in your permanent family records. If you have done your research properly, never again will it need to be re-done. Some one may challenge your conclusions but they will not challenge your research. You will have a genealogy — not just a hand full of assumptions but a complete genealogy. What you have done can be built upon.

General Search Research

General search research requires that information on all persons within the basic jurisdiction, who bear the same surnames as the ultimate objective families, be extracted from all sources created by the jurisdiction, for a carefully defined period of time. Using the data and clues provided by this search, particular or specific searches are performed in jurisdictions subordinate (local) or higher (state, national, or national) in authority. A general search is never undertaken in an inferior or superior jurisdiction; comprehensive searches are made in basic jurisdictions only where the likelihood of relationship of persons bearing the same surnames exists.

General search research has distinct advantages which selective research cannot provide. Significant by-products of this approach to genealogical research can solve brick wall problems in one of two ways: either the needed proof will be plainly stated, or the necessary circumstantial evidence will be present to lead to the necessary proof. If this data is not located and if the dimensions of the search have been properly defined, if the search itself was correctly performed and if the post-search analysis was thoroughly completed, then you must assume that the information does not exist at this time. Let us briefly review these by-products.

Missing Maiden Surnames. If the general search does not provide direct evidence of missing surnames for female pedigree ancestors, systematically beat the bushes for them. A few years ago, when a man sought a wife, he went courting in the homes of his neighbors, his friends and his business associates. Before trains, planes and hot rods this was the only practical approach. If general searches have been properly done you have the names of the people with whom your ancestors were closely connected. Check worksheets compiled from probates, land records, home sources, newspapers and other sources you have searched. All names of witnesses and associates are now available. Take these references and go searching in these households, on a particular search basis, to find the maiden surname. Note especially masters of apprentices, employers of farmhands and court judges with their legal assistants and court clerks.

Migrational Problems. No society is ever stagnant; populations are always on the move. These migrations usually have patterns and definite directions. Ancestors do not parachute out of the blue, seemingly from nowhere, and rarely do they travel alone. Where did the people come from who were living in the jurisdiction? Why did they come? How many came at one time? History and geography will furnish answers to these questions. This is why it is so important to study the historical background of the jurisdiction. Instead of hunting aimlessly, you can determine the migrational patterns of the people coming into and leaving the jurisdiction and know where to search.

Immigrant Ancestry. Sources of origin constitute another problem often difficult to solve. If the general search does not provide direct statements of origin, the following clues may lead to it: signatures in a foreign language on wills, deeds and other property records; names of children or middle names of pedigree ancestors. Place names or areas where ancestors settled, bequests of property, goods or money to a school, charity or other institution located in another area or country, may lead to a previous place of settlement. Photographs or paintings showing landmarks, scenery and the names of photographers or artists may also indicate immigrant origins.

YOU SHOULD NEVER TRY TO LOCATE AN IMMIGRANT ANCESTOR IN THE COUNTRY OF HIS ORIGIN UNTIL YOU HAVE PERFORMED GENERAL SEARCHES IN ALL OF THE JURISDICTIONS WHERE HE LIVED IN THE COUNTRY OF DESTINATION.

If direct evidence exists, general searches will provide it. If it does not exist, use what you have the best you know how. Every clue is needed and only through general searches can every clue be obtained in the most efficient way. Armed with a systematic approach, essential background knowledge and good common sense, you can solve origin problems and identify your ancestry.

Substitute Evidence. If you perform general search research, burned courthouses, bombed record offices and destroyed records do not stop your research. You have many substitute records which can provide the needed information. If certain record categories cannot be found or do not begin until way past your period of time, you can use the information from other, perhaps less well-known, records to provide the data. If the county clerk in a southern state tells you the records were destroyed during the Civil War, check the Southern Claims Commission files and the numerous records which claims investigators confiscated to substantiate claims. These are on file among federal records in Norfolk, Virginia[3].

If the naval records are missing, substitute the merchant shipping records (private documents) for the same period of time. If the parish registers are gone, substitute Bishop's transcripts, the minister's personal daybook or the poor law records. If the vital statistics for your area do not begin early enough, substitute the daybooks of physicians or midwives who practiced in the area, Bible records, newspapers, home sources and cemetery records. The account books of local carpenters and joiners who built coffins for burials are often local death registers.

If the court files are not available, use the appellate court files for that jurisdiction to obtain the data in cases appealed to a higher judicial body or check the briefs, case files and daily journals or day books of lawyers or solicitors who practiced in the area. Local newspapers publish case summaries in their legal notices. If the census schedule which you need is missing, use corresponding agricultural, industrial, mining, mortality, slave schedules, state and local censuses, local tax assessments and exemption lists. If your research is performed with general searches in the basic jurisdiction first, then particular searches in jurisdictions subordinate to and higher than the basic jurisdiction, these substitute sources will be searched as a matter of course. If the data is preserved, you will have found it and you will have the data necessary for complete and correct records. If you perform selective searches, looking for one ancestor at a time in only those sources "most likely to provide the information," you will have to make a series of additional searches to provide substitute data at a much greater expenditure of time and money. The general search researcher does not have to hunt for his information, he finds it easily — if it is preserved — as a result of his systematic search techniques.

Incomplete Records. In the past, most genealogists relied on the integrity of the sources they used, assuming that if the law stipulated a record must be kept, local and state officials were diligent in keeping it. If the law stipulated that a man must have a will or send his property through probate, any man who had property must have complied. If the law stipulated that children must be christened in the local church, the parents were diligent enough to comply. But recent studies in demography (the study of population and its changes from one period to another) have proven such assumptions to be highly dangerous. Demographers and historians in the New England area, studying wills and probates for evidence on local populations, have concluded:

> Depending on the values assigned to such variables as total population, death rate and the proportion of deaths which were deaths of adult males, recorded wills account for some *5 to 60 per cent* and recorded inventories account for some *10 to 80 per cent* of adult males who died during these periods. These are extreme limits, and in most periods the highest plausible figures are close to *20 per cent* of adult male deaths for wills and *40 per cent* in the case of inventories.

> Since the figures for most counties in most periods fall within a narrow range and since the probate records of almost all counties show great chronological integrity, it is extremely unlikely that missing records are the cause. Rather, *it would seem that few men left legally recognized wills* and that, the law notwithstanding, *inventories were recorded for less than half of the men* in the society.[4]

The picture is not any better for English parish registers, too often held inviolate by genealogists. The registers of Kempston (Bedfordshire) show that fully one-fourth of all burials in the churchyard between 1801 and 1812 were of unbaptized persons — mostly children. For Cardington (Bedfordshire), the figure was 17 per cent. The most accurate registers are those prior to 1750; those from 1750 to 1850 become more and more incomplete. There are several reasons for this: growth of nonconformity; poverty of parents who could not afford to pay christening, marriage and burial fees; opening of non-Anglican burial grounds; the great number of "unchurched" (those who had never set foot inside a church from the time they were born to the time they died) in industrial and mining areas; the growing irrelevance of the church and its sacraments to the problems of life; the increase in the number of hospitals and workhouses with chaplains of their own (the people in these are those most likely to die); delayed christenings which increase the likelihood of the child dying before it could be baptised. Statistics show that 73 per cent of all known burials in the city of Manchester (England) were in non-Anglican burial plots — many not affiliated with any church group. Marriage laws broke down, large numbers of couples were not married in their home parishes but elsewhere.[5]

These are but two examples of record inadequacy. Numerous others exist, the importance of which has not been realized by genealogists in the past, but which must be taken into consideration if family records are to be complete and correct.[6] To avoid the problems from incomplete sources, do not perform selective searches but organize your research into well-defined general searches first, with particular searches in all other jurisdictions. In this way, sources supplement each other.

STEP FIVE: RE-SURVEY

CHAPTER TWELVE
STEP FIVE: RE-SURVEY

When you began genealogical research for the first time, you made a preliminary survey on the whole pedigree. You systematically collected the data and conclusions, compiled by others, on every ancestor on your pedigree chart by exhausting the survey jurisdictions one by one in a logical sequence: You organized all the data you had in your own possession. You contacted your parents asking to see all of the information they had concerning your ancestors. You went to other relatives and family friends for the information they could give. Taking the references from these data, you carefully searched those institutional jurisdictions (genealogical and historical societies) pertinent to your pedigree. You gathered this information to prevent duplication of research effort, to exhaust secondary source materials and to provide a solid foundation for research.

Each new ancestor added to the pedigree during research must be surveyed as well. This process we call the *re-survey*. You have no way of knowing at the beginning of research when you will tie into the work of others. It is often a source of considerable chagrin to a researcher who, unable to find any compiled records relating to his grandparents in his original preliminary survey, embarks on a research program and identifies them. Then without further consideration, he proceeds to seek out the remainder of his ancestry through difficult and expensive research only to find that his great-grandfather was the subject of a biography in a printed family history tracing his ancestry several generations back. To avoid such a situation, it is essential to *re-survey* with each new pedigree ancestor.

The *re-survey* is performed in the same jurisdictions as the original preliminary survey — home and institutional jurisdictions. The discussions in Chapters Four and Five above should be applied at this time. There are a few differences however. If the preliminary survey was performed properly, there will be no need to consult immediate families or close relatives again because you have already exhausted the written records they had in their possession. The only reason for contacting them would be to obtain information contained in their memories and not as yet upon paper. The third category of the home jurisdiction — distant relatives and old timers — you reserved until this point in your research program. Now you have sufficient knowledge of the family to interview and question them intelligently.

Distant Relatives and Old Timers

As a survey source, distant relatives and old timers should never run out. Each new ancestor added to the pedigree opens up a whole new field of contacts through that ancestor's descendants. These unknown relatives should be contacted for the information they have concerning your new ancestors. When dealing with distant relatives and old timers, always be more interested in the living than in the dead. Equal doses of interest, patience and friendliness will pay off in genealogical data. Impatience, an air of brusqueness and being in a hurry will defeat you every time.

* Each genealogical contact you make, ask for names and addresses of other family members. A chain-reaction of new descendants can be made in this way.

* Subscribe to the newspaper published for local consumption. Each small community will have a separate column giving personal details about local community members, their travels, their day-to-day activities, their visitors and their vital statistics. Write to those who bear the same surnames you do.

* Advertise for relatives in local newspapers. A good way to locate lost cousins is through a carefully prepared inquiry placed in the local paper. Use a *display ad* rather than the classified type. Rates are not a great deal higher and it is certainly easier to create an eye catcher when you have a space two or three columns wide and three or four inches deep with a full selection of lettering sizes to choose from. Attract attention by printing the surname in large, bold

letters across the top of the ad, followed by the information you are seeking in the two columns below.

Display Ad.

ATTENTION
Members of the
MORRISON
FAMILY

We are compiling a family history on John Morrison, his wife Jane Anne Gunn, who lived and died in Gooseneck, Maine and their descendants.

If you are related or have information on this family, please CONTACT: Joseph A. Morrison 812 West Peach Drive Appleby, Ohio.

WE NEED YOUR HELP!

Classified Ad.

WANTED: Sewing done for the public in my home. Also sewing lessons given. Call Mrs. Manning 885-2180. Morrison Family: We are compiling a family history on John Morrison and his wife Jane Anne Gunn. If you have information on him please contact: Joseph A. Morrison, 812 W. Peach Drive, Appleby, Ohio.

WANTED: A working farm manager on cattle farm in producing hay and ensilage, and fencing. Monthly salary plus house and other subsidies. Only those with references and experience need apply to Mr. D. E. Kelly, Farm Manager, Spring Lake Farms, Route 2, Box 154, Moneta, Virginia.

Which would you read first (or at all)?

* Avoid large, daily papers. The people who read them are not likely to be interested in genealogical queries. The county or community weekly however, is read cover to cover by those who subscribe and those readers rarely miss a thing. Many people who have moved away to other localities still subscribe to keep in touch with home.

* Obtain names and addresses of newspapers and their advertising rates in directories at all advertising agencies or press associations. In fact, these commercial agencies are most

cooperative in assisting with the preparation of an effective ad as well as placing the request with the publisher of the newspaper. These directories are also available in many research libraries:

Weekly Newspaper Representatives, Inc. *National Directory of Weekly Newspapers.* Published annually.

N. W. Ayers and Sons. *Directory of Newspapers and Periodicals.* Published annually.

Advertiser's Aid. London: Newspaper Society, 1956. Other editions available.

Benn and Co. *Mitchell's Newspaper Press Directory.* Published annually in England.

Willings Press Guide. Published annually in England.

* Check current local directories. Telephone directories for almost any area in the world can be obtained through your local telephone exchange. Large libraries will also have collections of these. Current business, city, commercial and professional directories of the area in which your ancestors resided may be of help. The following guides will lead you to these:

Catalog of City, County and State Directories Published in North America. New York: Association of North American Directory Publishers, 1967.

Guide to American Directories. New York: McGraw-Hill, 1954. Published annually.

Klein, Bernard. *Guide to American Directories.* Englewood Cliffs, N. J.: Prentice-Hall, 1962.

* Write to the local postmaster. He is usually well acquainted with the area and its people. Tell him you wish to contact distant relatives who may still live in the area and ask him to pass your inquiry on to the most likely prospect.

Oral History

One of the most genealogically significant record sources to become available recently are oral history tapes. Oral history is really a combination of memoirs, diary, local history, family history and travelogue. Eye witness accounts are liberally sprinkled with anecdotes and personal opinions on almost every conceivable subject.

Illiterate peoples have long used oral tradition and memorization of important dates and events to preserve their tribal heritage. Genealogies have been transmitted from generation to generation orally among Polynesians, Indians, Eskimos and other peoples.[1] Interviews with old timers and important local personalities; army, navy and air force veterans; American Indian tribes; politicians; police chiefs; famous people; pioneers of the Far West and numerous others are being recorded on tape and filed for the use of individual researchers. Individual genealogists have used oral history techniques to recapture the memories of older family members, but the tapes are usually not saved nor the interviews completely transcribed.

* Use personal interviews whenever possible to obtain data from old timers and distant relatives. You have better control over the information they give and you are more apt to obtain what you desire. Consult the following references for oral history techniques which have proven to be effective.

Baum, Willa K. *Oral History for the Local Historical Society.* Nashville: American Association for State and Local History, 1971.

Fry, Amelia R. "The Nine Commandments of Oral History," *Journal of Library History,* III (1968), 63-73.

Lieber, Joel. "The Tape Recorder as Historian," *Saturday Review,* XLIV (1966), 98-99.

"Oral History: Columbia's Library on Tape," *Library Journal,* LXXXV (January 1, 1960), 36-37.

Rosenfield, Albert. "The Wild West Lives Again," *Colliers,* CXXXIV (Nov., 1954), 48-56.

Schippens, Donald J. and Tusler, Adelaide G. *A Bibliography of Oral History.* Los Angeles: Oral History Association, 1967.

Shumway, Gary, *Compendium of Oral History Projects in the United States.* New York: Columbia University Press, 1971.

Swain, Donald C. "Problems for Practioners of Oral History," *American Archivist,* XXVIII (1965), 63-69.

* Prepare a second copy of any interviews you hold with old timers and present it to the local historical society. Tapes, unless they have personal significance, could also be donated after the data has been transcribed.

Institutional Jurisdictions

Take the clues and references from home jurisdiction contacts and search those institutional jurisdictions which pertain to your new pedigree ancestors. Be sure to include those which are located in or near the areas where your ancestors lived.

Table Six summarizes the *re-survey*. Note that particular searches only are used during the *re-survey*. NEVER MAKE A GENERAL SEARCH IN A SURVEY JURISDICTION.

Table Six.

Step	Jurisdiction	Names	Search Procedure
Re-Survey: Systematic collection of genealogical data concerning pedigree ancestors and their families which has been previously compiled by others.	**Home:** Old timers and distant relatives **Institution:** Genealogical societies Hereditary societies Historical societies Archaeological societies Record societies	New pedigree ancestors New pedigree ancestors	Particular searches Particular searches

The question arises: "Will *re-survey* data provide enough information to lay a solid foundation for my next research objective?" Refer back to our discussion concerning general searches. As you seek data on the ultimate objective, you adjust your period of time to include the parents of the ultimate objective. It is here that new surnames are identified and other clues obtained, which enable you to continue research. This is a very important by-product of the general search. It provides identifying information for future ultimate objectives. If the general search does not, then you did not define the dimensions of that search properly and you may need to re-do it. The period of time for each general search should be defined to provide data concerning the next pedigree ancestors or the known cannot lead to the unknown. If the search was properly done, that data, combined with the information from the *re-survey* should be ample as a foundation for research on new ultimate objectives.

CONCLUSION

CONCLUSION
THE JURISDICTIONAL APPROACH

Genealogists are dependent upon preserved records for information concerning their ancestors.

These records are produced and preserved by jurisdictions.

These two facts dictate that research must be jurisdictional — you must know the jurisdictions which are responsible for the records upon which you are dependent. The most efficient and successful method to use in exploiting these jurisdictions and their records is the scientific method followed by other research disciplines. Scholars, regardless of cultural heritage or language barriers, communicate through research techniques understood by all.

The contribution of the *Jurisdictional Approach* is the application of this tried and proven method to genealogy to provide a step-by-step system:

Step One: Preliminary Survey. The *preliminary survey* is the systematic collection of genealogical information relating to pedigree ancestors and their families which has been previously compiled by others. It is wise to survey the entire pedigree before new research is undertaken. If properly completed, the *survey* will prevent unnecessary duplication, it will provide the foundation for new research and it will discipline you, temper your judgment and season you in the science. Armed with this experience and knowledge, you can properly seek additional evidence on your ancestors.

230

Table Seven.

Step	Jurisdiction	Names	Search Procedure
Preliminary Survey: Systematic collection of genealogical information concerning pedigree ancestors and their families which has been previously compiled by others	**Home:** Immediate family and friends Close relatives and associates	All pedigree ancestors	Particular searches
	Institution: Genealogical societies Hereditary societies Historical societies Archaeological societies Record societies	All pedigree ancestors	Particular searches

Step Two: Pre-Search Analysis. Upon completion of the survey, you analyze the data collected, decide which pedigree families are complete and correct and divide the pedigree into geographic segments. In the *pre-search analysis,* you define research objectives and outline thoroughly the means of logically reaching them.

Step Three: Outlined Research: A well prepared research outline is the guide to follow for executing searches in all of the sources produced by, for or about ancestoral families. In this step, you carefully gather all of the existing information which pertains to your progenitors.

Table Eight.

Step	Jurisdiction	Names (Ultimate Objectives)	Search Procedure (Immediate Objectives)
Outlined Research: Systematic collection of information from primary and secondary research sources	**Basic:** Town Independent City Borough Manor Parish Mining District County City-county City-state	All surnames	General searches
	Local: Municipal Ecclesiastical Employment Professional Social Institutional	All surnames or pedigree ancestors	Particular searches
	Higher: District State Territory Province Colony Country	Pedigree ancestors	Particular searches

Step Four: Post-Search Analysis. When the searches, as outlined during the pre-search analysis, have been completed, you perform careful evaluations of the information collected. You compare it with other data in your possession, resolve discrepancies which have arisen and record the conclusions on standard family group forms and pedigree charts. The evidence to substantiate those conclusions is placed in completed case history files.

Step Five: Re-Survey. Pedigree ancestors, newly identified during the post-search analysis are *re-surveyed* in order to outline the next set of research objectives. The whole process begins again.

Table Nine.

Step	Jurisdiction	Names	Search Procedure
Re-Survey: Systematic collection of genealogical data concerning pedigree ancestors and their families which has been previously compiled by others.	**Home:** Old timers and distant relatives **Institution:** Genealogical societies Hereditary societies Historical societies Archaeological societies Record societies	New pedigree ancestors New pedigree ancestors	Particular searches Particular searches

Notekeeping. Throughout these steps, disciplined *research notekeeping* provides the foundation for the entire system. There can be no system without this base; each step is performed by comparing and evaluating the data collected and organized (notekeeping) in the preceding step.

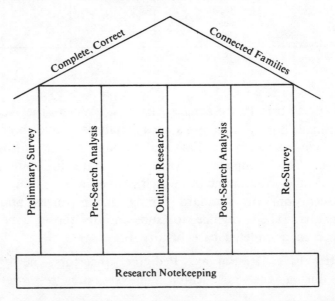

The *Jurisdictional Approach* is a step-by-step system of research procedures. To isolate any one step from the others is destructive. Each is completely dependent upon the preceding step and should be followed in proper, logical sequence. It is impossible to assume that the application of any one step, isolated from the others, would result in any more than coincidental success. The system has been designed and outlined in an attempt to bring order to research and to enable you to enjoy success with a minimum expenditure of time, effort and resources. If the procedures outlined are followed and the data exists, you will find it — we guarantee it. Your efforts will be a real contribution to knowledge and your posterity can build upon it with confidence.

APPENDIXES

APPENDIX ONE
FAMILY ORGANIZATION*

Genealogists are usually so preoccupied with the dead that they overlook the living. In the interest of balance and perspective, it seems proper to devote a portion of this work to *genealogy for the living*. If living families were bound today as many of our ancestral cultures centuries ago, the world would be a better place in which to live and future generations would inherit from you the history and records for which you are now searching. To that end, we suggest genealogy for the living through organized family activity today.

The primary purpose of the family organization is to help family members develop a family consciousness and a feeling of brotherhood. The family should foster respect and deference for one another. It is in family life that you should learn to love most deeply, sacrifice most completely, share with each other most often and develop the greatest amount of charity.[1]

The Individual Family

Just as the pedigree begins with YOU — YOUR FAMILY — so should the family organization begin with YOU — YOUR FAMILY. But genealogical research should not be the only reason for organizing the family. Genealogical work may serve to unite in common bond some family members, but those having no interest in genealogy will remain apart. Genealogical work needs to be put in its proper perspective as one of the important functions for which each family should provide, but not the only one. The individual family organization should provide for all of the following family needs: Government, Com-

*We owe a special debt to Kathryn E. Miller and the Jeremiah Leavitt and Sarah Shannon Family Organization, Inc., for applying these principles to their organization and for sharing their experience concerning legal incorporation and to William O. Tolman, President of the Thomas Tolman Family Organization, for reviewing this section and for permitting us to pattern parts of it after that organization. We also thank Dr. Lloyd R. Hicken for his suggestions for its improvement.

munications, Membership, Finance, Social Activity, Temporal
Welfare, Fellowship, Historical Facts and Genealogical Training
and Research.

Government. The government of each family unit should
consist of a president, vice president or special advisor and a
board of directors, who meet as frequently as necessary to insure the success of the organization. The father is the president
of the family organization. If he is dead, his children as the
board of directors, should select one from among themselves to
serve in their father's place and to assume his presidential
responsibilities:

1. Determine what method of operation will best accomplish the goals of the family.

2. Determine in what capacity the various board members
   will serve to insure the accomplishment of family duties
   — matching talent to position.

3. Seek counsel from the board of directors regarding the
   effectiveness of family programs.

4. Supervise and preside over all meetings and activities of
   the family.

The mother serves as a special advisor to the president; if
she is dead, this position may be deleted from the organization
or one of the children may be appointed to serve in this capacity.

The children consitute the board of directors. If any are
dead, their descendants will select a representative to serve. Each
director will be responsible for:

1. Supervising and directing at least one family responsibility or need of the organization.

2. Preparing an annual report of the activities under his
   direction during the year. These annual reports should
   be printed and distributed to all family members.

3. Preparing an annual budget and cost estimate which the
   activities of his office will incur, to submit to the
   treasurer for incorporation into the family budget.

Communications (Secretary): An effective family organization realizes that family members respond to planning, direction

and leadership. Each member should be included in the planning of family activities and be regularly informed of the progress and accomplishments made. This is the secret of success. The following duties are the responsibility of the family secretary:

1. Keeping accurate minutes of meetings and activities of the organization.

2. Preparing and distributing communications and reports to all family members.

If family members are living away from home, two additional duties should be filled:

3. Compiling and maintaining a complete up-to-date register of all members and their addresses.

4. Sending out notices of all meetings to those who should attend.

Membership: Family groups that get things done are made up of members who care about each other, respect each other and enjoy being with each other. They have had a part in family decisions and family accomplishment. To feel that someone is depending upon you and regards you with affection is to have a rebirth of desire to give of your time and effort in support of the family. Duties of family members:

1. All family members should be expected to participate in some way. Maximum success requires cooperation.

2. Each member should know the history of the family, the purpose of the organization, the activities planned, working procedure, the relationship between individual family and larger organizations of which it may be a part.

3. Each family member should feel free to express himself in regard to family activities. In a truly democratic family, all members have a right to be heard; and each can benefit by being permitted to make decisions in keeping with his age, ability and experience.

Finance: Family happiness and success depend upon the importance family members place on money and their wise management of it. To become a wise manager of money one must have training and experience in the handling of money.

These should be included in the education of children as soon as they have a consistent need of money so that a good foundation will have been laid to meet the more important money problems that arise in later years — planning for college, marriage, business.

Some families feel that financial affairs are the sole responsibility of the parents. While they have the responsibility of supervising the family budget, children should be included, both as a privilege and a responsibility, in planning the use of family resources. They will be more understanding about things they can and cannot have when they have been taught why money is needed, where it comes from, how it is spent, how the budget is prepared and how the records are kept.

Plans for earning, saving and spending should be discussed and prepared by all family members and will depend upon: family goals and activities, type and amount of income (wages, allowances, babysitting, doing odd jobs, etc.), number in family, family spending habits, health of family, housing conditions, debts and obligations. Through wise money management, a family may have a moderately small income and still enjoy an abundant life, if all family resources are profitably used.

Family financial affairs are managed by the treasurer under the supervision of the governing board. His responsibilities include:

1. Keeping an account of all receipts and expenditures.

2. Supervising and directing all fund raising activities.

3. Ordering and distributing supplies.

4. Preparing and managing the budget.

Social activities: The old adage: "The family that plays together stays together" is especially true of family organizations. For this reason, the most fun-loving member of the family should be in charge of recreation.

The social director will be responsible for planning, advertising and directing all home evenings, meetings, and other social activities concerning the family. Activities should be planned with the individual family members in mind. Be a do-it-yourself family, recreationally speaking. Homemade happiness costs less, lasts longer and is worth more than any other kind. It is nice to have imported talent, but believe it or not, everyone has some talent, and everyone needs and wants recognition for what he can do. Family activities are excellent places for the development of these abilities.

Include projects that will unite the family. Have activities that all will enjoy — even baby: songfests, contests, games, taffy-pulls, water fights, ice skating, tugs of war, hay rides, variety programs, story hours, record parties, genealogical excursions and historical sight-seeing.

If all members of the family participate in these family-centered activities, new consideration and understanding, greater use of family talents and greater love among family members will be fostered.

Temporal Welfare: Responsibility for economic maintenance rests first upon the individual, second upon the family and last upon one's church or government. Each individual family unit, under the direction of the board member in charge of temporal welfare, should provide the following:

1. Storage in anticipation of need: This should include water, food, fuel, clothing, basic medical supplies and bedding.

2. Encourage thrift and industry: The family should maintain its financial independence and security by wise management of its monetary affairs.

3. Care for their own needy: Individuals should be able to call upon their families for help before going to their church or government. If the family is united and prudently prepared, there will usually be no need to draw upon the other agencies.

4. Preparation for the future: In this day of adult education, vocational guidance and professional opportunities, there is no need for any family member — adult or youth — not to have a trade or vocation.

Many families have the mistaken idea that when the children marry and are no longer living with their parents, family responsibility for the temporal welfare of the family members ends. This is not so. The individual family relationship does not end with the marriage of the children. True, the children should stand upon their own feet and be responsible for their own actions, but the parents still have a right to offer counsel and assistance and the children still have a right to seek help from their parents. When the children need additional resources to provide necessities of life or to meet emergencies which arise, who should be more willing to give assistance than the parents. When the parents become aged and are in need of tender, loving care, who should be more obligated and better able to give it than the children which those parents raised to adulthood. In this way the family members work as partners. The family which retains the same warm relationship which existed when the children were small is fortunate indeed.

Historical Fact: The family historian should supervise and direct the compiling of complete, correct and up-to-date biographical, historical and genealogical records on all living family members.

1. Every family member should compile a record of the happenings of his own life — a personal diary, journal or book of remembrance containing important events. If it is accurate and interesting, it will serve to inspire and guide posterity. This he owes them.

2. A current and up-to-date record should be kept by the family on each member — vital statistics, important accomplishments — to serve as a reference for the family.

What you say of the exemplary lives of your family members will be forgotten with the passing of years. But what you record will be rich source material for future generations.

Genealogical Training and Research: Genealogical research is not an individual activity; it is a family concern. Each member can accomplish more through well organized family effort than he could ever hope to do on his own. Regardless of what position is held in the family organization, each member should know systematic methods of performing research and preserving records so that the quality of the work done may be efficiently evaluated. The director of genealogy is responsible for the following:

1. Encouraging all members to learn how to perform research systematically and providing training classes where necessary.

2. Directing and correlating all research activity in the family. *Plan what has to be done* and make assignments to family members.

3. Hiring field researchers or full-time researchers as needed. These should be family members if possible — they are more interested in devoting their time to the family.

4. Collecting, preserving and organizing the genealogical, biographical, and historical data from all sources.

5. Compiling all data collected into correct and connected family groups.

6. Preserving, cataloging and making available for family use, all valuable family papers and historical possessions (or copies of them): letters, diaries, news clippings, old books, pictures, documents, family heirlooms, dishes, firearms, household items, furniture, jewelry and others.

Procedure: The actual organization of the family unit will depend upon the number of family members and their ages. In a family where there are 9 children, each child will assume responsibility for one activity, as a member of the board of directors; in a family with only 5 children, each child will be in charge of at least 2 functions. In families where children are still too young to assume responsibility, the parents will have to carry the full load. But regardless of the size of the family or the ages involved, each individual family organization should provide for *all* family needs.

Because each family is different, with distint personalities involved, there is no definite procedure to follow in organizing your own family unit. But perhaps a few suggestions will be helpful:

* **Plan a Family-Night Activity:** This is especially good if the children are small or still living at home. The father should gather his children around him and formally organize his

own family with the mother as his special advisor and those children old enough to assume responsibility serving as board members with definite assignments (this includes bed-making and dish-washing). In this way, the children can be taught, while still young, to respect parental authority, to learn obedience and to accept responsibility.

* **Annual Get-Together:** Nearly every family who has married children, some of whom may be living away, arranges to meet together at least once a year — at Thanksgiving, vacations or Christmas. The next time they are all at home, organize them under the leadership of the father.

Once you have your own family unit organized and functioning smoothly, you should encourage your brothers and sisters, as parents, to organize their own families in a like manner. Once this has been done, these family units can form the organization of the next generation — your father's family.

If your father is still living and able to serve in this capacity, he automatically assumes the position of president, your mother the office of vice president or special advisor, and you and your brothers and sisters serve as the board of directors. You are now ready to encourage the formation of the next link in the chain, the family of your grand-parents.

Expanding the Family Organization

Each individual family unit should be organized and able to function on its own before becoming an active part of the large organizations of subsequent generations. Parents are responsible to unite their own families under the leadership of the husband and father so they are cooperatively communicating and working together. Then they can encourage brothers and sisters to do the same, as parents of their families.

By organizing from the bottom up, the formation of each link in the family chain is expedited in the following ways: First, the presidents of the individual family units already organized provide a ready-made potential government which has had *experience* in supervising and directing family activities, and which can convene the next generation to join in an organization at that level. If you follow this order correctly, then it will be impossible to organize a family from the top or common ancestor down, because there will be no one to lead until the bottom families are organized and functioning. Second, part of the families to be included in the next generation are already organized, getting along with each other and accomplishing something. Organizations already exist, they are *active* and *dynamic;* they need only join together to provide a working nucleus around which to organize the next generation and so on up the pedigree. In this way, a proper chain of command is established and each individual family unit automatically fits into its proper place within the whole.

With this sort of sound basis beneath each successively organized generation, the duties of the organization designed to encompass all of the descendants of an early immigrant ancestor, become simple tasks of coordinating the smoothly functioning subordinate groups for functions best met with massive united effort.

Organization. Uniting many individual families into a large organization is dependent upon the population involved, the number of branches represented and the responsibilities provided. The organization of five family units could place all responsibility for family needs on a few people, while one with hundreds of families may require extensive committees for each activity. While the individual family unit must provide for all family functions, the large family organization, consisting of many individual family units, may *select* those responsibilities which the members deem appropriate for united effort.

Each generation back on the pedigree increases the possibility of death having removed the father and increases the number of potential family members. In order to handle the affairs of succeeding generations, the organizational structure changes.

Governing Board: The government of the large organization consists of a president and a board of directors who will meet at least 4 times a year or more often if necessary. One meeting per year is not sufficient to adequately coordinate the activities of the family. If the father is still alive, by virtue of his position of father, he is the president.[2] If he is dead, the board of directors should select one from among themselves to serve in his place as president and chairman of the board to supervise and preside over all meetings and activities of the organization. If the mother is still alive, she serves as vice president or special advisor; if she is dead, this position may be omitted.[3] A proportionate number from each major branch[4] of the family, with a minimum of one, should be selected by that branch to represent them in all matters pertaining to the family organization. These representatives constitute the board of directors.

Each member of this governing board shares in the following responsibilities:

1. Determining what method of operation will best accomplish the ultimate goals of the family.

2. Determining in what capacities the various board members will serve to insure the accomplishment of family duties — matching talents to position.

3. Supervising and directing at least one function of the organization.

4. Preparing an annual report on the activities under his direction. These annual reports should be printed and distributed to all family members.

5. Preparing an annual budget and cost estimate on the activities of each department to submit to the treasurer for inclusion in the organization budget.

In the event that any responsibility of the governing board, as outlined, becomes too large for one person to perform, a committee should be formed with the approval of the board to carry out the tasks assigned. If this is done, the responsible board member will serve as chairman of that committee and will meet at least once per month with those family members on his committee. In cases where the members are scattered geographically, contact will have to be by mail or telephone, but nevertheless, monthly contact is suggested. Likewise, special committees may be needed from time to time and should be formed in a similar manner.

All members of this representative governing board should serve terms of at least 3 years. Provision can be made to select 1/3 annually if desired.

This leadership responsibility should be defined and delegated early in the formation of the organization. The group should choose the best leadership available because accomplishment is directly proportionate to quality of leadership. Selection on the basis of seniority or popularity alone is not wise. Each officer should know specifically what he is responsible for and must be willing to devote the necessary time to carry out his duties.

Some points to consider when choosing family leaders are: 1) willingness to learn and grow. A good leader should be constantly striving to develop necessary qualities — sense of humor, genuine liking for people and the ability to accept another's point of view. 2) Firm conviction and support of the purpose of the organization. Leaders should sincerely feel that the group can accomplish its goal and that the purpose of the organization is valid. 3) Ability to communicate with others. A leader should be on the same wave length as other family members. He should possess friendliness, optimism, and warmth. These qualities will enable a leader to work with others and help prevent discouragement when the going gets tough.

Communications (Publicity and Correspondence): The board member in charge of communications is the secretary of the organization and responsible for the following duties:

1. Keeping accurate minutes and proceedings of meetings and activities of the organization.

2. Preparing and distributing communications and reports to all family members.

3. Compiling and maintaining a complete up-to-date register of family members and their addresses.

4. Sending out notices of all meetings to those who should attend.

Family members respond to well-planned, well-publicized events. A continuous, year round program of frequent contact is necessary to recruit new members, to inform members of planned activities, to encourage attendance at family gatherings, to build unity and morale, to give recognition for a job well done and to gain support and backing for family programs.

248

> He who whispers down a well
> About the things he has to sell
> Will never glean the golden dollars
> Like he who climbs a tree and hollers.

Plan your campaign carefully. Political organizations realize that people and activity must be brought together. They spend much time and energy to persuade people to participate and back their groups. Among the tactics they use are:

1. Letters: personal, open, confidential.

2. Door Bell Ringing: members personally call upon other members to deliver literature, collect dues, issue invitations.

3. Chain Telephone Calls: each person calls another to enlist support or to invite him to a special activity.

4. Mass Petitions: people are asked to sign and openly declare their backing.

5. Personal Contact: personal visits to members, handshaking.

6. Mass Media Advertising: notices and platforms published in newspapers or broadcast over radio.

If the average large family organization would devote just a portion of the time and effort that political groups spend, using some of these ways of establishing close contact, they would be overwhelmed with the results.

Membership-Fellowship: The building and maintaining of an active, dynamic membership is fundamental to the large organization. The first effort should be a series of well planned membership drives. A careful estimate of the anticipated population should be made; the generation to be organized will dictate how many to expect. Each member should be *individually contacted and personally invited* to join. The initial contact is the all important one. The response to that first invitation will depend upon the reaction to it. Never mention genealogy in this initial contact — especially to those whom you have never met before. If you do, they may refuse. Not everyone is as interested in genealogy as you are and many family members may be antagonistic toward it.

Outline the benefits members will receive through joining and participating in the family organization. Let them know that they have much to gain by joining and much to lose if they do not join.

1. You will become better acquainted with all of your relatives as you share experience and accomplishment with them.

2. You will become more creative in thinking and expressing yourself through the stimulation of minds and hearts working toward a common goal. Nothing is quite so satisfying as successful family achievement.

3. You will get a great deal of fun and enjoyment by participating in family-centered activity. Everyone will have a job to do commensurate with his time and ability. Those family members who have talents and know-how will be more willing to serve.

4. You will participate in a vigorous, active family dedicated to uniting the complete family in a program of brotherhood.

5. You will have the security of knowing that every financial contribution will be used wisely and efficiently for the accomplishment of family projects.

Close liaison with communications is needed to be sure that all potential members are included.

All family members should be expected to participate in the family organization in some way by giving of their time or means according to their ability. Some may not be in a position to devote man hours in planning social activities or searching records and may prefer to participate through contributing money and attending activities. Others may lack the finances but they can participate by mailing letters to members, writing histories, organizing individual family units or raising money through planned projects. In this way, all family members can work together.

Finance: Any organization must have enough income to carry out its activities; especially the large organization. Without financial support, success is impossible. When financial affairs of the organization are handled with good management, the group remains solvent and healthy. For this reason, it is suggested that the director in charge of financing — the family treasurer — should be experienced in accounting and bookkeeping. This becomes very important if the family incorporates. The treasurer is responsible for:

1. Keeping an account of all receipts and expenditures.

2. Supervising and directing all fund raising activities.

3. Ordering and distributing supplies.

4. Preparing and managing the budget of the organization.

5. Filing income tax returns.

Some organizations feel that finances are the sole responsibility of the treasurer. While he has the job of preparing and managing the budget, all of the family members should understand why money is needed, where it comes from, how it is spent, how the budget is prepared and how the records are kept. Members who understand these things are not as demanding and better able to economize.

Many family organizations collect dues from their members to finance the organization, but these are seldom sufficient to engage in extensive research, to provide temporal support to needy family members or to publish histories. Additional funds are needed.

Fund raising can be a major factor in strengthening the organization if the family members are willing to fulfill their obligations. They can participate by contributing money or by donating time. It may be helpful to list some ways that have proven effective for other families raising extra money:

An organization of 100 families each gave $100 to build a swim club. They constructed a large swimming pool, concrete patio, bath houses, wading pool and a sheltered picnic area. The boys of the family who were over 16 years of age took life-saving courses so they could be employed as lifeguards. These facilities are available for rental by other groups for parties. The profit from this enterprise is given to the family organization to support its activities.

One of the branches of another family donated 25 acres of land to the family organization. The teen-agers of the family farmed it for wages and the profit was given to the organization for its use.

One family installed soda pop and candy vendors at the city park. Each machine nets about $2.00 per day or a total of $60.00 per month.

Another family organization collectively purchased 40 acres of unused government land for almost nothing and planted it in Christmas trees. When they had matured, they ran a local ad: "Cut your own Christmas trees — $2.00. Free hot chocolate." Enough money was raised to bulldoze a lake, build picnic and camping facilities. This family-operated park is used for family outings, swimming and fishing. It is also rented to groups and the income donated to the organization.

A family organization took a year's lease on an ice cream and candy store. The family members took turns serving, soda-jerking and cleaning for wages. The profit was given to the organization to support full-time researchers on the family genealogy.

A family published a quarterly bulletin, selling subscriptions to all individual family units. The organization netted 66% of the price for use by the family to support its activities.

Family organizations can think of numerous additional ways to raise money needed. The important thing is that *every member* should be included and expected to fulfill his obligation. Through this cooperative effort, sufficient financial support becomes possible.

Social Activities: The most lively member of the family should be placed in charge of this department. He is responsible for planning reunions, parties and gatherings. He arranges time, place and program of activities. He prepares notices to be mailed by the communications committee to all family members. He works closely with communications, membership-fellowship to be sure that all family members are individually invited to attend.

The family should meet together often under enjoyable circumstances to socialize and renew acquaintances. Once-a-year contact is not sufficient to foster closeness. If the family is spread over large geographical areas, one large reunion could be held in a central area annually with all families invited and smaller, more intimate socials could be held more frequently in each of the major localities where family members live.

Some of the cardinal rules to remember in planning group social activities are: First, the activities should arise out of the needs and interests of family members. Listening attentively and observing family members as they participate will help to determine their likes and dislikes. Second, consideration should be made of the age, experience and background of family members. Include activities which all will enjoy — even grandma. "We do not stop playing because we are old; we get old because we stop playing." Finally, activities should be varied and flexible to permit maximum individual participation and well within the abilities of the family so they can enjoy immediate satisfaction.

Since the earliest days, games have been among the most popular activities. Hikes, cookouts and camping trips have universal appeal, offering challenge and adventure. Nothing serves to unite a group more quickly and easily than singing together; no other art is as powerful in changing the mood of the group. If the social activities are carefully planned and well directed, recreational participation as a family will develop a greater feeling of kinship and closeness.

Temporal Welfare: When a family is truly united, responsibility for economic maintenance rests collectively upon all family members and all share in the closeness which comes from service unselfishly rendered. It is important to realize that the family contains not only the father, mother and children but also parents, brothers, sisters, aunts, uncles and cousins. Brothers and sisters should be able to look first to each other for assistance. Aunts, uncles, cousins, grandparents should be able to visit freely with each other and give aid and assistance when it is needed.

If a woman is left widowed with a young family to care for, train and educate, who is better qualified than her own family, to assist in time of need?

When a man loses his job because of some physical disability, who is better able to assist that man in finding some other means of livelihood or to help his family until he again begins earning support, than his own family?

When a family member is given a civic assignment that requires participation away from home, who is better able to assist in the care of children left at home than the members of the family?

The welfare committee is responsible to encourage and assist in the following:

1. Storing in anticipation of need: This should include food, water, fuel, clothing, basic medical supplies and bedding. Each family unit should be encouraged to provide for their own needs.

2. Encouraging thrift and industry: The family should maintain its financial independence and security by wise management of its monetary affairs.

3. Caring for their own needy: Individuals should be able to call upon their families for help, before going to their church or government. If the family is united and prudently prepared, there will usually be no need to draw upon these agencies.

4. Preparing for the future: In this day of adult education, vocational guidance and professional opportunities, there is no need for any family-member — adult or youth — not to have a trade or vocation.

5. Placing in gainful employment those who are able to work.

6. Providing employment within the family (either in the organization or in private enterprise owned or operated by family members) for those who cannot be otherwise placed.

7. Supplying needy family members with the necessities of life.

In this way, the family serves to implement the welfare programs of church and government, whose primary aims are to make the family self-sustaining and solvent, *before* an emergency arises. The family becomes strengthened as all members enjoy a full, more rewarding life.

Historical Fact: The family historian should supervise and direct the following activities:

1. Compiling complete, correct and up-to-date biographical, historical and genealogical records on each living member. Every individual family member should compile a record of his own life — keep a personal diary, journal, book of remembrance containing important events. If it is accurate and interesting, it will serve to inspire and guide his posterity. This he owes them. In addition, a current record should be kept by the family organization on each member — vital statistics, important accomplishments — to serve as a reference for family use.

2. Compiling accurate, fully documented histories or life sketches of the descendants and progenitors of common ancestors. In the years to come, these histories may be the only record future generations will have of these people. This makes it even more important that the information they contain is authentic. The completed research case history compiled by the genealogical committee is an excellent source of accurate data for each pedigree ancestor and his family.

3. Directing the publication of family histories so they will be available to all family members.

What you say of the exemplary lives of your family members will be forgotten with the passing of time, but what you write will live on, constituting rich source material for future generations.

Genealogical Training and Research: Genealogical research is not an individual activity; it is a family concern. Each member can accomplish more through well-organized family effort than on his own.

For genealogical research to be successful with a minimum expenditure of time and money, it must be planned and performed in a systematic way. The director of genealogical training and research should be well-trained in order to compile accurate and complete records. He is responsible for:

1. Encouraging members to learn how to perform research systematically. Training classes as needed should be conducted for both adults and youth, either through home study, group study or both. These training classes could

be held under the direction of the central committee in every locality where family members reside.

2. Directing and correlating all research activity in the family. The director should plan what has to be done and make assignments to family members.

3. Hiring field and full-time researchers as needed. These should be family members if possible. They are more willing to devote their full time to the family genealogy.

4. Collecting, preserving and organizing the genealogical data.

5. Preserving, cataloging and making available for family use all valuable family papers (or copies of them) and genealogical records: letters, diaries, temple record books, news clippings, old books, pictures, documents, family heirlooms, dishes, firearms, household items and clothing.

Procedure: The presidents of the individual family units which are already organized will form the working nucleus or temporary governing board for the organization of the next generation. They should select someone from among themselves to serve as temporary president and chairman of the board. This temporary board has had experience in supervising and directing activities in their own families and they are in a position to create the organization of the next generation. They should meet together as many times as necessary to draft concrete plans for the organization: the number of officers needed, the anticipated population, tentative constitution and by-laws, family responsibilities to be included and place of meeting.

Only when definite plans have been decided upon and are ready for presentation should the entire family membership be called together. At this time, the plans should be proposed by the temporary president for questions, changes and sustaining vote. Each major family branch should then select at least one representative for the permanent board of directors. This board will in turn choose its own president.

With this sound basis provided, the duties of the organization designed to encompass all of the descendants of an immigrant ancestor, become merely tasks of coordinating the smoothly functioning sub-ordinate groups for those functions best met with united effort.

Productive Business Meetings

The best leadership in the world will fail if they meet at the wrong time, in the wrong place, have the wrong people present and follow the wrong agenda. The governing board of the family organization should meet frequently to correlate activities, plan work and fill assignments. A good meeting can be very satisfying and productive, but a meeting that is poorly conducted can be most discouraging. The following items should be considered in planning and conducting business meetings.[5]

Place of the Meeting. Physical surroundings contribute to your attitude and the way you work at solving your problems. The place of meeting should be convenient to the members, comfortable to use, free from distraction and have ample parking facilities. The time should be arranged to fit the schedules of those expected to attend. Meetings scheduled in connection with meals are usually unproductive and unenjoyable. It is better to eat and then meet, or meet and then eat, but do not try to do both at the same time.

Notify those Concerned. Determine who should attend and then notify them about the meeting far enough in advance to permit them to attend. Every member who is expected to participate should be notified in advance and be given a copy of the agenda. In this way, he will know what he is expected to present, how much time he is allotted and the relationship of his topic to the rest of the program. An attractive and catchy notice will often get people to attend who might otherwise stay at home. This should be followed with a last minute reminder: postcard or telephone call.

Preparing the Agenda. A good meeting must have a good agenda; an orderly, logical sequence of items to be discussed and decided upon.

1. It should be realistic in time. Be sure enough time is allotted for each item to be discussed.

2. The items should require thought. There is little point in discussing items that could better be covered in a news bulletin.

3. Items should be arranged in logical order. Bring the members up to date on past activities by a brief report or reading of minutes. Then proceed with the main items for discussion and planning. End the meeting with mention of assignments and announcements for the next meeting.

4. It should contain suggestions on how the group should react to the items for discussion — necessity for discussion, type of solution needed, approvals, changes.

Careful planning must go into the preparation of this agenda; it should act as a *stimulus* and a guide to thoughtful and productive group discussion. The more effort and thought that goes into this preparation, the better the meeting will be.

Conducting the Meeting. The meeting should *start* and *stop* on time. Allot time for the people present to become acquainted with each other *before* the meeting begins. In this way, they can feel at ease with one another. This will facilitate discussion in the actual meeting.

The presiding officer should call the meeting to order using acceptable parliamentary procedure, make any introductions needed and explain the reason for the meeting. Review the agenda. The issues should be clarified and defined; suggestions should be made as to what the group should do about them. The chairman must be sure that focus is upon the point at hand and that all members participate. The discussion should be controlled so that the group does not go off on tangents. The chairman is responsible for the conduct of the meeting and should be in charge at all times. Do not "turn the meeting over" to anyone. Permit the various reports to be made, but do not relinquish the chair.

Guiding Group Discussions. People know how to talk to each other but very seldom know how to talk with each other. Group discussions, where each member participates, are the most productive and satisfying type of meeting for small groups, but certain elements should be kept in mind: Everyone should be permitted and expected to comment. The subject should be adequately discussed so each member has a clear understanding of it. The presiding officer should direct the discussion so that the point of the topic is kept in focus. The goal or final objective should be known by all participating. Everyone should feel at ease and relaxed with one another. The discussion should not be allowed to dwell on personalities or gossip.

Making Assignments. When an assignment is given, *expect* that it will be done, but stand by to offer assistance if necessary. Be sure that people know *what* is to be done, *who* is to do it and *when* it is to be finished. Set a reasonable time limit. It is a good idea to put assignments in writing and inquire frequently about the progress made. This will serve as a reminder to the one assigned. Commend in public the people who have done a good job; censure in private. Be prepared for those who fail to come through; not everyone who accepts an assignment will fill it.

Conducting Large Group Meetings. Meetings of large groups (reunions) have great potential but they require greater planning and preparation. They must have a concrete purpose: to share information, to inspire and unify, to gain backing and support or to make broad or long-range plans.

When large groups are involved, it is always easier to limit group participation, but some of the ways that have proven effective for audience preparation are:

1. Dividing into small discussion groups — a chairman should be appointed to serve as a spokesman. After the main presentation, each small group can discuss and decide: Do we agree? Do we have further questions? The decision will be made known by the group chairman.

2. Informal discussion during socials — appointed family members informally question other family members to learn their feelings on the matter. Then the results of this period are tabulated and studied.

3. Use of microphones in the audience — any member having a question or comment may post it by using one of the microphones in the audience. This is effective, but somewhat expensive to set up.

4. Listening groups — the audience is divided into groups and asked to listen for specific things. A chairman is selected to speak for each group and give their reaction to the subject assigned.

5. Follow-up questionaires — each member is given a questionaire to use during the meeting, upon which he jots down his reactions or questions and hands them in (unsigned if desired) at the end of the meeting.

The ability of a political organization to accomplish anything in the short time it meets in convention, comes from the preliminary planning which takes place prior to it. If the thousands of political delegates met together without this preparation — nothing would be done. Likewise, the meetings of the family organization will be successful only if proper planning and preparation are made *before* the meetings take place.

Strengthening Already Existing Organizations

You have organized your own immediate family and the members are working together in harmony; but you belong to an already existing large family organization beset by the following problems: 1) Only a few people are interested and those few must shoulder the entire workload of the family. 2) Individuals in the group lack clarity of purpose; they meet once a year for punch and cookies and a few handshakes, then go home for another year, oblivious to the true purposes of the group. 3) Dues usually collected are not sufficient to support the organization. All of the emphasis is placed on genealogical work; other family needs are neglected.

It is not possible for you to disband this group and start all over from the bottom, nor would this be wise. Every attempt should be made to strengthen the existing large organization. By incorporating the functions of an effective organization as already outlined, and by encouraging and assisting each individual family unit to organize themselves as outlined above, it is possible to increase the effectiveness of the existing large organization.

Since you are the one proposing that improvements be made, contact the executive committee of the existing organization. Present your proposals to them and enlist their support. At the next regularly scheduled reunion, obtain the necessary time to present your ideas to the family at large. Prepare an agenda containing the proposals to be considered as a guide for group discussion. Encourage family members to discuss the type of organization presented and the programs they are willing to support. Help select a temporary committee to prepare a formal organization for the family to ratify. If the agenda is presented in an enthusiastic manner, the family will respond. Remember that reform takes longer and is usually harder than prevention. So do not become discouraged if results seem slow. Keep at it and through persistence the existing large organization can become an effective one.

Legal Incorporation

Benefits. It is suggested that family organizations legally incorporate to provide a more efficient organization and one which is better able to cope with the financial and legal affairs of the family. Under certain circumstances non-profit status can be obtained. The following benefits should be considered:

1. Exclusive right and use of name or title.

2. Closer compliance with federal and state tax laws — withholding taxes for researchers and clerical help, filing tax returns.

3. More efficient organization — all officers must submit expense accounts, but none may receive wages or other remuneration for services (if non-profit organization) and financial records must be open for examination by all members, federal and state authorities.

4. Legal protection — legal indemnity for officers and members (protection from personal loss or damage for corporate liabilities) and protection of property belonging to the corporation.

5. Tax exemptions (for non-profit corporations) — all contributions and donations are tax deductible; all income and purchases are tax exempt. Sales of any items by the organization are subject to sales tax only.[6] Checking accounts have no service charge regardless of the number of checks written or balance maintained.

6. Organization can function in any state or foreign country under the laws of the state in which the corporation is formed.

7. Postal rates are greatly reduced for bulk mailing.

The laws governing non-profit corporations vary from state to state and country to country. Obtain a copy of the current laws which pertain to your area. Legal advice is recommended for those sections you do not fully understand. Government officials usually require copies of your constitution and by-laws, articles of incorporation and the names and addresses of the original trustees or governing board of the organization. They must also be satisfied that your income is truly non-profit and not for the benefit of any private interest, that all assets are dedicated to non-profit purposes should your group dissolve and that your income will not be used to influence legislation or political campaigns.

APPENDIX TWO

THE L.D.S. PRELIMINARY SURVEY

The Church of Jesus Christ of Latter-day Saints (L.D.S.) has encouraged genealogical research for many years to accomplish certain doctrinal objectives. The chances that someone has compiled information on your ancestors as part of this program is high. For this reason, you should begin the institutional section of your preliminary survey in the records preserved by the Church before searching other institutional jurisdictions.

Composite Records

Composite genealogical records produced by the L.D.S. Church are housed in the Genealogical Society Library in Salt Lake City, Utah. These include pedigrees, family group records, family histories and biographical references on millions of individuals from all countries of the world. These records do not pertain to L.D.S. members only; the majority refer to persons never connected with the Church during their lives. The Library also contains published family and local histories, biographies, periodicals, publications of institutional jurisdictions and special genealogical manuscript and printed collections which should be consulted during the preliminary survey. The quality of these composite records varies according to the diligence of the compiler and the source materials upon which they are based. Consult them as part of the survey regardless of the religious affiliation of your ancestors.

Archives

The Church Historian's Office (Salt Lake City, Utah) is the official depository for the denominational records of the L.D.S. Church. Some records and indexes on deposit there are in constant demand, so they are also available on microfilm at the Genealogical Society. Inasmuch as these records pertain solely to members of the Church, consult them only if pedigree ancestors or their families were members of the L.D.S. Church during their lives.

The following guides contain detailed descriptions of the many L.D.S. Church records, their contents and their genealogical application.

Brown, Mary L. *Handy Index to the Holdings of the Genealogical Society of Utah.* Logan: Everton Publishers, 1972.

Cunningham, Ronald and Evans, Evan. *A Handy Guide to the Genealogical Society.* Logan: Everton Publishers, 1965. New edition in preparation.

Genealogical Society. Research Paper Series F. No. 1. *L.D.S. Records and Research Aids,* No. 2. *A Brief Guide to the Temple Records Index Bureau.*

Jaussi, Laureen R. and Chaston, Gloria D. *Fundamentals of Genealogical Research.* Salt Lake City: Deseret Book, 1966. Chapters 10 to 20.

———————————— *Register of L.D.S. Church Records.* Salt Lake City: Deseret Book, 1968. This includes call numbers at the Genealogical Society Library. At the Library reference desk is a list of corrections and additions to this register which should be consulted in connection with it.

Kimball, Stanley B., *Sources of Mormon History in Illinois, 1839-48: An Annotated Catalogue of the Microfilm Collection at Southern Illinois University.* Carbondale: Southern Illinois University Press, 1964.

New York Public Library. *List of Works in the New York Public Library Relating to the Mormons.* New York: Public Library, 1909. Reprinted from *New York Public Library Bulletin,* XIII (1909), 183-239.

Union Catalog of Mormon Americana located at the Utah State Historical Society.

Procedure

* Make a personal visit to the Genealogical Society. The following search outline contains a listing of the sources which should be checked during the preliminary survey.

L.D.S. CHURCH RECORDS
SEARCH OUTLINE
(Copyright, 1972, Genealogical Copy Service)

PEDIGREE ANCESTORS   BIRTHDATE AND PLACE

_____

_____

_____

_____

_____

_____

_____

JURISDICTION:

INSTITUTION	ADDRESS	METHOD OF SEARCH	REMARKS
Genealogical Society of Utah	Salt Lake City	___Personal ___Correspondence ___Research Survey ___Researcher	No restrictions Copy facilities available
Church Historian's Office	Salt Lake City	___Personal ___Correspondence ___Researcher	Permission is required to use some records
Daughters of Utah Pioneers	Salt Lake City	___Personal ___Member	All records restricted to members only Brief abstracts of records only permitted, no copy facilities

SOURCES:

Records are arranged in the order in which they should be searched. Check (___) each record as you **search** it. Write additional sources in the empty blanks.

COMPOSITE RECORDS: Search these, regardless of religious affiliation of ancestors.

(GENEALOGICAL SOCIETY)

Church Records/Archives

___ Main Records Section
... Patron's Section
___ Pedigrees
___ 3-4 Generation Sheets
___ Pedigree Referrals

Other

Temple Ordinances

___ Endowments (Temple Index Bureau)
___ Nauvoo Baptisms
___ Baptisms for Dead*
___ Baptisms for Living*
... Re-Baptisms*
... Salt Lake Tabernacle Baptisms
... Sealings*

Secondary Sources

___ Pedigrees
___ Genealogies
___ Family Histories
___ Local Histories
___ Biographies
___ Genealogical Collections
___ Family Organization File
___ Family Organization Bulletins
___ Bibliographies
___
...
..

*Search only if other records provide proxy names or family representatives. Search last so every possible proxy is available.

L.D.S. ARCHIVES: Search only if ancestors were L.D.S. members.

(HISTORIAN'S OFFICE)

Special Indexes

_____Early Church Information File*
_____Miscellaneous Marriage Index*
_____Deceased Members
_____Scandinavian Deceased Members
_____Obituary (Deseret News and Tribune)*
_____Missionary
_____Patriarchal Blessing*
_____Biographical
_____Journals
_____Diaries
_____Excommunications
_____Mormon Battalion
_____Journal History
_____British Mission Journal History

Ward and Branch Records*

_____Records of Members
_____Blessing
_____Baptism
_____Confirmation
_____Ordination
_____Mission
_____Divorce
_____Excommunication
_____Death
_____Form E Annual Report*
_____Form 42 F-P Mission Annual Report
_____Children Under 8
_____Minute Books
_____Roll Books
_____MSS Histories
_____Printed Histories
_____Miscellaneous Membership File (British and Utah Wards)*

Church Censuses*

_____1846-47
_____1852   _____1940
_____1914   _____1950
_____1920   _____1955
_____1925   _____1960
_____1930   _____1965
_____1935   _____1970

Priesthood Records

_____Membership Rolls
_____Ordinations
_____Minutes
_____Biographies
_____Histories

Miscellaneous Records

_____Pioneers and Prominent Men of Utah
_____Jensen's Biographical Dictionary
_____Salt Lake City Directories
_____Delayed Birth Certificates
_____Documentary History of the Church (Roberts)

Periodicals, Newspapers
(Most of these are indexed)

_____Evening & Morning Star (1832-34)
_____Messenger & Advocate (1834-37)
_____Elders Journal (1837-38)
_____Times and Seasons (1839-46)
_____Millenial Star (1840--)
_____Warsaw Signal (1840-53)
_____Gospel Reflector (1841)
_____Wasp (1842-43)
_____Nauvoo Neighbor (1842-45)
_____The Prophet (1844-45)
_____Hancock Eagle (1846)
_____Frontier Guardian (1849-52)
_____The Seer (1853-54)
_____The Mormon (1855-57)
_____Deseret News (1850--)*
_____Instructor (1866-1970)
_____Improvement Era (1897-1970)
_____Children's Friend (1902-70)
_____Liahona, Elders Journal (1903-48)
_____Relief Society Magazine (1914-70)
_____Ensign (1971--)
_____New Era (1971--)
_____Friend (1971--)
_____Saints and Herald (Reorganized, 1860--)
_____Young Women's Journal (1889-1929)
_____Women's Exponent (1884-1901)

Emigration Records*

_____Emigration File
_____British Mission (Liverpool Office)
_____Scandinavian Mission
_____Danish Mission (Copenhagen Office)
_____Danish Mission (Forsgren Company)
_____Netherlands Mission
_____Swedish Mission

_____Pioneer Card File (Crossing the Plains)
_____Perpetual Emigrating Fund
_____Pioneer Company Journals
_____Handcart Company Journals
_____Emigration to Zion Records of Members

Non-L.D.S. Wagon Trains

_____Diaries
_____Letters
_____Logbooks
_____Account Books
_____Oral History
_____Newspapers

Overland Train Passenger Lists

_____Southern Pacific
_____Union Pacific

Ships Passenger Lists*

_____Boston
_____New York
_____Philadelphia
_____Charleston
_____New Orleans
_____San Francisco
_____Seattle

*Microfilm copies are available at the Genealogical Society

UTAH PIONEERS RECORDS: Search only if ancestors were Utah Pioneers.

(D.U.P. MUSEUM)

Camp Minute Books
MSS Pioneer Histories
County Histories
Camp Histories

Index to Relics
Pioneer Index File
Rare Books

Heart Throbs of the West
Treasures of Pioneer History
Our Pioneer Heritage

* Visit a branch library of the Genealogical Society located near you. Any survey record on microfilm can be obtained on loan through the branch library.

* If you cannot visit in person, use the Research Survey provided by the Genealogical Society. This service includes searches of the Temple Records Index Bureau, Church Records Archives, Early Church Information File, Miscellaneous Marriage Records File, Nauvoo Baptisms and if time permits, other composite records. It also includes a report, a recommendation for future research and a list of others engaged in research on the same ancestry (if any). The fee charged allows for approximately three hours of search time. Include with your request: pedigree chart, detailed outline of the part of the pedigree to be surveyed, family group sheets you may have for each marriage union on that part of the pedigree, list of sources you wish checked, type of report desired and the appropriate fee.

When you receive the finished report, describe each search on your calendar. If the genealogical data has not already been placed on family group worksheets, this should be done. Xeroxed copies of family groups sheets on file at the Society can be used as worksheets to prevent re-copying. Then give the report a number and file it in the enclosure file. In this way it becomes a permanent part of your note-keeping system.

Never request a Research Survey until you have organized the genealogical data in your own possession and have contacted your immediate relatives for information they may have on your family.

* Only a portion of the L.D.S. Church records are included in the Research Survey of the Genealogical Society. The remainder should also be consulted before the preliminary survey is complete. Obtain the name of an accredited researcher from the Genealogical Society. They maintain a list of individuals who are acquainted with L.D.S. Church records and who will perform survey searches for you.

* Control survey searches made in L.D.S. Church records as you would any other search. Consult Chapter Ten above for detailed instructions for hiring field researchers.

268

When this portion of your survey is finished, consult the other institutional jurisdictions as described in Chapter Five above.

APPENDIX THREE
RECORD ARCHIVES AND RESEARCH AIDS

It is beyond the scope of this volume to discuss research sources in detail. They vary from country to country and from jurisdiction to jurisdiction within each country. To understand source materials, however, you must be aware of the kinds of archives and depositories where they are preserved and the research aids pertaining to their use. This appendix will help you. You will want to refer, in addition, to the studies dealing with source materials in various countries listed in the bibliographies to this book.

Record depositories can be found at all levels of human activity from the ruler of a nation to the homes of his subjects. Table Ten lists the most common types.

Table Ten.

Kind of Depository*	National	State	Local	Public	Quasi-Public	Private	Remarks
National Archives	x			x			
National Libraries	x			x			
Federal Records Centers	x			x			On district
Presidential Libraries					x		level
Copyright Libraries	x			x	x		
State Libraries		x		x			
State Archives		x		x	x		
Historical Commissions		x		x			
Secretary of State Offices		x		x			
State Historical Societies		x		x			
County Record Offices			x	x			
County Courthouses			x	x			
Borough Chambers			x	x			
Town Halls			x	x			
City Halls			x	x			
Parish Chests			x	x	x		
Monastic Archives			x			x	
Manorial Archives			x			x	
Mining Districts			x	x			
Committees of Safety			x		x		
Family Muniment Rooms			x			x	
Newspaper Offices			x			x	
Boards of Health	x	x	x	x			Restricted by
Morticians Offices			x			x	law
School Boards		x	x	x			
Cemetery Archives	x	x	x	x	x	x	
Business Firms	x	x	x			x	
Universities		x		x	x	x	
Church Historical Societies	x	x	x		x	x	
Church Libraries	x	x	x		x	x	
Church Records Archives	x	x	x		x	x	
Historical Societies	x	x	x		x	x	
Archaeological Societies	x	x	x		x	x	
Record Societies	x		x		x	x	
Friendly Societies	x	x	x		x		
Political Parties	x	x	x		x		
Labor Unions	x	x	x		x		
Commercial Clubs	x	x	x			x	
Fraternal Lodges	x	x	x			x	
Research Libraries	x	x	x		x	x	Sometimes restricted

*Public and quasi-public depositories usually place no restrictions on access unless those restrictions are imposed by law. Private depositories can withhold souce materials and admit or reject scholars at will.

Local Archives and Depositories

Record depositories on the local level are as varied as the jurisdictions themselves. Efficient use requires a certain amount of knowledge of the jurisdiction and often a search for the depository which preserves the documents.

Public Archives. Basic jurisdictions in the United States include county, parish (Louisiana), town (New England), independent city, city-county, mining district, committee of safety (Revolutionary War) and military commander (Civil War period in the South). Basic jurisdictions in England include shire (late nineteenth and twentieth century), civil parish, manor, borough, peculiar, monastery (Middle Ages) and the English Crown (nobility). Continental Europe is quite similar. Which jurisdiction is basic depends upon geographical location, period of time and social status. There is, however, only one basic jurisdiction which exercises power over an individual at any given period of time. Each basic jurisdiction has created records which form the basis of its authority over the people within its boundaries. The question of creation of these basic records and the question of their preservation are often separate and distinct considerations. In America, there is a tendency toward the collection of basic records into central depositories — usually state archives or state libraries. This is especially true of colonial records (prior to 1790). They were created by basic jurisdictions but they are now preserved in state archives as manuscript collections. In England, many basic records are deposited in county record offices regardless of their original creating authority. Parish archives, manor rolls and documents of peculiars are also found housed in these shire offices.

Private Archives. Private archives in England and America constitute a largely untapped, but extremely valuable, source of genealogical information. Private archives include home and family records (home sources). Because of the landholding system which existed in England and the rest of Western Europe before modern times (and still exists in some places), the most important of the basic records — land, court and tax — are to be found in private or family archives. They also contain public documents which should be deposited in public archives but which have been retained for various reasons by the creator or the custodian of the records. Local officials, such as justices of the peace, coroners and medical officers, often retained their records and did not surrender them to public archives. Business firms, churches and many institutional jurisdictions (genealogical and historical societies, fraternal clubs and lodges), newspapers, insurance companies and morticians are also the creators of private archives. Some of the records created find their way into local libraries where they are catalogued for use. Hundreds of others remain in the possession of the orginal owners or their heirs. Many more end up at the local dump or as fuel for winter fires. To use these valuable sources it is necessary to trace the personal collections in which they are located. The following bibliographies will help to locate and use records of local jurisdictions in the' U. S. and England:

American Historical Association. "Inventories of State and Local Archives," *Annual Report of the American Historical Association, 1900-1915.* These cover every state in the United States at that time and were the forerunners of the W.P.A. Inventories (see below).

Gross, Charles, "Bibliography of Town Records of Great Britain," *American Historical Review,* II (1896-97), 191-200.

Hall, Hubert. "Welsh Local Records: Details and Classified Topographical List," *Cymmodorion Society Transactions,* (1914-15), 477-483.

Hardacre, Paul. "County Record Offices in England and Wales; A List of Guides and References," *American Archivist,* XXV (1962), 477-483.

Hodgson, James S. *The Official Publications of American Counties, A Union List.* Fort Collins, Colo.: 1937.

Humphreys, Arthur L. *A Handbook to County Bibliography, Being A Bibliography of Bibliographies Relating to the Counties and Towns of Great Britain and Ireland.* London: Strangeway & Sons, 1917.

Institute of Historical Research. "Guide to Accessibility of Local Records of England and Wales." *Special Supplement* to the *Bulletin* I and II (1923-34).

"Local Archives of Great Britain," *Archives,* #1-29. Descriptions of the county record offices, their holdings and services.

Local Records Committee. *Report on the Collection and Custody of Local Records.* London: H.M.S.O., 1902.

Phillimore's *Directory for Genealogists and Local Historians.* 1963.

In addition to these references, there are some special research projects on the local level of great significance to the genealogist.

Genealogical Society. The Genealogical Society of the Church of Jesus Christ of Latter-Day Saints (Salt Lake City), has millions of feet of microfilmed land, probate, court, tax, census, vital statistics and church records from many areas of the world. The greatest number of rolls apply to America, Great Britain and the Scandinavian countries but France, Canada, Poland, Czechoslovakia, Spain, Italy, Germany and other countries are also included. Microfilm crews are still at work in all of these areas and records are coming in at regular intervals. No other library in the world can match the scope nor the quantity of local primary source materials. Many researchers avoid this great depository because of its religious affiliation. Mistaken ideas that only L.D.S. members can use the facilities and that the records preserved apply only to members of the Church keep others away. The library is a research library open to all researchers. Its broad world coverage and its microfilm program of original records make it unique among archives.

For a nominal fee, any microfilm in the main library may be borrowed on loan or purchased for use in local branch libraries. Branch libraries are scattered throughout the United States and are open to all researchers regardless of religious affiliation. For a more detailed description of the branch library system and its services consult:

> Bennett, Archibald. "The Day of Branch Genealogical Libraries is Here," *Instructor* (July, 1965), 293 ff.

> "Branch Genealogical Libraries," *Improvement Era* (Sept., 1966), 790-91.

The research department of the Society is presently compiling a series of *major source papers* for each state and country which list types of records created, dates covered, locations, limitations and genealogical use. These valuable guides can be obtained at the Society at nominal cost. Through a controlled name-extraction program, the Society has transcribed and computerized the birth registers for a number of English parishes. These are available for searching in computer print-outs at the library. They are arranged in alphabetical order and provide master name indexes for each parish included. For more complete information on this program and its source coverage, write for Research Paper Series F. #3. *The Genealogical Society's Name Extraction Program.* See also C. Derek Harland, "What About Electronics in Genealogy?" *Instructor* (August, 1963), 272-73.

Historical Records Survey of the Works Progress Administration (1936-42). The Roosevelt administration, to counteract the effect of the Great Depression, employed 3000 clerical workers to examine local and state record archives and to prepare calendars, guides and inventories of them for publication. Rough forms on which the local workers inventoried the archives were sent to state agencies to be edited in standard format.

In 1939, the federal project ended. Some local governments and private authorities appropriated necessary funds to complete the job. Some did not and the project died for lack of support. By 1942, 836 separate publications were printed for county, town and municipal archives, state record collections, church and federal archives, local manuscript collections and imprints. Each inventory is prefaced with a historical sketch of the area involved, an analysis of the government structure, laws affecting its operation and reports of the housing and care of the records. While the quality of the work varies, the error factor is less than 15 per cent. These inventories are remarkable examples of mass scholarship and researchers owe a debt of gratitude to those who did the work.

The printed inventories can be found in most large research libraries. Unpublished ones, in manuscript form are located in state and local archives, university libraries and historical societies. These references will provide a better understanding of the project and help to locate inventories:

> Child, Sargent B. and Holmes, Dorothy P. *Bibliography of Research Project Reports: Checklist of Historical Records Survey Publications.* Washington: Works Progress Administration Techinical Series, 1943. Bibliography #7, revised.

> Colby, M. E. *Final Report on Disposition of Unpublished Materials of the W.P.A. Writer's Program.* Washington, D.C., 1943.

> Hoyt, Max E. "Unpublished Historical Records Survey Inventories," *National Genealogical Society Quarterly,* 33 (1945), 33-35.

> Kidder, Robert W. "The Historical Records Survey: Activities and Publications," *Library Quarterly,* XIII (1943), 136-49.

> Smiley, David L. "The WPA Historical Records Survey," *In Support of Clio: Essays in Memory of Herbert A. Kellar,* ed. by William B. Hessletine and Donald R. McNeil. Madison: University of Wisconsin Press, 1958.

The Historical Manuscripts Commission was founded in 1869 to locate and describe the local and private record collections of England and Wales. Consult these references:

Baillie, H. M. G. "The Use of the Resources of the Historical Manuscripts Commission," *Journal of the Society of Archivists,* III (1969), 462-66.

Beckham, Jessie E. "The British Historical Manuscripts Commission," *American Archivist,* VII (1944), 41-48.

Dopson, Laurence. "The Historical Manuscripts Commission," *History Today.* (1952).

Ellis, R. H. "The Historical Manuscripts Commission, 1869-1969," *Journal of the Society of Archivists,* II (1962), 233-42.

"Historical Manuscripts Commission: Untraced Collections" *Bulletin of the Institute of Historical Research,* XIX (1944), 116-20.

Roberts, R. A. "Concerning the Historical Manuscripts Collections," *Royal Historical Society Transactions,* 3rd S. IV (1910), 63-81.

The Commission is responsible for three important source aids:

1. **Reports and Calendars** (250 volumes to date) which contain extensive appendices of transcribed documents and catalogues in addition to source descriptions. Later reports briefly list the major documents and describe their contents but do not include transcripts. A full list of these reports is found in E.L.C. Mullins, *Texts and Calendars* (London: Royal Historical Society, 1958), 61-90 and in *Publications of the Historical Manuscripts Commission, Sectional List No. 17.* (H.M. S.O., 1967). Each volume is separately indexed and the entire series is indexed by general name and topographical entries.

2. **National Register of Archives** formed in 1945 to list and describe the local and private record holdings of England and Wales. A master list of all inventories is maintained in the search room at Quality House, London. An annual *Bulletin* includes accessions and migrations of manuscripts from one archive to another.[1] The following references present a more detailed description of this great finding tool:

Dopson, Lawrence. "Scotland's National Register of Archives," *Amateur Historian,* I (1954), 374-78.

Ranger, Felicity. "The National Register of Archives, 1945-1969," *Journal of the Society of Archivists,* III (1969), 452-66.

3. **The Manorial Documents Register** gives a short description and location for manorial documents — court rolls,

surveys, maps, tax and boundary records — arranged by name of manor and parish in which it is situated.

State Record Depositories (United States)

The public record depositories on a state level were originally established to provide reference services for government officials and to preserve the documents created as a by-product of government functions. They constitute a valuable source for genealogical data. In some states, archives and library are combined into one, in others they are separate in both buildings and functions. The following guides list some of the records created by state executive, legislative and judicial agencies.

Jenkins, William S. and Hamick, Lillian A. *A Guide to Microfilm Collections of Early State Records.* Washington: Library of Congress, 1950 and *Supplement,* 1951.

Hasse, Adelaide R. *Materials for a Bibliography of the Public Archives of the Thirteen Original States Covering the Colonial Period and State Period to 1789.* First published as *Annual Report to the American Historical Association* 1906 (1908), II. Reprinted, New York: Argonaut Press, 1966.

Keitt, Lawrence. *An Annotated Bibliography of Bibliographies of Statutory Materials of the United States.* Cambridge: Harvard University Press, 1934.

Maxwell, W. Harold and Brown, C. R. *A Complete List of British and Colonial Law Reports and Legal Periodicals.* 3rd ed. Toronto: University of Toronto Press, 1937.

National Association of State Libraries. *A Checklist of Legislative Journals of States of the U.S.A.* Providence: Oxford Press, 1938. Two *Supplements,* 1943 and 1955.

——————————— *Checklist of Statutes of States of the United States, Including Revisions, Compilations, Digests, Codes and Indexes.* Providence: Oxford Press, 1937.

Special Research Aids. A valuable research aid on a state basis is found in the imprint checklists begun by the W. P. A. Sixteen million titles of American Imprints published by local presses all over America were collected between 1936 and 1941. The files were deposited in the Library of Congress and added to the National Union Catalog. Many of the regional and local checklists have been published. Consult Douglas McMurtie, "Locating the Printed Source Materials for United States History," *Mississippi Valley Historical Review*, XXXI (1944), 369-78.

Charles Evans devoted his entire lifetime to the collection of information on all the known books printed in the United States from 1639 to 1800. These books are being made available on microprint through the American Antiquarian Society, which has the largest collection of early American books in the United States. The project is completely indexed and will continue until all known works have been included. Each group of microprints is indexed in a separate volume but there is a master index containing a complete description of each imprint. Roger P. Bristol has prepared a supplement published by the University of Virginia Press (1970) and Ralph R. Shaw and Richard H. Shoemaker have continued the project in their *American Bibliography: A Preliminary Checklist, 1801-1819* in 22 volumes published by the Scarecrow Press (1958-66). Most large libraries have complete sets of these.

The imprint checklists are valuable because they contain references to early maps, diaries and journals, state statutes, legislative publications and many other sources for genealogical research.

National Record Depositories (United States and England)

The United States Government is the largest publisher of records in America. These records can be found in complete sets in most research libraries throughout the country but they are rarely used by genealogists. The printed volumes — records of Congress, military records, census and numerous other categories are classified under the special system of "Government Documents." They are usually located all together in a special section of the library. The following two references explain this classification system and the categories of records included.[2]

Boyd, Anne Morris. *United States Government Publications: Sources of Information for Libraries.* New York: H. W. Wilson, Co., 1941.

Schmeckebier, Lawrence F. and Easton, Roy B. *Government Publications and Their Use.* Washington: Brookings Institute. 1969.

The government also underwrites or co-sponsors the publication of its record holdings. Examples include the *Territorial Papers* and the publication of the papers of the Presidents of the United States and important American Statesmen. See Clarence E. Carter, "Territorial Papers of the United States: A Review and Commentary," *Mississippi Valley Historical Review,* XLII (1955-56), 510-24; Richard B. Morris, "The Current Stateman's Papers Publications Program," *American Journal of Legal History,* XI

(1967), 95-106; and Buford Rowland, "The Papers of the Presidents," *American Archivist*, XIII (1950), 195-211.

The Federal Government also produces literally tons of archival manuscripts annually. Most of these are deposited for preservation after their current use is over, in the National Archives or Federal Record Centers (see below). The records and record groups into which they are divided are described in the following publications:

Beers, Henry P. *Guide to the Archives of the Government of the Confederate States of America*. Washington: National Archives, 1968.

Colket, Meredith B., Jr. and Bridgers, Frank E. *Guide to Genealogical Records in the National Archives*. Washington: National Archives, 1964. New edition in preparation.

Federal Records of World War II: Civilian and Military Agencies. 2 vols. Washington: Government Printing Office, 1950.

Johnson, Everly and Price. *Index to the Manuscripts and Printed Opinions of the Supreme Court, 1808-73*. 2 vols. Washington: Government Printing Office, 1965.

National Archives. *Guide to the Records in the National Archives*. Washington: National Archives, 1948. Shortened version issued in 1950 as *Your Government's Records in the National Archives*. A new edition of the *Guide* is in preparation.

Muncken, Kenneth W. and Beers, Henry P. *Guide to Federal Archives Relating to the Civil War*. Washington: Government Printing Office, 1962.

National Archives. *Accessions to the National Archives*. 1940 to date.

_____ *Preliminary Inventories*. #1-365. In Progress.

_____ *Prologue:* Journal of the National Archives. 1969 to date.

_____ *Publications of the National Archives and Records Services*. Washington: Government Printing Office, 1969.

The majority of these can be readily found in research libraries or they can be obtained from the creating agency or the Government Printing Office free or at nominal cost.

Federal Record Centers. These have been established in many sections of the United States as regional branches of the National Archives. Centers are located in Boston, New York City, Philadelphia, Mechanicsburg (Pa.), Alexandria (Va.), East Point (Ga.), Chicago, Kansas City (Mo.), St. Louis, Fort Worth, New Orleans, Denver, San Francisco, Bell (Calif.), Seattle and Honolulu. Records of government agencies pertaining to that particular section of the country, formerly housed in the National Archives, have been transferred to these district centers for more efficient preservation and easier access. Guides to the materials in each center are being prepared to aid the researcher in their use.[3]

Presidential Libraries. These libraries are another feature of the archival system in the United States. They house the public and personal papers of the twentieth century Presidents of the United States and several executive members of their administrations. The libraries are built with public and private funds in the home state of each president. The records are available, with some limitations, to scholars. Consult Wayne C. Grover, "Presidential Libraries: A New Feature of the Archival System of the United States," *Indian Affairs,* II (1957), 1-6 and "The Presidential Library System," *Palimpset* XLIII (1962), 387-92.

Special Research Aids. Between 1906 and 1932, the Carnegie Institute of Washington, D. C., in collaboration with the American Historical Association, financed the compilation and publication of guides to manuscript materials relating to American history located outside the continental United States. The bulk of this material, however, remains in foreign depositories.[4]

Andrews, C. M. *Guide to the Materials for American History, to 1783, in the Public Record Office of Great Britain.* 2 vols. Washington, 1912-14.

Andrews, C. M. and Davenport, F. G. *Guide to the Manuscript Materials for the History of the United States to 1783, in the British Museum, in Minor London Archives, and in the Libraries of Oxford and Cambridge.* Washington, 1908.

Bell, H. C. *et al., Guide to British West Indian Archive Materials in London and in the Islands, for the History of the United States.* Washington, 1926.

Bolton, H. E. *Guide to Materials for the History of the United States in the Principal Archives of Mexico.* Washington, 1913.

Chapman, C. E. *Catalogue of Materials in the Archivo General de Indias for the History of the Pacific Coast and the American Southwest.* Berkeley, 1919.

Faust, A. B. *Guide to the Materials for American History in Swiss and Austrian Archives.* Washington, 1916.

Fish, C. R. *Guide to the Materials for American History in Roman and Other Italian Archives.* Washington, 1911.

Golder, F. A. *Guide to Materials for American History in Russian Archives.* 2 vols. Washington: 1917-37.

Hill, R. R. *Descriptive Catalogue of the Documents Relating to the United States in the Papeles procedentes de Cuba. Deposited in . . . Seville.* Washington, 1916.

Jameson J. F. ed., "Guide to the Items Relating to American History in the Reports of the English Historical Manuscripts Commission," Am. Hist. Assoc., *Reports,* 1898, 611. — Addenda to 1927 are in the *Cambridge History of the Empire, I,* 837.

Learned, M. D. *Guide to the Manuscript Materials Relating to American History in the German State Archives.* Washington, 1912.

Leland, W. G. and Meng, J. J. *Guide to Materials for American History in the Libraries and Archives of Paris.* 2 vols. Washington, 1932-43. — Two more volumes remain to be published.

Matteson, D. M. *List of Manuscripts Concerning American History Preserved in European Libraries.* Washington, 1925.

Parker, D. W. *Guide to the Materials for United States History in Canadian Archives.* Washington, 1913.

Paullin, C. O. and Paxson, F. L. *Guide to the Materials in London Archives for the History of the United States since 1783.* Washington, 1914.

Paz, Inlian *Catalogo de manuscritos de America existentes en la Biblioteca Nacional.* Madrid, 1933.

Perez, L. M. *Guide to the Materials for American History in Cuban Archives.* Washington, 1907.

Report on American Manuscripts in the Royal Institution of Great Britain. 4 vols. London, 1904-09. — Many of these have since been transferred to American repositories.

[Milton Rubicam], ed., "Materials in Foreign Archives for Writing Pennsylvania History," *Pennsylvanian,* II (1944-45), 17.

Shepherd, W. R. *Guide to the Materials for the History of the United States in Spanish Archives.* Washington, 1907.

Recent additons to these guides include:

Beers, Henry P. *The French and British in the Old Northwest: A Bibliographic Guide to Archives and Manuscript Sources.* Detroit: Wayne State University Press, 1964.

Crick, B. R. and Alman, Miriam. *A Guide to the Manuscripts Relating to America in Great Britain and Ireland.* London: Oxford University Press, 1961.

Gipson, L. H. *Guide to Manuscripts Relating to the History of the British Empire, 1748-1776.* New York: Alfred J. Knopf, 1970.

The Public Record Office is the English equivalent to the National Archives. It houses most of the national public records of Great Britain and its Empire. Significant categories of records, however, are also to be found in Somerset House. These publications describe the records kept and their contents:

Bond, Maurice. *List of the Main Classes of Records in the House of Lords Records Office.* London: H.M.S.O., 1966.

Ford, Percy. *Guide to Parliamentary Papers — What they Are, How to Find and Use Them.* Oxford: Blackwell, 1955.

Guiseppi, M. S. *Guide to the Contents of the Public Record Office*. 3 vols. London: H.M.S.O., 1963-1970.

Powicke, F. F. and Fryde, E. B. "Bibliographical Guide to the Lists of English Office Holders to 1800," *Handbook to British Chronology* (London: 1961), xxi-xxviii.

Public Record Office. *Lists and Indexes*. Several volumes have been published to date.

——————————————. *Record Publications. Sectional List*. #1964.

——————————————. *List of Colonial Office Records Preserved in the Public Record Office*. New York: Kraus Reprint Corp. 1963.

National Copyright Libraries

The Library of Congress was originally established to provide information and book collections for the use of American government officials. Its collections have grown until it is one of the largest research libraries in the world. It is entitled to two copies of every book copyrighted in the United States. These are catalogued, along with numerous other books, in the *Subject Catalogue* and *Printed Catalogue Cards of the Library of Congress,* available in most large libraries.

The Library is the central supervising agency of the *National Union Catalogue,* a locating device for printed books in the libraries of the United States. Printed editions of the *National Union Catalogue* can be found in most research libraries. The Library also has a large manuscript collection and other special collections. The following list of aids will help you to determine those items pertinent to your pedigree.

Handbook to Manuscripts in the Library of Congress. Washington: Library of Congress, 1918.

Garrison, Curtis W. "List of Manuscript Collections in the Library of Congress to 1931," *Annual Report of the American Historical Association,* 1930, I (1931), 123-249.

Vanderbilt, Paul. *Guide to Special Collections of Prints and Photographs in the Library of Congress*. Washington: Library of Congress, 1955.

Roberts, Martin A. "Records in the Copyright Office of the Library of Congress Deposited by the U. S. District Courts, 1790-1870," *Papers of the Bibliographical Society of America,* 31 (1937) 81-101.

Powell, C. Percy. "List of Manuscript Collections Received in the Library of Congress, July 1931 to July 1938," *Annual Report of the American Historical Association,* 1937, I (1938), 113-45.

Library of Congress, *Report of the Library of Congress. Quarterly Journal of Current Acquisitions,* 1943 — .

Griffin, Grace G. *A Guide to the Manuscripts relating to American History in*

282

British Archives Reproduced for the Division of Manuscripts of the Library of Congress, Washington: Library of Congress, 1946.

The British Museum is entitled to two copies of each book licensed for printing or copyrighted in the United Kingdom and these are listed in the *Printed Catalogues of the British Museum* and the *Subject Catalogue of the British Museum.* The library also houses a large collection of manuscripts. Among the most important for genealogy and local history are the Cotton, Harleian, Royal, Sloane, Lansdowne, Hargrave, Burney, Egerton, Kings, Arundel and Additional Manuscripts Collections. Separate printed catalogues are available for each of these collections. Consult:

Gilson, Julius P. *A Student's Guide to the Manuscripts of the British Museum.* London: S.P.C.K., 1920.

Sims, Richard, *Handbook to the Library of the British Museum.* London: John Russell Smith, 1854.

Skeat, T. C., *The British Museum: Catalogues of the Manuscript Collections.* Rev. ed. London: British Museum, 1962.

Another valuable copyright library is the *Bodleian Library of Oxford University.* It boasts a printed book and manuscript collection of English history second only to the British Museum. Falconer Madon's seven volume, well indexed *Summary Catalogue of the Western Manuscripts in the Bodleian Library,* (Oxford: University Press, 1953) is a valuable guide to its MSS holdings.[5]

General Guides to Records

Guides to record holdings differ in form and arrangement. *Lists* usually give titles and publication data only. *Indexes* are alphabetical arrangements of subjects, places and names. *Inventories* list documents in the order of finding or receipt with brief descriptions. *Calendars* are arranged by date and describe each document listed. *Catalogues* are orderly, systematic guides to searching. They are arranged alphabetically or chronologically and contain descriptions and additional comments as to location, printed editions, special studies and other references.[6]

Many record depositories have prepared guides and catalogs to their holdings. Some have been published or are available in typescript, others are card indexes only. A survey of archives made in 1961 by the Library Association of England indicated that 214 English libraries had published articles on their collections. The results of the survey are on file at their central offices in London.[7] The Cambridge University Library in Cambridge England has several volumes of printed catalogs to manuscript collections preserved in the individual colleges of the university. These valuable guides were compiled by M. R. James between 1895 and 1925. The following list will lead the researcher to other manuscript catalogs and indexes.

Ash, Lee and Loring, Denis. *Subject Collections.* New York: R. R. Bowker, 1967.

Billington, Ray A. "Guides to American Historical Manuscript Collections in Libraries of the United States," *Mississippi Valley Historical Review,* XXXVIII (1951-52), 467-96.

Brooks, Philip C. *Research in Archives: The Use of Unpublished Primary Sources.* Chicago: University of Chicago Press, 1969.

Brubaker, Robert L. "Publishing Historical Sources: Recent Projects in the United States," *Library Quarterly,* XXXVII (1967), 195-99.

Burnett, Edmond C. "A List of Printed Guides to and Descriptions of Archives and other Repositories of Historical Manuscripts," *Annual Report of the American Historical Association,* 1896, I (1897), 481-512.

Burnette, Lawrence O. Jr. *Beneath the Footnote: A Guide to the Use and Preservation of American Historical Sources.* Madison: State Historical Society of Wisconsin, 1969.

Clark, G. Kitson and Elton, G. R. *Guide to Research Facilities in History in Universities of Great Britain and Ireland.* 2d ed. Cambridge: Cambridge University Press, 1965.

Downs, Robert B. *American Library Resources: A Bibliographical Guide.* Chicago: American Library Association, 1951. *Supplement,* 1950-61. See also the author's *Resources in North Carolina Libraries,* in *Southern Libraries* and in *New York City Libraries.*

Eagle, Selwyn. *Library Resources in London and South East England.* London: Library Association, 1969.

Elton, G. R., ed. *The Sources of History: Studies in the Use of Historical Evidence.* London: Hodder and Stoughton, Ltd., 1968. In progress. 4 volumes have been issued with 15 more announced for publication in the future.

Evans, Frank B. *The Administration of Modern Archives: A Select Bibliographic Guide.* Washington: National Archives, 1970.

Graphic Historical Society of America. "A Survey of Picture Collections Relating to Individual States," *Eye to Eye,* II (1953), 36-40.

Hale, Richard W., Jr. *Guide to Photocopies of Historical Materials in the United States and Canada.* Ithaca: Cornell University Press, 1961. The Institute for Colonial Studies at the State University of New York is working on an up-dated edition of this valuable guide.

Hamer, Philip M. *A Guide to Archives and Manuscripts in the United States.*

New Haven: Yale University Press, 1961. Superseded largely by the *National Union Catalog of Manuscript Collections* of the Library of Congress.

Handlin, Oscar. *Harvard Guide to American History.* Cambridge: Harvard University Press, 1954.

Hepworth, Philip. *Archives and Manuscripts in Libraries.* 2d ed. London: Library Association, 1964.

Hobbes, John L. *Local History and the Library.* London: Andre Deutsch, 1962.

Ireland, Norma O. *Local Indexes in American Libraries: A Union List of Unpublished Indexes.* Boston: F. W. Faxon Co., 1947.

Morris, Richard B. and Greene, Evarts B. *A Guide to the Principal Sources for Early American History in the City of New York.* 2d ed. New York: Columbia University Press, 1953.

Mullins, E. L. C. *Texts and Calendars: An Analytical Guide.* London: Royal Historical Society, 1958.

Museum of Modern Art Film Library. *The Film Index: A Bibliography.* New York: Museum of Modern Art, 1941.

Richardson, Ernest C. *A Union World Catalog of Manuscript Books. III. List of Printed Catalogues of Manuscript Books.* New York: 1935.

Vormelker, Rose L. *Special Library Resources.* New York: Special Libraries Association, 1941-47.

Annual reports of archives and libraries usually contain lists of their recent acquisitions. Some are complete descriptions, some brief lists, some include selective collections only. These reports are available in most large libraries or copies can be obtained from the archives themselves.

Many archives and large research libraries also publish quarterly journals which list acquisitions of documents and contain valuable articles on their use. Some of the most important are:

American Library Association, *R Q* (1960 —)
Newberry Library, *Bulletin* (1944 —)
Harvard Library, *Bulletin* (1947 —)
Huntington Library, *Quarterly* (1931 —)
National Archives, *Prologue* (1969 —)
American Antiquarian Society, *Proceedings* (1812 —)
New York Public Libary, *Bulletin* (1897 —)
Folger Shakespeare Library, *Reports* (1948 —)
Bodleian Library, *Quarterly Record* (1914 —)
John Rylands Library, *Bulletin* (1903 —)
National Library of Wales, *Journal* (1939 —)
British Museum, *Journal* (1926 —)

Library Association, *Record* (1936 —)
Cambridge University, *Historical Journal* (1923 —)
London University, Institute of Historical Research, *Bulletin* (1923 —)

For others, check the list of periodical indexes and guides on pages 80-81 above.

Specific Guides to Basic and Local Records

The following bibliographies often include the locations of the records discussed.

Business Records.

Larson, Henrietta M. *Guide to Business History: Materials for the Study of American Business and Suggestions for their Use.* Cambridge: Harvard University Press, 1948.

Census.

Franklin, W. Neil. "Availability of Federal Population Census Schedules in the States," *National Genealogical Society Quarterly,* L (1962), 19-25, 100-09. "Addendum," LI (1963), 16.

——————————— "Availability of Federal Mortality Census Schedules, 1850-85," *National Genealogical Society Quarterly,* LII (1964), 205-09.

——————————— "Availability of Name Indexes to Federal Population Census Schedules, 1790-1890," *National Genealogical Society Quarterly,* LI (1963), 165-67. "Supplement," pages 167-68 by Milton Rubincam.

Census Library Project. *State Censuses, 1790-1948.* Washington: Government Printing Office, 1948.

A Census of Pensioners for Revolutionary or Military Services. Washington: Blair and Rives, 1841. Published by Act of Congress. Reprinted, Baltimore: Southern Book Company, 1954. The Genealogical Society of the L.D.S. Church has compiled a name index to this Census published by the Genealogical Book Company in Baltimore in 1965.

National Archives. *Federal Population Censuses, 1790-1890.* Washington: National Archives, 1965.

Texas University. *International Population Census Bibliography.* Austin: Bureau of Business Research, 1965.

U. S. Bureau of Census. *A Century of Population Growth, 1790-1900.* Washington: Government Printing Office, 1909. Reprinted, New York: Johnson Reprint Corp., 1966.

Charters.

Ellis, Henry J. and Brickley, Francis B. *Index to the Charters and Rolls in the Department of Manuscripts of the British Museum.* 2 Vols. London: Trustees of the British Museum, 1900. Reprinted, 1965-67.

Davis, G. R. C. *Medieval Cartularies of Great Britain: A Short Catalogue.* London: Royal Historical Society, 1958.

286

Sawyer, P. H. *Anglo-Saxon Charters: An Annotated List and Bibliography.* London: Royal Historical Society, 1968.

Church Records.

Allison, William H. *Inventory of Unpublished Material for American Religious History in Protestant Church Archives and Other Resources.* Washington: Carnegie Institute, 1910.

Barrow, John Graves. *A Bibliography of Bibliographies in Religion.* Ann Arbor: University of Michigan, 1955.

Binsfield, Edmund L. "Church Archives in the United States and Canada: A Bibliography," *American Archivist,* XXI (1958), 311-32.

Marchant, L. R. "The Archives of Protestant Missions from London to Australia, 1787-1850: A Survey," *Journal of the Society of Archivists,* I (1959).

—————————. *A Guide to the Archives and Records of Protestant Christian Missions from the British Isles to China, 1796-1914.* Perth: University of West Australia, 1966.

Mode, Peter G. *Source Book and Bibliographical Guide for American Church History.* Boston: J. S. Canner and Co., Inc., 1964.

Pilgrim Trust. "Survey of Ecclesiastical Archives." Unpublished report of a Committee appointed to keep record of church archives and their record holdings. 2 vols. 1946-52. Copies located at the National Register of Archives and British Museum in London.

Suelflow, August R. *A Preliminary Guide to Church Records Repositories.* N. P.: Society of American Archivists, 1969.

Blair, Lawrence. *A List of Churchwarden's Accounts.* Ann Arbor: Edwards, 1939.

Blomfield, Kathleen and Percy-Smith, H. K. *National Index of Parish Register Copies.* London: Society of Genealogists, 1939.

Burke, A. M. *Key to the Ancient Parish Registers of England and Wales.* Baltimore: Genealogical Book Company, 1962. Reprint of 1908 edition.

Commissioners of Parochial Registers. *Report of Non-Parochial Registers for England and Wales, 1838 and 1857.* London: H.M.S.O., 1838 and 1857.

Karr, Nola M. "Detailed List of Old Parochial Registers of Scotland," *National Genealogical Society Quarterly,* XLIV (1956), 134-42; XLV (1957), 10-16, 73-76, 144-54.

Phillips, E. "Bibliography of Published Churchwarden's Accounts," *English Historical Review,* XV (1900), 335-41.

Society of Genealogists. *A Catalogue of Parish Register Copies in the Possession of the Society of Genealogists.* London: 1963. Revised edition.

Steel, D. J., general editor. *National Index of Parish Registers.* London: Society of Genealogists, 1968. 3 vols. have been published to date with several more to come.

Court Records.

Barnes, T. G. and Smith, A. Hassell. "Justices of the Peace for 1558 to 1688: A Revised List of Sources," *Bulletin of the Institute of Historical Research,* XXXII (1959), 221-42.

Becker, Harold K. and Felkenes, George T. *Law Enforcement: A Selected Bibliography.* Metuchen, N. J.: Scarecrow Press, 1968.

Hunnisett, R. F. "The Medieval Coroner's Rolls," *American Journal of Legal History,* III (1959), 95, 205, 324, 383.

Jeffrey, William, Jr. "A Bibliography of Published Materials on Early New England Court Records," *Boston Public Library Quarterly,* VI (1954). Also printed separately by Harvard Law School, 1954.

Kimball, Elisabeth G. "A Bibliography of the Printed Records of the Justices of the Peace for Counties," *University of Toronto Law Journal,* VI (1946), 401-13.

Morris, Richard B. "Early American Court Records: A Publication Program," *Anglo-American Legal Series,* 1. New York: New York University School of Law, 1941.

Prager, Herta and Price, William W. "A Bibliography on the History of the Courts of the Thirteen Original States, Maine, Ohio and Vermont," *American Journal of Legal Hisotry,* I (1957), 336-62; II (1958), 35-52, 148-54.

Putnam, Bertha. "Justices of the Peace, 1558-1688," *Bulletin of the Institute of Historical Research,* XXXII (1959), 221-42.

Stair Society. *An Introductory Survey of the Sources and Literature of Scots Law.* Edinburg: MacLehose, 1936.

Diaries.

Kaplin, Louis, *et. al. A Bibliography of American Autobiographies.* Madison: University of Wisconsin Press, 1961.

MacPike, Eugene F. "English, Scottish and Irish Diaries, Journals, Commonplace Books, 1550-1900: A Bibliographical Guide to Selected Source Material," *Bulletin of Bibliography,* XVII (1941), 183, 213. Also issued separately.

Matthews, William. *American Diaries: An Annotated Bibliography of Those Written Prior to the Year 1861.* Boston: J. S. Canner & Co., 1959.

_____ *British Autobiographies: An Annotated Bibliography of British Autobiographies Published Before 1951.* Berkeley: University of California Press, 1955.

_____ *British Diaries: An Annotated Bibliography of British Diaries Written Between 1442 and 1942.* Berkeley: University of California, 1950.

Directories.

Burton, Robert E. "City Directories in the United States, 1784-1820: A Bibliography with Historical Notes." Unpublished M.S. Thesis, University of Michigan, 1956.

Davis, Marjorie V. *Guide to American Business Directories.* Washington: Public Affairs Press, 1948.

Goss, C. W. F. *London Directories, 1677-1855: A Bibliography with Notes on their Origin and Development.* London: Archer, 1932.

Moriarity, John H. "Directory Information Material for New York City

Residents, 1626-1786: A Bibliographic Study," *Bulletin of the New York Public Library,* XLVI (1942), 807-64.

Norton, Jane E. *Guide to National and Provincial Directories of England and Wales, Excluding London Before 1856.* London: Royal Historical Society, 1950.

Enclosures.

Beresford, Maurice W. "Bibliography of Enclosure Commission Minutes," *Bulletin of the Institute of Historical Research,* XXI (1946), 62-69.

Tate, W. E. *Handlist of English Enclosure Acts and Awards.* A Series of articles appearing in appropriate local historical society journals in the 1950's and 1960's, for each English county.

———————— "A Note on the Bibliography of Enclosure Acts and Awards," *Bulletin of the Institute of Historical Research,* XVIII (1940-41), 97-101.

Guilds.

Unwin, George. *The Guilds and Companies of London.* London: Allen & Unwin, 1908. Reprinted 1938. 2d edition, 1962.

Manorial Records.

Davenport, Frances G. *A Classified List of Printed Original Materials for English Manorial and Agrarian History During the Middle Ages.* Boston: Radcliffe College, 1894.

Genealogical Society, L.D.S. Church. *Location of Manor Court Rolls.* Typescript. 1968. 5 vols.

National Library of Wales. *A County List of Manorial Records and Other Manuscript Material Relating to Manors and Lordships of Wales.* Aberyswyth: National Library of Wales, 1936.

Public Record Office. *Register of Manorial Documents and Their Locations.* Kept current by the Master of the Rolls.

Museums.

Museums Directory of the United States and Canada. Washington: American Association of Museums, 1965.

Katz, Herbert. *Museums U.S.A.: A History and Guide.* Garden City: Doubleday, 1965.

Newspapers.

Brayer, Herbert O. "Preliminary Guide to Indexed Newspapers in the United States, 1850-1900," *Mississippi Valley Historical Review, XXXIII (1946), 237-58.*

Brigham, Clarence S. *History and Bibliography of American Newspapers, 1690-1820.* 2 vols. Worcester, Mass.: American Antiquarian Society, 1947.

———————— "Additions and Corrections to History and Bibliography of American Newspapers," *Proceedings of the American Antiquarian Society,* LXXI, N. S. (1961), 15-62.

Crane, Ronald S. and Kaye, Frederick B. *A Census of British Newspapers and*

Periodicals, 1620-1800. Chapel Hill: University of North Carolina Press, 1927.

Cranfield, G. A. *Handlist of English Provincial Newspapers and Periodicals, 1700-1760.* Cambridge: Cambridge Bibliographical Society, 1952. Corrections and Additions in *Cambridge Bibliographical Society Transactions,* II (1956), 269-74, 385-89.

Gregory, Winifred. *American Newspapers, 1821-1936: A Union List of Files Available in the United States and Canada.* New York: 1937.

Library of Congress. *A Checklist of American Eighteenth Century Newspapers in the Library of Congress.* Washington: Government Printing Office, 1936.

——————————— *Checklist of American Newspapers in the Library of Congress,* Washington: Government Printing Office, 1900.

——————————— *Checklist of Foreign Newspapers in the Library of Congress.* Washington: Government Printing Office, 1929.

——————————— *Newspapers on Microfilm.* Washington: Library of Congress, 1967.

Tercentenary Handlist of English and Welsh Newspapers, Magazines and Reviews, 1620-1920. London: Dawsons, 1966. Facsimile reprint of 1920 edition.

Weed, K. K. and Bond, R. H. *Studies of British Newspapers and Periodicals from Their Beginning to 1800: A Bibliography.* Chapel Hill: University of North Carolina Press, 1946.

Passenger Lists.

Bridgers, Frank E. "Passenger Arrival Records in the National Archives," *National Genealogical Society Quarterly,* L (1962), 140-45.

Lancour, Harold. *A Bibliography of Ships Passenger Lists, 1538-1825: Being a Guide to Published Lists of Early Immigrants to North America.* 3d edition. New York: New York Public Library, 1963.

Rasmussen, Louis J. *Railway Passenger Lists of Overland Trains to San Francisco and the West.* San Francisco: San Francisco Historic Records Society, 1968. In progress.

Probate Records.

Camp, Anthony J. *Wills and Their Whereabouts.* London: Society of Genealogists, 1963.

Genealogical Society of the L.D.S. Church. "English Probate Jurisdictions." *Research Papers* Series A. 42 pamphlets.

Schools.

Baird, William R. *Manual of American College Fraternities.* Menasha, Wisconsin: G. Banta Co., 1879.

Jacobs, Phyllis M. "Registers of the Universities, Colleges and Schools of Great Britain and Ireland," *Bulletin of the Institute of Historical Research,* XXXVII (1964), 185-232.

Johnson, Marjorie. "Bibliography of Printed Registers of the Universities, Inns of Court, Colleges and Schools of Great Britain and Ireland," *Bulletin of the Institute of Historical Research,* IX (1931), 19-30, 65-83, 154-70. "Addenda," X (1932-33), 109-15.

Locating Archives and Libraries

To determine the names and addresses of libraries and other depositories in the areas of your ancestry, check the following references:

American Library Association. *American Library Directory.* Chicago: American Library Association, 1968-69.

Aldrich, Ella V. and Camp, Thomas E. *Using Theological Books and Libraries.* Englewood Cliffs, N. J., Prentice-Hall, 1963.

Historical Manuscripts Commission. *Record Repositories in Great Britain: A List.* 4th ed. London: H.M.S.O., 1971.

H. M. Treasury, Organization and Methods Division, *A Guide to Government Libraries.* London: H.M.S.O., 1958.

Kruzas, Anthony J. *Directory of Special Libraries and Information Centers.* Detroit: 1968. Supplement, 1970.

Lewanski, Richard C. *European Library Directory: A Geographical and Bibliographical Guide.* Furenzi, Italy: Leo S. Olschki, 1968.

Library Association. *Complete Address List of Public Libraries . . . with a Select List of University and Special Libraries.* London: Library Association, 1961. Supplements are issued. Subsequent editions are available.

Ruoss, G. Martin. *A World Directory of Theological Libraries.* Metuchen, N. J.: Scarecrow Press, 1968.

Saur, Klaus G. *World Guide to Libraries.* New York: R. R. Bowker C., 1968.

Society of American Archivists. *College and University Archives in the United States and Canada.* 1966.

_____ *Directory of State and Provincial Archivists,* 1968.

_____ *Directory of Business Archives in the U.S. and Canada.* 1969.

Suelflow, August R. *A Preliminary Guide to Church Record Repositories.* Society of American Archivists. 1969.

U.S. Library Survey: over 600 libraries, historical societies, archives and ethnic societies contacted by the Cache Genealogical Library to determine the extent of genealogical holdings and services available through correspondence. Summary and tabulation in Table 3, *Handbook for Genealogical Correspondence.*

Wales, A. P. *International Library Directory: A World Directory of Libraries.* London: A. P. Wales, 1969-70.

Some libraries are too small to be included in the above lists. They are too small to own buildings of their own; they share the physical facilities of another library, school or archives. To locate these, get a list of local libraries in the area from the state library.[8]

Libraries and archives, as never before, are making their collections available for research. Reliable catalogues and guides to these collections have increased in number in the past fifteen years and are available for purchase, loan or use through local libraries. Centralization of records, microfilming of documents, the collection of oral history, the building of beautiful and functional research centers, the use of electronic computers for information storage and retrieval, and the ready availability of copy facilities make document searching almost as easy as "library research" has been in the past. No longer need genealogists confine themselves to wills, censuses, church records and marriage certificates. Legions of documents are waiting to disclose their treasures. Use them!

FOOTNOTES AND BIBLIOGRAPHIES

FOOTNOTES.

Chapter One.

[1]See Bibliography of Books on Genealogical Research and Notekeeping.

[2]Derek Harland, *Basic Course in Genealogy, Volume II: Research Procedure and Evaluation of Evidence* (Salt Lake City: Bookcraft, 1958. Reissued in 1963 as *Genealogical Research Standards*) and Ethel W. Williams, *Know Your Ancestors: A Guide to Genealogical Research* (Rutland, Vt.: Charles E. Tuttle Co., 1960).

[3]See Colonel Carleton E. Fisher, "Quality Assurance," *National Genealogical Society Quarterly*, LIII (1965), 243-50 and Dr. Wayne C. Grover, "Genealogy and American Scholarship," *Ibid.*, XLII (1954), 105-07.

[4]Norman F. Cantor and Richard L. Schneider, *How to Study History* (New York: Thomas Y. Crowell, 1967), chap. i.

[5]*English Ancestry* (Oxford: Oxford University Press, 1961), chap. x.

[6]Richard D. Altick, *The Art of Literary Research* (New York: W. W. Norton & Co., 1963), 203-08.

[7]See Donald L. Jacobus, "Is Genealogy an Exact Science: Methods of Research," *American Genealogist,* X (1934), 65-69 for some of the reasons genealogists settle for second-best.

[8]F. Ashley, "The Scientific Method and Historical Research," *Industrial Arts and Vocational Education,* XXVI (1937), 173-75.

[9]Williams, *Know Your Ancestors*, 271. Dr. Williams has included many other important guidelines in her book, based upon her own wide experience in genealogical research.

[10]Wagner, *Ancestry*, 11.

Chapter Two.

[1]This notekeeping system first appeared in the *Instructor* (Oct. 1963), 372-74 and in the *Teacher's Supplement* to Howard S. Bennion, *Genealogical Research: A Practical Mission* (Salt Lake City: Deseret News Press, 1964). It was also issued separately by the *Instructor,* 1964. There are many notekeeping systems in use by genealogists and local historians. Consult the bibliographies at the end of the book for reference to most of those in print. Those examined personally or previously used by the authors themselves have some weaknesses and some strengths. The system offered here, however, is based upon the principles recommended in most historical training manuals and has proven to be the most simple, the most efficient and the easiest to use under a wide variety of circumstances. It has been used effectively in American, Canadian, French, English, German and Scandinavian genealogical research. It is readily adaptable to modern technological advances in data processing and photography. It is one of the systems most compatible with the Name Tabulation program of the Genealogical Society of Utah. We invite all researchers who desire to organize their materials efficiently and effectively to put this system to the test — you'll not be disappointed.

²Other pedigree charts are available. See David E. Gardner, Derek Harland and Frank Smith, *Basic Course in Genealogy, Volume I: Introduction to Record Keeping and Research* (Salt Lake City: Bookcraft, 1958), 233-56. Except for special research projects or wall display they do not present a true picture and are often complicated to fill out.

³Some married couples prefer to place one of their children on line 1, the husband on line 2 and the wife on line 3. They then pursue their research as a cooperative venture. If both sets of ancestors come from the same geographical area, this is usually the most economical and efficient way to proceed.

⁴Few genealogical books deal with the intricacies of how to enter data on genealogical forms. Two have been prepared by the Church of Jesus Christ of Latter-day Saints. Both are now out of print but they can be found in many research libraries. See Gardner, Harland and Smith, *Basic Course I* and *Genealogical Instruction Manual* (Salt Lake City: Genealogical Society, 1965).

⁵The use of electronic computers in genealogy can simplify notekeeping but the expense is still quite high. Punched cards of uniform size can be used as worksheets and sorted on a mechanical sorter at a local computer center. As these become more numerous the cost may come within the range of practicability for note-taking. See A. C. Foskett, *A Guide to Personal Indexes Using Edge-Notched and Peek-a-boo Cards* (Hamden, Conn.: Archon Books, 1967) for the procedures to follow in coding and punching the cards.

⁶Altick, *Literary Research*, 176.

⁷Wagner, *Ancestry*, 11. See also C. G. Crump, *History and Historical Research* (London: Routledge and Sons, 1928), 2-11.

⁸Some researchers prefer to have photocopies of each document they search in the enclosure file. If there is any question concerning the extract on the worksheet the document is available for easy reference. In this case, there will be an enclosure number for every search. Wide-spread access to copy facilities in most record repositories and inexpensive cost for legible reproduction brings this adaptation within the reach of anyone interested. The use of a standard camera by the researcher himself or his agent reduces the cost considerably. See Otto R. Croy, *Camera Copying and Reproduction* (London: Focal Press, 1964) for photocopying non-book records — coins, paintings, wood, stone, stained glass or textiles. Robert Simmons, *Close-up Photography and Copying* (Philadelphia: Chilton, 1961) discusses specific techniques to copy books and manuscripts. The photo reflex or contact photography process is another alternative. Using sensitized paper, a sheet of glass to hold the paper in contact with the document and a 100 watt light bulb, even the most inexperienced can reproduce documents for genealogical research inexpensively. See particularly W. C. E. Hartley, "Document Copying," *Amateur Historian*, II (1956), 311-12 and H. W. Greenwood *Document Photography* (London: Focal Press, 1947). Consult also Laurence A. Cummings, "Pitfalls of Photocopy Research," *Bulletin of the New York Public Library*, LXV (1961), 97-101 for some of the disadvantages and problems of working with photocopies rather than extracts or originals.

⁹Several varieties can be obtained from genealogical supply dealers. Write Genealogical Copy Service, 1010 West 1500 South, Woods Cross, Utah 84087 for the dealer nearest you from whom the forms illustrated in this book can be obtained.

Chapter Three.

¹Vincent L. Jones, "Make A Preliminary Survey," *Instructor*, XCV (1960), 172-73.

[2]Some pedigrees can be efficiently surveyed all at one time because the people involved come from the same general locality and have similar backgrounds. Some pedigrees are so diverse, however, that it is better to split them into sections and survey them one at a time. This requires greater planning and care. Be sure that ancestors are grouped together for efficient searching in each jurisdiction you search to avoid needless re-visiting of relatives and re-checking of *survey* sources.

[3]Write Genealogical Copy Service, 1010 West 1500 South, Woods Cross, Utah, 84087 for the dealer nearest you from whom the survey outline pictured in this book may be obtained.

Chapter Four.

[1]One exception exists: relatives who are actively engaged in genealogical research themselves. See page 61 below.

[2]Donald Lines Jacobus, "Traditions and Family History," *American Genealogy,* IX (1932-33), 1-4.

[3]Harland, *Basic Course II,* 22.

[4]Adapted from the original in the author's possession.

[5]Arthur Ponsby, *English Diaries from the Sixteenth to the Twentieth Centuries* (London: Metheun, & Co., 1922).

[6]Many diaries, memoirs and autobiographies have been published. Consult Louis Kaplan, *et. al., A Bibliography of American Autobiographies* (Madison: University of Wisconsin Press, 1961); Eugene F. MacPike, "English, Scottish and Irish Diaries, Journals, Commonplace Books, 1550-1900: A Bibliographical Guide to Selected Source Material," *Bulletin of Bibliography,* XVII (1941), 183, 213. Also issued separately. William Matthews, *American Diaries: An Annotated Bibliography of Those Written Prior to the Year 1861* (Boston: J. S. Canner & Co., 1959); *British Autobiographies: An Annotated Bibliography* (Berkeley: University of California Press, 1955) and *British Diaries: An Annotated Bibliography* (Berkeley: University of California Press, 1950). Davis Bitton, Professor of History at the University of Utah, is presently compiling a bibliography of manuscript and printed pioneer diaries and journals with their locations. Preliminary lists are available in the Western Americana Room at the University and in the L.D.S. Church Historian's Office.

[7]The student may wish to learn more about these unique documents of the past in Edward Chiera, *They Wrote on Clay: Babylonian Tablets Speak Today,* ed. by George C. Cameron (Chicago: Chicago University Press, 1938).

[8]Frances Baker, "Romance from an Old Account Book," *Instructor,* (Jan. 1964), 20-22.

[9]See W. V. Bingham and B. V. Moore, *How to Interview* (3rd edition. New York: Harper & Brothers, 1941) and Stewart Harral, *Keys to Successful Interviewing* (Norman: University of Oklahoma Press, 1954).

[10]The student might enjoy reading Robin W. Winks, *The Historian as Detective: Essays on Evidence* (New York: Harper & Row, 1968). This is a fascinating collection of readings from famous historians on the investigation of historical evidence with references to detective and mystery who-done-its which use similar techniques.

[11]For additional details consult, Archibald F. Bennett, *A Guide for Genealogical Research* (Salt Lake City: Genealogical Society, 1951. 2d edition, 1956), 44 ff; Cache Genealogical Library, *A Handbook for Genealogical Correspondence* (Salt Lake City: Bookcraft, 1963) and J. R. Gobble, *What to Say in Your Genealogical Letters: Do's and Don't's in Genealogical Correspondence* (Idaho Falls: For the Author, 1967).

298

¹²The current directory can be obtained from 108 Sea Lane Ferring, Sussex, England.

Chapter Five.

¹Printed in *Visitation of Warwick, 1619 by William Camden, Clarenceux,* edited by John Fetherston (London: Harleian Society, 1877).

²During the Tudor period in England, heralds of the College of Arms were commissioned to examine evidences of right to bear coats of arms and to prevent unlawful assumptions of arms and titles. These heralds visitations created pedigrees as by-products of their official duties — public records. Many printed volumes are called visitations, but few of the official records have appeared in print. Some early ones were published by the Camden Society (1849) and the Surtees Society (1859). In 1869, the Harleian Society began publishing visitation pedigrees and many volumes to date have appeared. Many of those printed are based upon copies three or four times removed from the originals. Others are based on comparison of the originals with manuscript copies and are carefully edited. These considerations influence their reliability. Consult Wagner, *Ancestry* and G. D. Squibb, "Visitation Pedigrees and the Genealogist," *Genealogist's Magazine,* XIII (1960), 225-36, 266-73. Squibb compares the printed ones with the originals to assess their accuracy.

³Edward A. Fitch, "Historians of Essex: Nicholas Tindal," *Essex Review* II (1893), 177.

⁴This is discussed in greater detail in Chapter Eight.

⁵Arlene H. Eakle, "Fieldwork in History: Research Techniques of Three Renaissance Local Historians," *Aspects of English History: Three Studies* (M. A. Thesis, University of Utah, 1971), 36-68.

⁶Consult the following references for coverage and contents: H. A. Doubleday and William Page, *A Guide to the Victoria History of the Counties of England* (London: A. Constable & Co., 1903); R. P. Pugh, "The Structure and Aims of the Victoria County Histories of the Counties of England," *Bulletin of the Institute of Historical Research,* XL (1967), 65-73. For an assessment of the accuracy of the volumes, see Lawrence Stone, "The Elizabethan Aristocracy — A Restatement," *Economic History Review,* 2d Series, IV (1952), 309-10.

⁷There is no comprehensive bibliography of these works but an annotated bibliography of printed and manuscript histories written in England, 1500-1800 is under preparation by Arlene H. Eakle. Nearly 3,000 titles have been listed. The Short Title Catalogues of books printed in England and Europe from the beginning of printing to 1700 include local and family histories. University Microfilms (Ann Arbor, Mich.) is microfilming English works and the University of Kentucky (Lexington) is microfilming Italian works. These copies are available in many large research libraries. Books in the series for France, Germany, Netherlands and the Scandinavian countries are also available.

⁸The reader may enjoy the experiences of John E. Cussans when he compiled his *History of Hertfordshire,* 3 vols., written between 1870-1881, as described by W. Branch Johnson, "Behind a County History," *Amateur Historian,* III (1957-58), 253-56.

⁹L. G. Pine, *Genealogists Encyclopedia* (Newton-Abbott: David & Charles, 1969), 221.

¹⁰See Randolph S. Churchill, *Winston S. Churchill: Youth, 1874-1900* (Boston: Houghton-Mifflin, 1966).

[11]The extensive collections of British landed and titled pedigrees published by the Burke family are discussed and evaluated in the following articles by L. G. Pine: "Introduction," *Burke's Landed Gentry,* 1952 edition. This edition contains a series of articles on the compiling of British pedigrees which do not appear in other editions. "Truth in Genealogy, the Work of Genealogical Reference Books," *Quarterly Review of London,* CCXCVIII (1960), 170-77. "The Work of Burke's Peerage, Ltd.," *Armorial,* I (1959), 29-34.

[12]See the *Catalogues of the Manuscript Collections of the British Museum,* 1962 edition. See also the section on guides to manuscripts in Appendix Three below.

[13]This section is necessarily brief because 1) these records are consulted only if you are led to them by clues in the preliminary survey, 2) they are considered primary sources, better searched during the research phase of genealogy and 3) they will be covered in greater detail in subsequent volumes in this series.

[14]See Appendix Two for institutional jurisdictions pertaining to the L.D.S. pedigree and how to search them.

[15]See Chapter Ten for effective use of libraries.

[16]See pages 200-03 below for guidelines to follow when using a field researcher.

[17]Sir Anthony R. Wagner, *English Genealogy* (Oxford: Oxford University Press, 1960), 359.

[18]The only exception to this rule comes if the collection will not be available for seaching after the pre-search analysis is completed. If this is the case, perform a brief analysis of the survey findings to date, on that portion of the pedigree affected. Consult directions in Chapters Six through Nine below and then outline your search in the collection. Realize that to search research sources prematurely is a compromise of research standards and can create walls on your pedigree. But if extenuating circumstances dictate the compromise, so state the situation on your calendar and proceed with the search as outlined.

Chapter Six.

[1]Tape or other kinds of recordings, motion picture films, still photographs and other products of the mechanical age in which we live are also primary sources.

[2]Genealogy has been compared to a court of law. While some similarities do exist, there are some essential differences due to the ultimate purposes of each. The judge must resolve a dispute between two parties, at the same time safeguarding the individual rights of both. He cannot break the legal rules imposed to seek the truth. The genealogist, however is bound by no such rules. In a court of law, public documents admissable before a judge must be produced in the line of duty; they must still be retained by the original creating authority. Evidence which does not point directly at the issue at hand is irrelevant. The genealogist is not forced to accept such rigid standards. Documents are admissable regardless of the depository in which they are found or the circumstances under which they were created. Those documents most often declared irrelevant in a court of law are those of most value to the genealogist. Squibb, "Visitation Pedigrees," 225. See also the table of evidence and its genealogical value in Noel C. Stevenson, "The Rules of Evidence: A Standard for Proving Pedigrees," *Genealogical Research: Methods and Sources* (Washington: American Society of Genealogists, 1960), 47-48. The genealogist, unlike the lawyer or judge, does not select "best" evidence or "best" documents. The genealogist searches *all existing sources* which pertain to the pedigree. He compares the evidence from each one and the only time "best" evidence has a determining say is when two or more documents are in conflict. The dependability of each, in terms of authenticity and credibility, is determined and that which is "best" is used to resolve the conflict. See Nicholas Rescher

and Carey B. Joynt, "Evidence in History and in the Law," *Journal of Philosophy*, LVI (1959), 561-78. Genealogy, like history, cannot always be answered with direct (demonstrable) proof but must be satisfied with probable or plausible proof. Critical analysis of all existing sources can provide a high degree of probability. See Cantor, *How to Study History*, 176-80.

[3]Cummings, "Pitfalls of Photocopy Research," 97-101.

[4]Robert P. Newman and Dale R. Newman, *Evidence* (Boston: Houghton-Mifflin, 1969), 71 and Winks, *Historian as Detective*, 52. Asking intelligent questions is an art which can be learned. Consult Stanley L. Payne, *The Art of Asking Questions* (Princeton: Princeton University Press, 1951) for directions in framing significant questions.

[5]This section is based on Altick, *Literary Research*, 43-44; George J. Lacey, "Questioned Documents," *American Archivist*, IX (1946), 267-75; Wilson R. Harrison, *Suspect Documents: Their Scientific Examination* (London: Sweet and Maxwell, 1958) and L. C. Hector, *Paleography and Forgery* (York: St. Anthony's Press, 1959).

[6]There is no manual of diplomatics in English. There are two foreign treatises which cover the subject in detail: Harry Bresslau, *Handbuch der Urkundenlehre fur Deutschland und Italien* (2 vols. Leipzig: 1912-13) and Arthur Giry, *Manuel de diplomatique* (Paris: 1849. Reprinted, 1925).

[7]To arrive at the correct date, consult: Helen L. Chatfield, "The Dating of Documents," *American Archivist*, XXIV (1961), 171-74; C. R. Cheyney, *Handbook for Students of English History* (London: Royal Historical Society, 1945); John A. Dahl, *Conversion Tables: Republican Calendar-Gregorian Calendar* (Salt Lake City: Service Press, 1968); Donald L. Jacobus, "Dates and the Calendar," *American Genealogist*, IX (1933), 130, 227; and D. A. MacKay, "The Dating of Records," *Amateur Historian*, II (1955), 176-80.

[8]For dating paper by weave or material content, see Gordon A. Johans, "A Brief History of Paper," *Book Collector's Quarterly*, XV (1934), 50 ff.

[9]Consult: Alfred J. Fairbank, *Renaissance Handwriting: An Anthology of Italic Scripts* (Cleveland: World Publishing Co., 1960); L. C. Hector, *The Handwriting of English Documents* (London: Edward Arnold, Ltd., 1958. Revised edition, 1966); Jerome B. Lauay, *Disputed Handwriting: With Illustrations and Expositions for the Detection and Study of Forgery by Handwriting of all Kinds* (Chicago: 1909); W. Le Hardy, "How to Read Seventeenth Century Handwriting," *Amateur Historian*, I (1953), 146-54; Roy Nash, *American Writing Masters and Copybooks . . . Through Colonial Times* (Boston: Colonial Society of Massachusetts, 1959); and K. C. Newton, "Reading Medieval Local Records," *Amateur Historian*, III (1956-57), 81-94.

[10]R. B. Haselden, in his *Scientific Aids for the Study of Manuscripts* (Oxford: Bibliographic Society, 1935), has prepared a checklist for the examination of manuscripts to determine their authenticity and validity as historical documents. He suggests the use of mechanical devices to detect forgeries and tampering. The genealogist would be well rewarded for time spent with this checklist. Far too many genealogists are ill-equipped to use original documents — unedited, uncopied and unevaluated. The volume also contains some excellent examples of reading manuscripts with the aid of ultra-violet light. For additional information on forgery and how to detect it, check C.N.L. Brooke, "Approaches to Medieval Forgery," *Journal of the Society of Archivists*, III (1968), 377-86; and D.A. MacKay, "The Historian and the Forger," *Amateur Historian*, III (1957), 105-08.

[11]This section is based on the following references: Richard Clayton, *Evidence in a Nutshell* (London: Sweet and Maxwell, 1970); Cantor, *How to Study History*, Chaps. iii-iv; Louis Gottschalk, *Understanding History* (New York: Alfred A. Knopf, 1961) chap. vii; Thomas Woody, "Of History and Its Method," *Journal of*

Experimental Education, XV (1947), 175-201; Newman and Newman, *Evidence,* chap. v; Carter V. Good, *Introduction to Educational Research* (New York: Appleton-Century Crofts, 1963), chap. iv and Davis Bitton, "Impact of the New World on Europe," Lecture for History 509, University of Utah, 20 Jan. 1971.

[12]Consult: Anglo-American Historical Committee, "Report on Editing Historical Documents," *Bulletin of the Institute of Historical Research,* II (1923-24), 6-25; British Records Association, *Notes for the Guidance of Editors of Record Publications: A Report . . .* (London: British Records Association, 1946); Lyman H. Butterfield, "Editing American Historical Documents," *Massachusetts Historical Society Proceedings,* LXXVIII (1966), 81-104; and Clarence C. Carter, *Historical Editing* (Washington: National Archives, 1952). These works are written to establish guidelines so that the printing of manuscripts might be quality-controlled. They will help the researcher understand the things considered important for quality editing and provide a basis for comparison with the work actually done.

[13]John Norden, *Speculi Britanniae Pars: A Topographical and Historical Description of Cornwall* (London: William Pearson, 1728. Reprinted, Newcastle-Upon-Tyne: Frank Graham, 1966).

[14]See J.W. Saunders, "The Stigma of Print," *Essays in Criticism,* I (1951), 139 ff and Henry Fishwicke, "Tim Bobbin versus John Whitaker," *Lancashire and Cheshire Antiquarian Society Transactions,* XIII (1895), 19-26.

[15]E.H. Bates, "Thomas Gerard of Trent, His Family and His Writings," *Dorset Natural History Society Proceedings,* XXXV (1914). 55-70.

[16]See Martin A. Roberts, "Records in the Copyright Office of the Library of Congress Deposited by the U.S. District Courts, 1790-1870," *Papers of the Bibliographic Society of America,* XXXI (1937), II, 81-101. For pseudonyms and pen-names consult: William Cushing, *Initials and Pseudonyms: A Dictionary of Literary Disguises* (Waltham, Mass.: Mark Press, Inc., 1963. Reprint of 1885 edition); Samuel Halkett and John Laing, *Dictionary of Anonymous and Pseudonymous English Literature* (4 vols. Edinburgh: 1882-88. Revised edition, Edinburgh: 1926-34); Richard Kleiner, *Index of Initials and Acronyms* (Princeton: Auerbach, 1971); and Archer Taylor and Frederic J. Mosher, *Bibliographic History of Anonyma and Pseudonyma* (Chicago: Newberry Library, 1950). For licenses to print consult: Edward Arber, *Transcript of the Registers of the Stationers' Company, 1557-1640* (5 vols. London: Privately printed, 1875-1894); G. E. B. Eyre, *Transcript of the Worshipful Company of Stationers from 1640-1708* (London: Privately printed, 1913-14); and W. W. Greg and E. Boswell, *Records of the Court of Stationers Company of London* (2 vols. London: Bibliographical Society of London, 1930).

[17]Winks, *Historian as Detective,* 541. This section includes material from Ralph G. Plumb, "County Histories," *Wisconsin Magazine of History,* XXXVI (1952-53); Donald L. Jacobus, "Errors in Genealogical Books," *American Genealogist,* X (1934), 129-33; Allan G. Bogue, "Iowa Claims Clubs," *Mississippi Valley Historical Review,* XLV (1958), 233 note; and Robert Douch, *A Handbook of Local History: Dorset* (Bristol: University of Bristol, 1962).

[18]Wagner, *Ancestry,* 151. Anthony a Wood, *Athenae Oxoniensis: An Exact History of all the Writers and Bishops Who Have Had Their Education in the Most Antient and Famous University of Oxford* (2 vols. London: 1691-92 and many subsequent editions). See J. Milton French, "The Reliability of Anthony Wood and Milton's Oxford M.A.," *Publications of the Modern Language Association,* LXXV (1960), 22-30 and J. B. Primrose, "The First Review of *Athenae Oxoniensis,*" *Bodleian Quarterly Record,* VIII (1936), 206-07.

[19]Edward A. Finch, "Historians of Essex: Philip Morant," *Essex Review,* III (1894), 238.

[20]*Transactions of the Essex Archaeological Society,* III (1865), 196.

[21]If you and your spouse are performing a preliminary survey as a joint project, the first sheet completed will show your husband or wife, yourself and your children. Your pedigree chart will begin with the name of one of your children and you and your spouse will appear on lines 2 and 3 of the chart. If your surveys are separate you will appear as a child on the first sheet compiled and your pedigree chart will begin with you. Your records, however, should also contain a fully documented sheet for your individual family unit — your husband or wife, yourself and your children.

Chapter Seven.

[1]By "existing" we mean those which are accessible with no restrictions placed upon them by the creator, the present owner or the depository in which they are preserved. Some records are closed because they are less than 100 years old, others are closed because of their poor physical condition and some are closed because the original creator or the present owner, for personal reasons, refuses to make them available. Obviously, the researcher is handicapped by such limitations. But there may come a time when these will be lifted, then the records should be searched and their data added. See also Gardner, *Basic Course I,* 327, 340 and Harland, *Basic Course II, 21.*

[2]See Frank Smith and David Gardner, *Genealogical Research in England and Wales* (Salt Lake City: Bookcraft, 1964) III, 129.

Chapter Eight.

[1]See also Philip C. Brooks, *Research in Archives* (Chicago: University of Chicago Press, 1969).

[2]See also Bruce Dickens, "The Progress of English Place-names Studies since 1901," *Antiquity,* XXXV (1961), 281-85; and Richard B. Sealock, *Bibliography of Place-names Literature in the United States and Canada* (2d edition. Chicago: American Library Association, 1967). *Bullinger's Postal and Shippers Guide* for the United States and Canada and *Directories of Post Offices* (American and English) are also very helpful. Al Smith's *Dictionary of City of London Street Names* (New York: Arco Publishing Co., Inc., 1970) is entertaining and valuable.

[3]Consult Edward M. Douglas, *Boundaries, Areas, Geographic Centers and Altitudes of the United States and the Several States with a Brief Record of Important Changes in their Territory and Government* (2d edition. Washington: Government Printing Office, 1932) and Joseph M. Kane, *The American Counties* (New York: Scarecrow Press, 1960) for changes in American national, state and county boundaries.

[4]The *Handbook for Genealogical Correspondence* prepared by the Cache Genealogical Library (1963) contains additional details on sources and descriptions of maps, atlases and gazeteers of the world.

[5]See R. E. Harrison, "Evaluation of Modern Maps," *Special Libraries,* XLIV (1953), 45-47.

[6]The following list of bibliographies will also help to locate contemporary maps:

> Chubb, T. *The Printed Maps in the Atlases of Great Britain and Ireland: A Bibliography, 1579-1870.* London: Homeland Association, 1927. Reprinted.

> *Civil War Maps in the National Archives.* Washington: National Archives, 1964.

> Goodman, Marie C. *Map Collections in the United States and Canada: A Directory.* New York: Special Libraries Association, 1954.

Ladd, Richard S. *Maps Showing Explorer's Routes, Trails and Early Roads in the United States: An Annotated List.* Washington: Library of Congress, 1962.

LeGeer, Clara E. *United States Atlases: A Catalog of National, State, County, City and Regional Atlases in the Library of Congress.* 2 vols. Washington: Library of Congress, 1953. This is a supplement to Phillips (see below).

Phillips, P. L. *A list of the Maps of America in the Library of Congress.* Washington: Government Printing Office, 1901.

_____ . *A list of Geographical Atlases in the Library of Congress.* 4 vols. Washington: Government Printing Office, 1909-1920.

Riston, Walter W. "What About Maps?" *Library Trends,* IV (1955), 123-39.

Rodger, E. M. *The Large Scale County Maps of the British Isles, 1596-1850: A Union List.* Oxford: Bodleian Library, 1960.

Shull, Tressie N. "County Atlases for Genealogical Use," *National Genealogical Society Quarterly,* XXXVII (1949), 4-11.

Skelton, Raleigh A. *County Atlases of the British Isles, 1579-1850: A Bibliography.* London: British Museum, 1964.

Wright, John K. *Aids to Geographical Research: Bibliographies, Periodicals, Atlases, Gazeteers and Other Reference Books.* New York: Columbia University Press, 1947.

[7]Write Genealogical Copy Service, 1010 West 1500 South, Woods Cross, Utah 84087, for the dealer nearest you from whom this research outline can be obtained.

[8]See Elizabeth B. Wood, "Pots and Pans History: Relating Manuscripts and Printed Sources to the Study of Domestic Art Objects," *American Archivist,* XXX (1967), 431-42.

Chapter Nine.

[1]Indexes to United States censuses are being prepared so rapidly that it is difficult to keep up with them. Gendex Corporation, Provo, Utah and the Association for Records and Census Indexing, Arlington, Virginia are directing large projects which appear in printed form as they are completed. State libraries and archives, historical societies and individual groups are also at work. Be sure to check for indexes which apply to the areas where your ancestors resided. They can be real time-savers.

[2]See Bibliographies at the end of this volume.

[3]Full instructions for calculating dates can be found in Harland, *Basic Course II,* 104-17.

[4]Similar source materials are available for other countries of the world (see Appendix Three). A research outline for English national sources is under preparation. Write Genealogical Copy Service, 1010 West 1500 South, Woods Cross, Utah, 84087 for the dealer nearest you.

Chapter Ten.

[1]The authors are presently compiling a detailed study of American source materials and their genealogical application. See also Appendix Three and the Bibliographies at the end of this volume.

[2]This section is based upon Hattie Knight, *The 1-2-3 Guide to Libraries* (Provo, Ut.: Brigham Young University, 1964).

[3]We are indebted to Delbert E. Roach, Librarian of the Genealogical Society Library in Salt Lake City for this material.

[4]Bennion, *Genealogical Research, a Practical Mission*, 26.

[5]Additional information on reading handwriting may be found in the following bibliography:

> Bennion, Howard S. *Genealogical Research, A Practical Mission*. Salt Lake City: Deseret News Press, 1964, Chapter 10.
>
> Bennett, Archibald F. *A Guide to Genealogical Research*. Salt Lake City: Genealogical Society, 1959, Appendix 2, 3.
>
> Bolton, C. D. "Colonial Handwriting", *Essex Antiquarian*, I (1897) 175-76.
>
> Emmison, F. G. *How to Read Local Archives, 1550-1700*. London: Historical Association, 1967.
>
> Johnasson, Carl-Erik. *How They Wrote; a Guide to the Baltic Script of Scandinavia; Denmark, Norway, Finland, Sweden*. Provo, Utah: Brigham Young University Press, 1970.
>
> Kirkham, E. Kay. *How to Read the Handwriting and Early Records of America*. Salt Lake City: Deseret Book, 1961.
>
> Martin, Charles T. *The Record Interpreter*. London: Stevens & Sons, Ltd., 1960. Reprinted, 1969.
>
> Parkes, M. B. *English Cursive Book Hands, 1250-1500*. Oxford: Clarenden Press, 1969.
>
> Smith, Frank and Gardner, David E. *Genealogical Research in England and Wales*. Salt Lake City: Bookcraft, 1965, III, 1-122. Includes valuable bibliography.
>
> Whalley, J. I. *English Handwriting, 1540-1853*. London: H.M.S.O., 1970.

[6]Williams, *Know Your Ancestors*, 273.

[7]Brooks, *Research in Archives*, 50.

[8]See William N. Bischoff, "Tracing Manuscript Sources," *Oregon Historical Quarterly*, LI (1950), 156-63.

[9]See G. Barraclough, "The Historian and His Archives," *History Today*, IV (1954), 412-20.

[10]Winks, *Historian as Detective*, 117-18.

[11]Robert J. Tarte, "New England Analysis," Lecture delivered at the Genealogical Research Seminar, August 4, 1971, Brigham Young University, Provo, Utah.

[12]Some researchers include a tape recorder or typewriter and a camera as essential research equipment. If you use these, be sure you know how to operate them properly and consult the library before using them.

[13]Roger C. Flick, "General U.S. Library Reference Materials," a lecture delivered at the Genealogical Research Seminar, August 4, 1971, Brigham Young University, Provo, Utah.

[14]Winchell, Constance M. *Locating Books for Interlibrary Loan with a Bibliography of Printed Guides which Show Locations of Books in American Libraries*. New York: H. W. Wilson, 1930.

¹⁵For Union Catalogs of other materials which are available, consult Arthur Berthold; *Union Catalogs: A Select Bibliography* (Philadelphia: Union Library Catalog, 1936). Reprinted in R. B. Downs, *Union Catalogues in the United States* (Chicago: American Library Association, 1942), 349-91.

¹⁶An abstract, if made properly, contains the essential information and clues in the document.

Chapter Eleven.

¹Wagner, *Ancestry*, 144. See Gardner, Harland and Smith, *Basic Course I*, chap. vii for a discussion of varying kinds of collateral relationships.

²In spite of the common belief among many genealogists today, church registers and vital statistics do not provide the best proof of relationship. Property records — land, probate, court, chattel and tax records — found in great abundance throughout the world, provide much better proof. Some of the problems associated with relationship and its designations in records are discussed in B. S. Bramwell, "Frequency of Cousin Marriages," *Genealogists Magazine*, VIII (1939), 305 ff; C. E. Gilliam, "Mr. in Virginia Records before 1776," *William and Mary Quarterly*, (1939); and Donald L. Jacobus, "Interpreting Genealogical Records," *American Genealogist*, X (1933), 2-6; XI (1934), 9-11; XIX (1942), 8-10.

³See Frank W. Klingberg, *The Southern Claims Commission* (Berkeley: University of California Press, 1955).

⁴See the statement by Kenneth A. Lockridge in *William and Mary Quarterly*, XXV (1968), 516-17, based on his study of the wills and probates of Essex, Middlesex, Suffolk, Berkshire and Hampshire counties in Massachusetts, Hartford and Fairfield counties in Connecticut and all of New Hampshire. Italics added for emphasis.

⁵J. T. Krause, "The Changing Adequacy of English Registration, 1690-1837," *Population in History*, ed. by D. V. Glass and D. E. C. Eversley (London: Edward Arnold, 1965), 379-93.

⁶For additional insight from demography see E. A. Wrigley, An Introduction to English Historical Demography (London: Weidenfeld and Nicolson, 1966) and T. H. Hollingsworth, *Historical Demography* (London: Camelot Press, 1969). See also *National Index of Parish Registers: Volume I, General Articles*, published by the Society of Genealogists (1968).

Chapter Twelve.

¹Welsh oral pedigrees, which date from the early medieval period, have finally been accepted as authentic by the College of Arms in England. We thank Dr. Lewis Marx, Professor of Biology at St. Joseph's College, Philadelphia for this note. The Genealogical Society of Utah is recording oral pedigrees and family histories of the Polynesians and some Indian groups. At the present time, the data is being fed directly into electronic computer bases and will be available for searching in the future.

Appendix One.

¹See Harold G. Clark, *Families, Families, Families: How Do You Keep Them Together?* (Provo, Utah: Brigham Young University, 1965).

²If the father becomes incapacitated or otherwise unable to function, the Board of Directors should make him Honorary President and select another to carry out his responsibilities.

³In very large organizations where the members are spread over wide geographical

areas, it is effective to create subordinate organizations comprising family units living within these areas. A chairman and secretary can be appointed to oversee and correlate activities. These chairmen may serve as vice presidents on the governing board of the large organization.

[3]Major branch: If there are 7 children, the family organization will have 7 major branches—each child and his posterity (spouse and descendants) constituting a major branch.

[5]Adapted from Audrey Frecker and Harleigh Frecker, *How to Work With Groups* (n.p., Y.M.C.A, n.d.). Used with permission from the Salt Lake City unit of Y.M.C.A.

[6]See also Charles L. B. Lourdes, "Tax Advantages of Charitable Gifts," *Virginia Law Review*, XLVI (1960), 409-12 and Martin M. Love, "When Not to Apply for Advanced Ratings from the Internal Revenue Service," *Journal of Taxation*, XII (1960), 244.

Appendix Three.

[1]Prior to 1955, accessions and migrations were published in the *Bulletin of the Institute of Historical Research* (London University).

[2]The next volume in this series, *American Research Sources* contains a detailed discussion of claims made against the United States Government. These records are located in government documents.

[3]Robert J. Tarte, "New England Analysis." Write for National Archives *General Information Leaflet* # 22, which is free upon request. Those records on microfilm can be borrowed on interlibrary loan through local university libraries or departments of history.

[4]Oscar Handlin, *et. al.*, *Harvard Guide to American History* (Cambridge: Harvard University Press, 1954), 87-88.

[5]For national libraries in other countries of the world, their collections and services, see the July, 1955 issue of *Library Trends*.

[6]Arthur J. Willis, *Introducing Genealogy* (London: Ernest Benn, Ltd., 1961), 17.

[7]See *Library Association Record* (1962), 269-83 for a tabulation of results.

[8]Tarte, *op. cit.*

BOOKS ON GENEALOGICAL RESEARCH
AND NOTEKEEPING

Aett Festskrift til Finne-Groun. Om Nordisk slegtforskning og Oslo byhistorie. Oslo: 1944.

Allende, Francisco de Cadensas y, *et. al.* Apuntes de nobiliaria y nociones de genealogia y heraldica, curso de grado. Madrid: Eliciones Hidalguia, 1960.

American Association for State and Local History. Genealogical Research: A Basic Guide. Technical leaflet # 14. 1969.

Beckman, Bjarne. Till medeltidsgenealogiens metodik. Linkoging: Ostgota correspondenten, 1959.

Bela, Kempeleon. A Nemesseg Utmutato az Osszes Nemessegi Ugyckben. Genealogiae es Heraldikai Kezikonyv. Budapest: Benko Gyula Knyvkereskedese, 1907.

Bennett, Archibald F. Advanced Genealogical Research. Salt Lake City: Deseret Book Co., 1959.

_____. Finding Your Forefathers in America. Salt Lake City: Deseret Book Co., 1957.

_____. A Guide for Genealogical Research. Salt Lake City: Genealogical Society, 1957. 2d edition, 1960.

Bennion, Howard S. Genealogical Research: A Practical Mission. Salt Lake City: Deseret News Press, 1964. Also Teacher's Supplement.

Bidlack, Russell E. First Steps in Climbing the Family Tree. Detroit: Detroit Society for Genealogical Research, 1962.

Bird, Jack. "Some Sources for French Genealogy and Heraldry," Genealogists Magazine, XIII (1960), 237ff.

_____. "Some Sources for German Genealogy and Heraldry," Genealogists Magazine, XIII (1960), 143.

Blakelock, M. P. Your Family History: How to Trace it and Record It. London: Wells Gardner, 1931.

Bolton, C. K. Genealogical Research in Libraries. Salem: 1895.

Borgomale, H. L. Rabino di. "Genealogical Research in France," Genealogists Magazine, X (1946), 1-7.

Boykin, Phyllis M. and Porter, Donna J. The Welding Link: A Training Course in Genealogy. Denver: Boykin-Porter, 1967.

Brenner, Alfred. Slaktforskning. Praktisk handbok for Finland. Helsinki: 1947.

Bushby, Gladys and Fish, Evelyn. Practical Research in Genealogy: A Compilation of Genealogical Research Data. Mesa, Arizona: Arizona Temple District Genealogical Library, 1955.

Camajari, Count Guelfo Guelfi. "Some Sources for Italian Genealogy," Genealogistš Magazine, XIV (1962), 66.

Cache Genealogical Library. Handbook for Genealogical Correspondence. Salt Lake City: Bookcraft, 1963.

Camp, Anthony J. Tracing Your Ancestors. London: Foyle's, 1964.

Campbell, Colin. [Articles in French and English on Genealogy and Heraldry reprinted from Various Periodicals], 1956 —.

Canyon Rim Stake. German Genealogical Research: Supplementary Materials. Used in a Course. N. p., n.d.

Cappon, Lester J. "Genealogy: Handmaid of History," National Genealogical Society Quarterly, XLV (1957), 1-9.

Clare, W. A Simple Guide to Irish Genealogy. London: G. E. J. Coldwell, 1938.

Clough, Wilson O. Ancestors All: A Simple, Scientific Method for Recording Ancestors. Laramie, Wyo.: n. p., 1960.

Colaneri, G. Bibliogragia araldica e genealogica d'Italia. Roma: 1904.

Cole, William A. and Jensen, Elwin W. Israel in the Pacific: A Genealogical Text for Polynesia. Salt Lake City: Genealogical Society, 1961.

Crofton, H. A. How to Trace a Pedigree. London: Elliott Stock, 1911.

Daughters of the American Revolution. Is That Lineage Right: A Training Manual. Washington, D.C.: National Society of Daughters of American Revolution, 1958.

Doane, Gilbert H. Searching for Your Ancestors. 2d edition. Minneapolis: University of Minnesota Press, 1952.

Dow, Earl W. Principles of a Note-System for Historical Studies. London: Century, 1924.

Dragsted, Ove. "The Marstrand System of Filing Genealogical Material," Genealogists Magazine, XI (1952), 61-65.

Durye, Pierre. La genealogie. Paris: Presses Universitaires de France, 1961.

E-Z Research Organizer. Salt Lake City: n.d.

Fabritius, Albert. Handbog i slaegtsforskning. Kobenhaven: 1943. 2d edition. Kobenhaven: J. H. Schultz, 1963.

Fahy, T. G. "Genealogical Research in the Netherlands," Genealogists Magazine, XIII (1961), 366.

———————————— "Some Sources for Dutch Genealogy," Genealogists Magazine, XIV (1962), 24.

Falley, Margaret D. Irish and Scotch-Irish Ancestral Research. 2 vols. Privately Printed, 1961-62.

Filby, P. William. American and British Genealogy and Heraldry: A Selected List of Books. Chicago: American Library Association, 1968.

Forst de Battaglia, O. Traite de genealogie. Lausanne: Editions Spes, 1949.

Fotheringham, Ila J. Genealogical Sources for Utah and L.D.S. Church Survey and Research. N. p., 1968.

Gardner, David E., Harland, Derek and Smith, Frank. A Basic Course in

Genealogy, Volume I: Introduction to Record Keeping and Research. Salt Lake City: Bookcraft, 1958.

Genealogical Associates. Genealogy and Local History: An Archival and Bibliographical Guide. Evanston, Ill.: n. p., 1958. In progress.

"Genealogical Research in German-Speaking Lands: A Symposium," National Genealogical Society Quarterly, XLV (1957), 117-29, 203-10. Also issued separately.

Genealogical Society. Papers presented at the World Conference on Records. Several volumes. Salt Lake City: 1969.

Ghens, A. Contribuo alla bibliografia genealogica Italiana. Roma: 1936.

Gobble, John R. Who's Where in Your Genealogical Records? A Filing and Finding System. Idaho Falls, Ida.: n. p., 1963.

Gooch, Roe Ann. The Note Keeper: Genealogical Research, Scientifically Systematized. Salt Lake City: Litho Graphics, 1966.

Gray, Nancy. "Compiling Your Family History: A Guide to Procedure," Descent Journal of the Society of Australian Genealogists, II (1965), 84 ff. Also issued separately.

Gregoire, Jeanne. A la recherche de nos ancetres: guide du genealogiste. Montreal: for the author, 1957.

Hamilton-Edwards, Gerald. In Search of Ancestry. London: Michael Joseph, 1966. Issued in the United States as Tracing Your British Ancestors: A Guide to Genealogical Sources. New York: Walker and Company, 1967.

Hansen, Niel T. Guide to Genealogical Sources: Australia and New Zealand. Melbourne: Melbourne Stake Presidency, 1962.

Harland, Derek. A Basic Course in Genealogy, Volume II: Research Procedure and Evaluation of Evidence. Salt Lake City: Bookcraft, 1958. Reissued as Genealogical Research Standards, 1963.

Heckscher, Ella. Sex kapitel om slaktforskning: kort handledning for amatores. Stockholm: Monnier, 1954. 6th ed. 1966.

Heydenreich, Eduard K. H. Handbuch der praktischen Genealogie. 2 vols. Leipzig: 1913.

Highland Stake. A to Z in Genealogy: Some Basic suggestions on Record Making. Salt Lake City: n. p., 1958.

Hildebrand, Bengt. Handbok i slakt: och personforskning. Stockholm: Wahlstrom & Widstrand, 1961.

Hodgson, P. F. How to Trace Your Own Pedigree. London: 1889.

Holben, Richard E. Researching the Family History for Beginners. Albequerque, N. M.: Family History, 1968.

Holmstrom, J. E. How to Take, Keep and Use Notes. London: Aslib, 1947.

Iredale, David. Your Family Tree: A Handbook on Tracing Your Ancestors and Compiling One's Own Pedigree. Tring, Herts.: Shire Publications, 1970.

Isenburg, Wilhelm C. H. von. Historische genealogie. Berlin: 1940.

Jacobus, Donald Lines. Genealogy as a Pastime and a Profession. New Haven:

Tuttle, Morehouse and Taylor Co., 1930. 2d rev. ed. Baltimore: Genealogical Book Company, 1968.

—————————. "Is Genealogy an Exact Science: Methods of Research," American Genealogist, X (1934), 65-69.

Jacquart, Joseph. Une bibliotheque de genealogiste-amateur; un inventaire un plan. Bruxelles: 1959.

Jaussi, Laureen R. and Chaston, Gloria D. Fundamentals of Genealogical Research. Salt Lake City: Deseret Book Co., 1966.

Johansson, Carl-Erik. Cradled in Sweden: A Practical Help to Genealogical Research in Swedish Records. Provo, Utah: Brigham Young University Press, 1970.

Jones, Frances T. D. "An Approach to Welsh Genealogy," Transactions Honorable Society of Cymmrodorion, 1948 (1949), 303-466.

Jones, Milton J. Genealogical Research Work Book. Salt Lake City: L.D.S. Aids, 1965.

Jones, Vincent L. "Effective Ways to Prepare and Preserve Research Notes," Instructor, (Oct. 1963), 372-74. Also issued separately.

—————————. "Make a Preliminary Survey," Instructor, XCV (1960), 172-73.

—————————. Stamp Out Chaos, Eliminate Confusion. Transcript of Lecture Given April 20, 1963, Mt. Hood Genealogical Forum, Oregon City, Oregon.

Jordan, D. S. and Kimball, S. L. Your Family Tree: Being a Glance at Scientific Aspects of Genealogy. New York: 1929.

Juestrich, Max N. Family History. West New York, N. J.: 1936.

Keech, Gertrude C. Persons, Places and Things. London: Mitre Press, 1961.

Kendall, Henry. The Kinship of Men: An Argument from Pedigrees on Genealogy Viewed as a Science. London: Kegan Paul, 1881.

Kent, D. B. G. "The Study of Ancestry," The Vermonter, XX (1915), 117-22, 141-48.

Kirkham, E. Kay. The ABC's of American Genealogical Research. Salt Lake City: Deseret Book Company, 1954.

—————————. Making the Genealogical Record: An Explanation of the O-Kay System of Record Keeping. Salt Lake City: Deseret Book Co., 1959.

—————————. Research in American Genealogy. Salt Lake City: Deseret Book Co., 1956.

—————————. Simplified Genealogy for Americans. Salt Lake City: Deseret Book Co., 1968.

Klocke, Friedrich von. Die entwicklung der genealogie vom ende des 19 hu zur mitte des 20 jahrhunderts. Schellenberg bei Berchtesgaden: Degener, 1950.

Komaiko, Jean and Rosenthal, Kate. Your Family Tree. New York: Parents Magazine Press, 1963.

Kraz-Ronne, Cato. Mine Forfedre. Anetaole i Listeform et Arbeidshefte. 2 opplag. Oslo: Grondahl & Son, 1959.

Kruimel, Herman L. Handeleiding voor stamboomonderzoek. Rotterdam: H. de Bot, 1952.

Langton, C. "Records and Record Searching in Jersey," Genealogists Magazine, V (1931), 314 ff.

Lea, James H. Genealogical Research in England, Scotland and Ireland: A Handbook for the Student. Boston: for the Author, 1906.

Leader, M. "Irish Records," Genealogists Magazine, XII (1958) 512-15, 549-59.

Library of Congress. Guide to Genealogical Research: A Select List. Washington, D.C.: Library of Congress, n.d.

Lorenz, O. Lehrbuch der gesammten urissenschaftlichen Genealogie. Berlin: 1898.

Lundgren, Victor. Indexing Names to Save Duplications When Researching. Provo, Utah.: J. Grant Stevenson, n.d.

MacLachen, John D. Family Record Book. New York: 1936.

MacPike, E. F. Romance of Genealogy. London: 1912.

Marsay, Jacques M. J. Vicmte de. Methodes critiques en genealogie. Paris: Societe du grand armorial de France, 1946.

Marstrand, Vilhelm. "[Notekeeping System,]" Personalhistorisk Tidsskritt. (1938).

Matthews, J. Hints for Tracing an Anglo-American Pedigree in the Old Country. London: 1902.

Meads, Dorothy M. "Searching Local Records," Review of English Studies, IV (1928), 173-90, 301-22.

Mears, Neal F. What is Up in your Family Tree? Chicago: n. p., 1928.

Mesa Tenth Ward, Primary Sources for Genealogical Research. Mesa, Ariz.: East Mesa Stake, 1965.

Michael, Prudence G. Don't Cry Timber. N. p., 1970.

Mills, William S. Foundations of Genealogy. New York: Monographs Publishing Co., 1899.

Mitgau, Johann H. Standische daseimsformen genealogisch gesehen. Gottingen: Heinz, 1953.

Moore, Russell F. The Family History Book: A Genealogical Record. New York: Simmons-Boardman Publishing Corp., 1961.

Morris, Louise E. B. Primer in Genealogical Research. Dallas: B. & W. Printing and Letter Service, 1965.

Nederhand, Erica H. Ancestral Research in the Netherlands, Textbook: Advanced Study in Dutch Records and Methods of Genealogical Research. N. p., n. d.

Newberry Library. Genealogy Beginners Manual. Chicago: Newberry Library, 1965.

Nerney, Mary C. "Excursion into Genealogy: Immortality in Reverse," Vermont History, XVI (1948), 37-52.

Nichols, Elizabeth L. The Genesis of Your Genealogy: A Simplified Step-by-step Instruction Book for the Beginner in Genealogy. Providence, N. J., for the Author, 1969.

Oates, Addison F. The Art of Collecting Genealogy and History. N. p., 1971.

O Connell, Basil M. [Articles on Genealogy Reprinted from Various Periodicals], 1955 —.

Owen, Joyce D. Let's Climb a Family Tree. N. p., 1967.

Olsson, Nils William. "Tracing Your Swedish Ancestry," Swedish Pioneer Historical Quarterly, XIII (1962). Reprinted Royal Swedish Ministry of Foreign Affairs, Stockholm: 1965.

P. P. The Genealogists Reference Journal. Leicester: P. P., 1925.

Parker, Donald D. Scottish and Scotch-Irish Ancestry Research. N. p., n. d.

Paul, James B. An Essay on How to Write the History of a Family. Edinburg: Oliver & Boyd, 1920.

Pender, S. Guide to Irish Genealogical Collections. Dublin: 1935.

Phillimore, W. P. W. How to Write the History of the Family: A Guide for the Genealogist. Boston: Cupples & Hurd, 1888. 2d ed. 1900. 3d ed. London: 1905 under title, The Family Historian: A Short Guide for Writing and Printing the History of a Family.

——————————— Pedigree Work: Handbook for the Genealogist. London: 1900. 3d ed. London: Phillimores, 1936.

Pine, Leslie G. American Origins. Garden City: Doubleday, 1960. Reissued, Baltimore: Genealogical Book Co., 1967.

——————————— The Genealogists Encyclopedia. Newton-Abbott: David & Charles, 1969.

——————————— Heraldry, Ancestry and Titles: Questions and Answers. Kingswood, Surrey: Elliott Right Way Books, 1965.

——————————— Trace Your Ancestors. London: Evans Bros., 1953.

——————————— Your Family Tree: A Guide to Genealogical Sources. Rev. and exp. ed. London: H. Jenkins, 1962.

Pitoni, Venanzio P. Guidex: Genealogical Research: A Guide to Principal Sources and Indexes. 2d ed. Annapolis: 1946.

Poli, O. de Essai d'introduction a l'histoire genealogique. Paris: 1887.

Powell, Thomas. Direction for the Search of Records. 1622. Reissued as Repertoire of Records. 1631.

Preece, Floren S. and Phyllis P. Preliminary Survey Workbook. N. p., 1966.

Public Archives of Canada. Tracing Your Ancestors in Canada. Ottawa: Public Archives, 1966. Reprinted, Genealogists Magazine, XV (1966), 293 ff.

Reed, Evan L. Ways and Means of Identifying Ancestors. Chicago: Ancestral Publishing and Supply Co., 1947.

——————————— Whence Came You and How to Provide the Answer. Chicago: Ancestral Publishing and Supply Co., 1936.

Reise, Heinz, ed. Quellen zur genealogie. Gottingen: 1965.

Roesler, Gofffried. Neuzeitliche darstellyngsformen familiengeschichtliche forschungsergebnisse am beispiel des debtschen familienarchives. Band 1-12. Neustadt an der Aisch: Verlag Degener, 1960.

Royer, Lucien P. Traite pratique de recherches genealogiques. Paris: Editions Aframpe, 1958.

Rubincam, Milton, ed. Genealogical Research: Methods and Sources. Washington, D.C.: American Society of Genealogists, 1960.

Rye, Walter. Records and Record Searching. London: J. G. Cupples & Co., 1888. 2d ed., 1897. Reprinted, London: Phillimores, 1968 and Baltimore: Genealogical Book Co., 1968.

Saffroy, Gaston. Bibliographie genealogique, heraldique et nobiliaire de la France des origines a nos jours. N. p., for the Author, 1968-1970. 2 vols.

Scheidt, Walter. Livre de raison: Directives et schemas pour establissement de l'histoire de la Famille. Bruxelles: La Roue Solaire, 1943.

Sere, J. Traite de Genealogie. Paris: 78, Rue D'anjou, 1911.

Shephard, Charles. "Genealogical Bibliographies and Handbooks," National Genealogical Society Quarterly, XII (1923), 25-27.

Sims, Richard. A Manual for the Genealogist, Topographer, Antiquary and Legal Professor. London: Edward Avery, 1888.

Smith, Frank and Gardner, David E. Genealogical Research in England and Wales. 3 vols. Salt Lake City: Bookcraft, 1956-1964.

Smith, Frank and Thomsen, Finn A. Genealogical Guidebook and Atlas of Denmark. Salt Lake City: Bookcraft, 1969.

Society of Genealogists. Genealogists Handbook. 3d ed. London: Society of Genealogists, 1961. 5th ed. 1969.

Song, Tal-che. (Korean Letterwriting, Rites and Ceremonies and Genealogy.) N. p., n. d. In Korean.

Slekhistorisk litteratur. Tilvakst, 1943-55. Stavanger, 1955.

Stetson, Oscar F. The Art of Ancestral Hunting: A Guide to Ancestral Research and Genealogy. Brattleboro, Vt.: 1936. 3d ed. New York: Stephen Daye Press, 1956.

Stevenson, J. Grant. A Genealogical Checklist. Provo, Ut.: Stevenson Supply, 1964.

———————————. A Genealogical Study Guide. Provo, Ut.: Stevenson Supply, 1962.

Stevenson, Noel C., ed. The Genealogical Reader. Salt Lake City: Deseret Book Co., 1958.

———————————. Search and Research: The Researchers Handbook. Salt Lake City: Deseret Book Co., 1951. 2d ed. 1959.

Stiles, Henry E. A Handbook of Practical Suggestions for the Use of the Student of Genealogy. Albany: Joel Munsell and Sons, 1899.

Stokvis, A. M. H. J. Manuel d'histoire de genealogie et de chronologie de tous les etats du globe. 3 Vols. Leyden: 1888-91.

314

Swedish Foreign Office. Finding Your Forefathers. Swedish Foreign Office Press and Information Service, 1957.

Tolman, William O. An Introduction to Record Keeping and Research. Provo, Ut.: n.d.

Tupiquy, Jacques Meurgey de. Guide des recherches genealogiques aux archives nationales. Paris: Impr. Nationale, 1953.

Unett, John. Making a Pedigree. London: George Allen & Unwin, Ltd., 1961.

Varennes, Kathleen. Bibliographie annotee d'ouvrages genealogiques a la bibliotheque du Parlement. Ottawa: Library of Parliment, 1963.

Vincent, Vincente de Cadenas y. Tratado de genealogia, heraldica y derech nobiliario curso de licencia; lecciones. Madrid: Hidalguia, 1961.

Wadham, Rex A. and Memmott, Evan H. Creative Genealogy. Provo, Ut.: Offset Copy Co., 1965.

Wagner, Sir Anthony R. English Ancestry. Oxford: University Press, 1961.

——————————. English Genealogy. Oxford: Clarendon Press, 1960.

Wall, Alexander J., "American Genealogical Research," Papers of the Bibliographic Society of America, XXXVI (1942), 305-14.

Wallace, Arthur and Bousfield, Shirley. Record Keeping in Genealogical Research. Los Angeles: Los Angeles Temple Genealogical Library, 1964.

Wasmansdorff, Erich. VDFF: Verzeichnis der familierforscher und familienverbande. Glucksburg: C. A. Starke, 1956.

Watabe, Masao. Our Ancestors. Manuscript on Japanese Genealogical Research. Translated from the Japanese. n.d.

Wecken, Friedrich. Taschenbuch fur familiengeschichtsforschung. Schellenberg bei Berchtesgaden: Degener, 1951.

White, David. Reference Manual for Genealogical Research. Penelyn, Pa.: n. p., 1954.

Willis, Arthur J. Genealogy for Beginners. London: Ernest Benn, Ltd., 1955.

——————————. Introducing Genealogy. London: Ernest Benn, Ltd., 1961.

Wolf, J. C. "Tools and Techniques of Genealogical Research," Indiana Magazine of History, XXXVIII (1942), 93-105.

Worthen, Joyce C. Handbook for Genealogical Research in Japan. n. p., n. d.

Wretman, Johan. Slakt-vetenskapen Med Hansyn till Svensk Forskning. Stockholm: P. A. Norstedt & Soners Forlag, 1924.

Wright, Norman E. Genealogy in America, Volume I: Massachusetts, Connecticut and Maine. Salt Lake City: Deseret Book Co., 1968.

——————————. Key to Genealogical Research Essentials. Provo, Ut.: Brigham Young University Press, 1966. Reissued Salt Lake City: Bookcraft, 1967.

——————————. "Orderly Preservation of Research Notes," Instructor, IC (1964), 412 ff.

Zabriskie, George O. Climbing Our Family Tree Systematically. Salt Lake City: Parliament Press, 1969.

RESEARCH TECHNIQUES
IN OTHER DISCIPLINES

Altick, Richard D. The Art of Literary Research. New York: W. W. Norton & Co., 1963.

Ashley, F. "The Scientific Method and Historical Research," Industrial Arts and Historical Research, XXVI (1937), 173-75.

Barron, H. M. Your Parish History: How to Discover and Write It. London: Wells Gardner, n. d.

Barzun, Jacques and Graff, Henry F. The Modern Researcher. New York: Harcourt, Brace and World, 1957.

Brickman, William W. Guide to Research in Educational History. New York: New York University Bookstore, 1949.

Cantor, Norman F. and Schneider, Richard L. How to Study History. New York: Thomas Y. Crowell Co., 1967.

Cox, J. C. "How to Write the History of a Parish," Local Gleanings, I (1879-80), 396-79 97. Also issued separately. 5th ed. London: 1909.

Crump, C. G. History and Historical Research, London: Routledge & Sons, 1928.

Drew, C. D. "On Writing a Parish History," Proceedings of the Dorset Natural History Society, LIII (1932), 236-46.

Fling, Fred M. The Writing of History. New Haven: Yale University Press, 1920.

Freedman, Paul. The Principles of Scientific Research. New York: Pergamon Press, 1960.

Good, Carter V. and Scates, Douglas E. Methods of Research: Educational, Psychological, Sociological. New York: Appleton-Century Crofts, 1954.

Gottschalk, Louis. Understanding History: A Primer of Historical Method. New York: Alfred A. Knopf, 1961.

Hanson, T. W. "Local Historical Research," Halifax Antiquarian Society, (1942), 1-7.

Hockett, Homer C. The Critical Method in Historical Research and Writing. New York: Macmillan Co., 1955.

Humphreys, Arthur L. How to Write a Village History. Reading: 1930.

Johnson, Allen, The Historian and Historical Evidence. New York: Scribner and Sons, 1934.

Johnson, C. The Mechanical Processes for the Historian. London: S.P.C.K., 1922.

Lach, Szyrma W. S. "How to Write Parochial and College Histories," British Archaeological Association (XVII).

Louissell, David W., Kaplan, John and Waltz, Jon R. Principles of Evidence and Proof. Mineala, N. Y.: 1968.

Marshall, R. L. Historical Criticism of Documents. London: S.P.C.K., 1920.

McAshan, Hildreth H. Elements of Educational Research. New York: McGraw-Hill, 1963.

Parker, Donald D. Local History, How to Gather It, Write It, Publish It. New York: Social Science Research Council, 1944.

Phillimore, W. P. W. Parish Historian: A Short Initial Guide For Writing, Printing and Illustrating the History of a Parish. London: Phillimore, 1905.

Pollack, Ervin H. Fundamentals of Legal Research. 3d ed. Brooklyn: Foundation Press, 1967.

Piggott, Sir F. T. "Practical Notes on Historical Research," Royal Historical Society Transactions, Ser. 4, V (1922), 132-49.

Pugh, R. How to Write a Parish History. London: Allen & Unwin, 1954.

Salzman, L. F. "The Writing of Local History," South East Naturalist and Antiquarian Society, LXII (1937), 10-15.

Shafer, R. J. A Guide to Historical Method. Homewood, Ill.: Dorsey Press, 1969.

Skipp, Victor H. T. "Amateur Study of Local History," Amateur Historian, VI (1964), 182-85.

Tuffs, J. E. "Hints on the Collection of Historical Notes and Other Materials," Amateur Historian, III (1957-58), 264-67.

Vincent, John M. Aids to Historical Research. New York: Appleton-Century, Co., 1934.

——————————————. Historical Research: An Outline of Theory and Practice. New York: Peter Smith, 1929.

Wake, Joan. How to Compile a History and Present-day Record of Village Life. Northampton: 1935.

Wigmore, John H. Student's Handbook of the Law of Evidence. Chicago: 1935.

Wilkinson, John. "On Parochial Histories," Wiltshire Magazine, III (1857), 57-67.

——————————————. "Parochial Histories of Wiltshire and Dorset," Wiltshire Magazine, IV (1858), 253-66.

Wilson, E. Bright, Jr. An Introduction to Scientific Research. New York: McGraw-Hill, 1952.

INDEX

INDEX

AMS Press, 197
Abstract, 92, 190
Abstracts of title, 53
Accounts, 48-49
Accreditation of genealogists, 3
Accurate records, 116
Addresses, 50
Administrative records, 82
Adoption papers, 53
American Antiquarian Society, 277
American Association for State
   and Local History, 99
American Historical Association, 99
American Institute of Genealogy, 61
American University, 3
*Ancient and Present State of the
   City of Oxford*, 110
Announcements, 50
Antiquarian societies, 64
Antiquities of Warwickshire, 111
Apprenticeship records, 54
Approaches to genealogy, 16-17
Archaeological societies, 64
Archives —
   acquisitions, 284
   journals published by, 284-85
   national, 277-82
   private, 271-72
   public, 271
   records, 82, 263-64
   state, 276
Archivists, 199-200
Arms of Krupp, 3
Assumed ancestors, 12, 67
Atkyns, Sir Robert, 103
Atlases, 50
Authorship, 102-04
Axioms, see research axioms
Baby books, 49
Basic jurisdiction —
   definition, 127, 146, 271
   formation, 137
   study of, 127-33
Bible, 44-46
Bibliographic centers, 197
Binding, 95
Biographies, 79, 47-48
Bodleian Library, 67, 82, 282
Book —
   marginal notations, 50
   physical make-up, 174-76
Book of remembrance, 22, 47
Book Review Digest, 109
Book reviews, 108-11
Books, 50
Brackets, 17-18, 19
Brasses, 64
Brigham Young University, 3

British Museum, 67, 82, 132, 282
British Records Association, 99
British Record Society, 64
Brook, Roy, 103
Boundary changes, 122
Bulletins of family organizations, 44
Burt Franklin Company, 197
Business records, 285
Calendar —
   cross references, 14, 23-24
   definition, 13
   how to compile, 14-15
   illustrations, 14, 15, 45, 51, 71, 85
Calligraphy, 94-95
Cambridge University Library, 283
Camden, William, 102
Canadian Historical Review, 109
Canterbury Tales, 184-85
Carbon copies, 60-61
Card catalogue, 178-79
Carnegie Institute, 279-80
Case histories, 20-21, 115, 210
Catholic Record Society, 190
Census, 285
Chainmarks, 95
Charters, 285-86
Chaucer, Geoffrey, 184-85
Church certificates, 53
Churchill, Lord Randolph, 79
Churchill, Sir Winston, 79
Church records, 286
Citizenship papers, 54
Clay tablets, 48
Clues, 7, 41-43, 50, 58, 83
Coats of arms, 50, 66
Code of ethics, 4, 6-9
Coker, John, 102
Collateral ancestors, 11
College of Arms, 7, 67, 82
Collier, John, 102
Common ancestor, 11
Commonplace books, 49
Composite records, 65-82, 263
Comprehension, 99
Comprehensive search, see general search
Cooperation, 8-9
Copied sources, 92-93
Copyright, 103
Correspondence —
   carbon copies, 60-61
   field researcher, 201-03
   form letters, 60
   Genealogical Society of Utah, 267
   known relatives, 59-60
   letters and letterbooks, 48
   record officials, 199-200
   rules, 59-60
   sending return postage, 60